VALLEY

506900:

W9-BWP-533

Gunning, Sally.
The rebellion of Jane
Clarke /

VALLEY COMMUNITY LIBRARY
739 RIVER STREET
PECKVILLE, PA 18452
(570) 489-1765
www.lclshome.org

ALSO BY SALLY GUNNING

Bound
The Widow's War

THE REBELLION OF JANE CLARKE

THE REBELLION
OF JANE CLARKE

Sally Gunning

wm
WILLIAM MORROW
An Imprint of HarperCollins*Publishers*

Valley Community Library
739 River Street
Peckville, PA 18452-2313

This book is a work of fiction. References to real people, events, establishments, organizations, or locales are intended only to provide a sense of authenticity, and are used fictitiously. All other characters, and all incidents and dialogue, are drawn from the author's imagination and are not to be construed as real.

THE REBELLION OF JANE CLARKE. Copyright © 2010 by Sally Gunning. All rights reserved. Printed in the United States of America. No part of this book may be used or reproduced in any manner whatsoever without written permission except in the case of brief quotations embodied in critical articles and reviews. For information address HarperCollins Publishers, 10 East 53rd Street, New York, NY 10022.

HarperCollins books may be purchased for educational, business, or sales promotional use. For information please write: Special Markets Department, HarperCollins Publishers, 10 East 53rd Street, New York, NY 10022.

FIRST EDITION

Designed by Lisa Stokes

Library of Congress Cataloging-in-Publication Data has been applied for.

ISBN 978-0-06-178214-5

10 11 12 13 14 OV/RRD 10 9 8 7 6 5 4 3 2 1

FOR ANDREA

The seeming truth which cunning times put on
To entrap the wisest.

—*The Merchant of Venice*, Act III, Scene 2

Acknowledgments

In writing *The Rebellion of Jane Clarke* I relied heavily on Hiller B. Zobel's *The Boston Massacre*, Frederic Kidder's *The History of the Boston Massacre*, *Legal Papers of John Adams*, *Diary and Autobiography of John Adams*, *Adams Family Correspondence*, and numerous accounts of the day found in the *Boston Gazette* at the Boston Public Library. Esther Forbes's *Paul Revere and the World He Lived In* was additionally helpful with general background.

My thanks to Kathleen Remillard, Nina Gregson, and the rest of the staff at Brewster Ladies Library, Lucy Loomis at Sturgis Library, Mary Sicchio at Cape Cod Community College, and Elizabeth Bouvier and Jennifer Fauxsmith at the Judicial Archives/Massachusetts Archives, for their assistance with the historical research.

My agent Andrea Cirillo always had my back but accepted no excuses, no matter how inventive they became. My editor Jennifer Brehl's patience and care saw that every word remained on track. My readers Nancy Carlson, Jan Carlson, Diane Carlson, and John Leaning were, as usual, ready, willing, insightful, and supportive. I don't have the words for all my husband, Tom, contributed to the cause, although the words "lobsters on the porch" do come to mind.

I would also like to thank doctors Monica Piecyk, Jane Watts, and Eric Woodard, massage therapist Barbara Coughlin, and the gang at Rehabilitation Hospital of Cape Cod—particularly, Jennifer Avery, Jennifer Hardigan, and Kristen Marston—for getting me back at the keyboard after a diagnosis of rheumatoid arthritis sidelined me for months. Without their fine care and concern this book would never have seen the light of day.

THE REBELLION OF JANE CLARKE

Satucket

Chapter One

JANE CLARKE STOOD in the sedge growth on the lip of the dune and looked out over the half-drained bay, the ribbons of sand rising up through the retreating water. Her cousin's sloop, the *Betsey,* had slipped in ahead of the falling tide and lay canted sideways in the channel, keel nestled in the mud. Already, the oxcarts rumbled over the sand loaded with barrels and crates full of salt, rum, molasses, and other more worldly goods—most of them legal—come to Satucket from Boston, but Jane wasn't there for goods. Jane was there for letters. Even at her distance Jane could identify the mail sack in the foremost oxcart, but she stayed where she was, half-camouflaged by the sedge, because Joseph Woollen was the one driving it shoreward. Was it worth facing Woollen's unblinking fish eyes just to get to the letters first?

Yes, she decided. She slid down the bluff and saw Woollen's head lift at the sight of her, saw him dive at the sack; by the time she'd reached the cart he had her letters sorted and ready. He thrust them at her with a formal, "Good-day, miss," as if he didn't know her name, as if at his cousin's wedding he hadn't pressed lips like cold chicken livers up and down her neck. Jane gave one nod to cover both greeting and good-bye, took the handful of letters, and hurried off toward the landing road, as if she were in a great rush to get them to her father, which she should have been, of course, as most of them were his. She proceeded along the landing road onto the King's road at an even pace, but at the cartway that led from the road to her father's house she walked faster, keeping one eye on alert for family or servants. She *should* go straight home—her father's letters aside, the day's work sat waiting—but two of the letters were for Jane, and the minute she stepped inside the house she would lose all chance of reading them in peace. The plan was to take the path along the millstream to her favorite rock above the millpond, where she might, for a time, keep her news to herself.

Such was the plan, but as Jane rounded the bend she came up against a knot of men standing in front of Thacher's tavern, their voices hot and sharp, the words flying back and forth like training-day musket shot.

"The *ears*?"

"Lopped off!"

"The devil! When?"

"Last night. Bangs Inn. Winslow paid a call after supper, tied his horse out front, left around ten and found the creature cut up."

"Bloody hell! Who did it?"

"Who did it! God's breath, man, who do you think? Name me another who'd carry an argument to a man's horse. Name me—" Whatever the speaker had in mind, it was cut short when he spied Jane. He snapped his jaw shut; the rest of the group turned, saw Jane, and likewise fell silent.

The talk had been bad enough, but the silence was worse. Jane might have pretended their silence had nothing to do with her, that the talk had cut short at her approach out of nothing but a gentleman's desire to shield a lady from an unpleasant subject, but the looks back and forth, the shifting feet, the sharp edge to the silence itself told her what she'd already guessed the minute the speaker had closed his mouth.

They blamed her father for the horse.

Griffith, her father's neighbor, braved the silence first. "Good-day, Jane."

"Good-day, sir."

The other men touched their hats or dipped their heads; Jane cricked her neck in response; but after she'd walked past she heard the steady *pock-pock-pock* of their lowered voices at her back. What cowards they were! Her rage began to pump her feet, but once she felt the ground rushing by underneath she checked her stride—they would not catch her in flight. She waited till she'd left the road and was out of sight before she picked up her skirts and bolted, following the millstream black with fish, past Winslow's fulling mill, all the way up to the milldam. Beyond the dam the millpond lay sleek and calm; below it the alewives pooled, resting for their final thrust through the turbulent floodgate into the pond to spawn; there Jane decided to rest as well, letting her heart catch up with her legs.

While Jane rested, she peered down into the vortex of circling fish. The annual spring migration of the alewives had long puzzled Jane—what was it that convinced generation upon generation of fish to fight their way around so many rocks and against such a powerful current to the millpond to shed their eggs? What did that particular pond offer over the bays and inlets and tide pools below that could be worth such injury and exhaustion, even death? Jane could not, would not ever, understand it.

After she had collected her breath, Jane pulled her skirt tight and continued along the wilder portion of path, used now only by a handful of children or the few remaining Indians who camped beyond the millpond. A large rock lay ahead, the water lipping at three sides of it, creating the illusion of a fortress; Jane hitched up her skirt and climbed on top of it. The dark rock had already stored up some of the fleeting May sun, and now that the clouds had returned Jane was glad enough for the heat of it; she settled as comfortably as she could on the warm stone and crossed her legs, spreading the letters in the basket her skirt had formed between her knees.

Of the two letters addressed to Jane she recognized both hands; she also noted that one of the writers had included a letter to her father. She picked up the other letter—the letter from her brother—already away from Satucket five years now, four at Harvard College and one clerking for the lawyer John Adams in Boston. She ran her finger under the fold and cracked the seal; the letter was short, but so were all her brother's letters.

10 April 1769

> My Dear Sister,
> I am in hopes this finds you well and should like to report the same, although yesterday I took a fall off a horse that should have been shot before it was ever put out to let. Of course, if Father had seen fit to set me up with my own horse I'd not be confined to this bed, but if the fool who fired the musket that shied the horse had aimed lower I'd not be confined to this life.

Jane read on in a fine alarm. Who was firing muskets so near a horse and rider? How badly was her brother hurt? He mentioned a sprained knee, a wrist—she continued reading in hopes of finding plans for her brother's recuperating in Satucket but found no hint of it. She put the letter aside and picked up the next.

1 May 1769

> My Dearest Jane,
> I hope this letter finds you in all your usual glowing health. I write to inform you that I expect to have completed all my town business by the 16th and have written to your father acquainting him with my dual intention, the one being to stop at Satucket on my return trip to Wellfleet on the 19th or 20th of this month. You know the second intention. Or perhaps I should say the first?

Having spent overlong on your father's epistle, I now have time for
a scant few lines to you, but suffice it to say that since I left you at your
father's you have been behind my every thought. I see your face each
time I blink and yet I could not describe it to a stranger—'tis all sum
over parts.

If it makes up in any way for the insufficiency of this letter, allow
me to assure you that I believe I have spent the time on your father's
letter to good effect, and that I am,

Ever your,
P. Paine

Jane folded up both letters and pushed the pair into her pocket out
of sight, feeling suddenly, explosively, out of sorts. That her brother's letter should disturb she understood well enough—he made no mention of
nurse or doctor, which meant any one of his sprains might indeed be a
break; he seemed more interested in blaming her father for the horse than
the stranger for the shot that had pitched him off it in the first place. But
what of Phinnie's letter? Halfway through the reading, she'd developed a
painful bubble in her chest that felt sure to erupt through her ribs at any
moment, and she had no idea what might have caused it.

Jane took the letters out of her pocket, opened Phinnie's, and read
it through again. At the second reading she could pick out a few trouble
spots; for instance, she might ask: *Was* she first or was she second on his
list of intents? She might also like to know why she should be *behind* all his
thoughts and not once out front. She might wonder too if she was expected
to take *sum over parts* as compliment.

Jane put the letters away again, threw her legs over the edge of the
rock, and dropped to the earth. She headed off without remembering to
haul in her skirt, and the grass and bullbriers pulled at it as she went; when
she'd reached the milldam, in a quarter of the time it had taken her to
walk up, the bubble in her chest had pushed into her lungs, making them

feel like the overworked gills of the fish that swam in exhausted circles at her feet. She stopped, put her hands on her hips, breathed in and out, and looked out over the mill valley.

The village of Satucket stretched east another six miles, encompassing a busy stretch around the meetinghouse that most villagers would have considered Satucket's heart, but Jane saw this part of it, her part of it, as the true source of village life. There was Winslow's fulling mill below her to the left; across the road were the herring men, their nets dipping and swaying under the usual cloud of gulls; below them was her father's tannery, the tanner just setting down his scraping blade to take up his paddle and stir his vats; across the millstream from the tannery was the big wooden wheel of her father's grist mill, rumbling under the fall of water like the village pulse. Beyond all of that lay the greening, snaking, salt marsh, and the ocean that forever pushed and pulled at the village's edge, filling the air with the piquant smell of life and death. Just so the mill valley had spread out before Jane all twenty-two years her life, and yet this time as she looked she saw something different. Two mills. One stream. Too many lawsuits.

For that was, of course, what lay behind the horse.

Jane couldn't say how many years the Clarkes and Winslows had been feuding over the millstream privilege, but she knew it dated back to a time before her birth, to the day Jane's grandfather sold his mill to the Winslows, built a new one on the other side of the stream, and dug the gutter that drew the water to the new site. The Winslows had accused Jane's grandfather of drawing off so much water that it hampered the operation of the old mill; Jane's grandfather, and her father as time advanced, claimed there was plenty of water for both. The Winslows took the Clarkes to court over the diversion of the water and won their case, although the settlement was insultingly small, or so Winslow said. He sued again, accusing Jane's father of failure to maintain his half of the milldam, blaming him for the flood that caused the fulling mill three hundred pounds in damage. The court again found for Winslow, but Jane's father appealed and received a considerable reduction in the damages. One might think that two judgments in his favor would put Winslow to rest, but it had not; only the week before another summons had arrived, a *qui tam* as Jane's father called it, two words Jane didn't understand and didn't dare ask to be translated, considering her father's state when he'd received it.

Those were the legal actions to date, but the legal actions were only half her father's troubles—the rest swarmed out of the busy hive of village rumor: Jane's father had got Winslow cast out of the church for evil-speaking; he'd gone out in the dead of night and ripped up Winslow's milldam; he'd set the fire that burned the old fulling mill to the ground; and now, supposedly, he'd cut off the ears of Winslow's horse.

There, again, the bubble rose upward in Jane's chest, now disrupting her swallowing, finally revealing its true source—not Phinnie Paine's letter, but the outrageous rumor that her father—her *father*—had cut off the ears of another man's horse. Yes, the other rumors had stung, but this was separate from all the rest. What kind of man could accuse another of such an act? What kind of man, on hearing it, could believe it and repeat it publicly, in the middle of the King's road, to anyone who happened to wander past?

Jane pulled her eyes back from the distant valley to the alewives at her feet; some of them had completed their rest and were beginning to fling themselves into the final wall of water, which was all that lay between them and peace. Jane watched several dozen fish pass through the floodgate, but she'd already been too long at her errand; she turned and worked her way back down the stream until she'd reached the steps that led up the hill to her father's house.

Chapter Two

WHEN JANE ENTERED the keeping room her father was sitting at table, reading a month-old *Boston Gazette*. When Jane had once commented to her brother on their father's tendency to read the radical *Gazette* more often than the conservative *Chronicle* Nate had said, "He would know his enemies better than his friends." As her father seldom read a paper in silence Jane took a quick glance over his shoulder to prepare herself for that morning's topic. The choices appeared to be three: the activities of the British troops stationed at Boston the past fall to keep the peace; the unruliness of the Boston inhabitants; the governor's speech. Jane predicted today's topic would be the unruly inhabitants—a mob had broken the windows of a loyalist merchant who had continued to import the British goods that the rebels had proscribed—and so it was.

"*This* they call defending a man's right to his life?" Jane's father cried. "*This* they call defending his liberty, his property?"

As Jane's father continued, it occurred to Jane that she might have predicted the rest: her stepmother, Mehitable, turning her face to her husband in that closed openness that meant he had her attention if not her understanding, her stepbrother Neddy slipping out the door to the barn like a starved cat, her stepsister Bethiah charging into the room in the full flood of a mindless jabber that drew her a swat, the little ones staring at their father like a pair of big-eyed, cornered foxes. After Bethiah's interruption there followed a brief calm where the only sound to be heard was her father's voice ratcheting up and down over the meaning of *liberty* versus *liberties* until the infant began to cry, at which her father broke off to ask why it was that a mother four times over had not yet learned how to stop up a babe's mouth with a tit.

All of it Jane might have announced in advance of the event except for one thing: the return of the bubble in her chest. She didn't know what should distress her in any of it, for none of it was any different from what she'd seen and heard every day of her life. Her father spoke as he thought; her stepmother did neither; Neddy would live in the barn if he could; the little ones froze to their seats whenever their father sneezed; Bethiah—fourteen now and old enough to know better—never did take the mood of a room before she charged into it.

Jane, who did know better, laid her father's letters down next to his right fist, picked up his mug, and refilled it in silence.

Jane's father looked up. "What's took you?"

"Some excitement in the road."

"Excitement in the road!"

She looked at her father. The room had already grown hot from the cooking fire and his long lip and short forehead shimmered with damp. She said, "Some kind of injury to Winslow's horse."

Jane's father leaped up. "You may spare me the rest! I've heard enough of Winslow for the week!" He picked up the pile of letters and the mug and retreated to his office.

———

THE SHOUT CAME JUST as Jane had put the vinegar to boil; she handed
Bethiah the spoon and turned for the office. Jane's father sat at his desk. He
was not an impressive man when standing—his proportions reminding
Jane much of the cider keg in the cellar—but when sitting his chest and
head took on the more inspiring lines of a marble bust. He looked up as
Jane entered and smiled at her as he smiled only at her; if her brother Nate
had grown into a more compliant boy Jane was sure that the son would
have held first place in their father's heart, but as Nate had chosen another
road, it was left to Jane to bask in the happy if sporadic warmth that shone
on the most favored.

Jane stood before her father and waited, his attention already gone
back to something in one of his letters, but Jane didn't mind the waiting.
She had always liked her father's office—the look of the great rows of books
on the shelves, the feel of the heavy wood desk, even the odor of musty
paper and pipe smoke and her father's sweat. When Jane was younger and
jealous of her brother's attention to his primer she'd once snuck into the
room, climbed up on her father's desk, and removed one of the books from
his shelf, but she'd found it a large disappointment—the "books" as she'd
thought them were in fact account ledgers full of nothing but names and
numbers marked off in pounds, shillings, pence. But an addition of a few
years had added to the significance of the ledgers, teaching Jane something
new about the man with whom she'd lived her entire life. Up to then she'd
known that his rule was law, that when he was not to be bothered it was
best not to bother him, and that when he wasn't bothered he loved her as
well as any father should. But inside the account books Jane discovered the
names of nearly every man in the village, and the numbers alongside each
name represented considerable sums of money, either paid or owed; from
this Jane learned that her father was also successful, important, smart.

Which was no doubt why men who were none of those things talked
about him the way they did around the village.

Jane's father finished his second examination of the letter in question
and raised it in the air. He smiled at Jane. "Well, daughter, my congratula-

tions to you—Paine has made his offer. How many visits has it been now, ten? A dozen?"

"Not near a dozen. And most on business with you."

"Hah! Business with me! Here is all his business with me: he'll have a house across the road as I promised for your marriage portion, half interest in the mill, full charge of both mill and tannery. You've picked yourself an able man, Jane; and an agreeable one; a clever man I'd even call him. I can talk politics with him without fear of disrupting my digestion as always happens whenever your brother engages me on the subject. But I expect you need no essay from me on Phinnie Paine's character; let me say, however, if I'd got this letter from Joseph Woollen he'd have got another answer. You're not planning to argue Woollen to me, are you?"

So her father had seen them at the wedding. "No, Papa," Jane said.

Jane's father leaned across and patted her cheek. "So we are agreed. I had little doubt of it. Paine says that pending my approval he'll speak to you when he arrives, but I'm not the fool he takes me; I know the modern way. No doubt 'tis all settled between you."

"Only as far as I could trust in your good opinion of him."

"Hah! Yes! Very pretty! You're a good child. Now leave me be. I've a letter to answer."

Jane left him.

AFTER DINNER THE MIDWIFE Granny Hall's neighbor boy came for Jane. It was a thing the old woman had begun to do of late, ever since an epidemic of dysentery had brought her to her bed along with the rest of the village, and Mehitable had offered Jane to go about delivering her cathartics. Since that time Granny Hall had got in the habit of calling on Jane for the more mundane tasks that occupied her practice—digging roots, planting herbs, brewing her decoctions—and Mehitable, a steady customer, had been willing enough to spare Jane from any household task in exchange for a poultice, an ointment, a tincture in payment.

Granny Hall lived in a half house covered with honeysuckle vines along the road to the Southside near the meetinghouse; in Jane's first remembrance of her the woman had been very old and had since only grown older. It was an irony of the old woman's age that her white hair had come around again to yellow, but it hadn't youthened her. Nor did the way she pulled out the chair and dropped into it, as if in doubt of ever rising. Indeed, she must have weakened, because for the first time, she allowed Jane to pay her calls with her. At the Snow house Jane administered the brandy while Granny Hall put three stitches in Jabez Snow's thigh where the bull had got him, but at Crowell's Jane was allowed to give a puke for a stomach complaint, and at the Bakers it was left to Jane to gargle the putrid malignant sore throats of all five of their children. To Jane's surprise and pleasure everyone except Jabez Snow felt better after her ministrations; as she worked her way home she made note to herself that next time she'd be more generous with the brandy.

JANE WALKED INTO THE HOUSE to the sound of her father barking in his office. She paused at the door long enough to identify the recipient of the bark as the nephew he'd taken on as his tanner's apprentice. Any such noise always brought on Mehitable's sick headache—Jane looked for her in her bed and found her there, eager for an application of the midwife's headache decoction, given to Jane in her last payment.

Jane returned below-stairs to find the apprentice gone and her father on his way to the tavern in no fine mood; Jane hurried the children's supper so she might have them in bed before he returned, it being her experience that the tavern had never improved a bad mood and indeed often ate up a good one. Bethiah—sometimes not so great a fool—followed the children to bed soon after they'd finished the clearing up, but Jane stayed below. If she made haste she might have time enough in the peace and quiet to answer her brother's letter.

Jane settled herself at the keeping room table, brought the candle close, and picked up her pen, but she watched the candle lose an inch of grease before she was able to make a single mark on the paper. She'd thought first to tell Nate of Phinnie Paine's letter to their father, but on reconsideration she decided it was better to wait till Phinnie had come and gone and they had, indeed, "settled the matter." She next thought to tell Nate of Winslow's horse, but Nate hadn't leaped as eagerly as his cousins into the next generation of feuding, and she worried that this last rumor might push him, if not to some regrettable action, then at least to some regrettable words. Nate had grown quite talented at regrettable words, especially around Jane's father. Or perhaps Jane should say he'd grown quite talented at words *Jane* regretted.

In the end Jane did as she so often did in her letters—she asked Nate a string of questions that he would no doubt ignore when he wrote his answer. Had he seen a doctor for his injuries? Wouldn't he like to take the next ship home to Satucket and recover under the care of a sister who'd been lately cultivating her skills at nursing? What was a *qui tam*? She folded the letter, sealed it, addressed it, and left it on the post table near the door to await the next likely conveyor.

JANE'S STEPMOTHER REMAINED IN BED the next day; Bethiah took over the babe, and Jane took the two little girls with her on her errand to the cobbler's. Both girls were in the high spirits that came with such a rare unleashing until they turned onto the King's road and saw the horse. Winslow had reined up at the side of the road in order to speak to the Indian Sam Cowett, and the horse bobbed and tossed its head, as if bothered by flies, or pain, or the whistling of the wind across the exposed stumps. Jane pulled the girls close and clucked them along the far side of the road as fast as she was able. She looked once more as she passed and noted that in contrast to the fretful horse its rider sat still and calm with his head held high;

he saw Jane and tipped his hat to her as politely as if her name were Snow
or Doane or Baker. Jane dipped her head in answer.

THE LITTLE GIRLS COULD not recover from the sight of it. They tugged
at Jane's skirt and peppered her with questions that she attempted to push
away by pointing out every distraction along the road. *Look there, the miller's cart . . . See here, the strawberries in blossom . . . Watch out for that rut . . .*
They'd gotten so little satisfaction from her that as they entered the house
they overcame their usual timidity and began to pester their father, who
sat at table being served a plate by Bethiah. *What happened to the horse's
ears, Papa? Where are the ears, Papa? Can it hear if we call it? Can it hear a wolf?
A crow?*

Throughout the questions the only sounds the girls received in answer
were Jane's orders to hush until Hitty braved one last question. "Would
you ride a horse with no ears, Papa?"

To Jane's surprise, her father chose to answer that one. "I would not."

"Why not, Papa?"

"Because such a man can have no dignity."

There, at last, the little girls quieted; they would not know what *dignity* was, but they knew enough of their father's face to know all ques-
tioning had ended. Jane, thinking of Winslow tipping his hat, thought she
did know what dignity was, and that her father was wrong about it. She'd
known her father to be wrong about a thing before, but for some reason
she found this instance of it more troubling. It made her want to ask her
own question. It made her not want to ask the question. It made her look
away as she collected the empty plate in front of him.

BY THE TIME JANE reached the bed she shared with Bethiah she found
that her sister's musty body had already dampened the sheets and she'd
locked her elbows around both bolsters. Jane eased in beside her and lay as

still as a pan of milk; it wasn't worth waking the girl and risking a stream of chat just to reclaim a bolster. She lay listening to the house: the tick of the clock in the front room, the *choonk* of a log settling into the fire, the breeze rattling her window. On another night these sounds might have soothed her into sleep, but tonight each one attacked her ears like a dog's bark. Thinking of dogs, she began to wonder if in her new house across the road she'd hear Paul Wing's dog, who barked every time a leaf dropped. Or did Phinnie have his own dog? Jane didn't know. She began to wonder what else she didn't know about Phinnie, outside of her father's testament. She remembered meeting Phinnie for the first time in her father's office and liking what she saw—features not too bold or too soft, clothes not too new or too old, the smile that stayed in the eyes after the mouth had given it over. She also remembered liking the way he stood with his hands at perfect ease at his sides, the way he measured his words without rush, the graceful way he mounted his horse as she watched from the window.

Horse. Just touching on the word brought it back again, the image of Winslow's horse tossing its head, the look of the blackened stumps. She yanked at the bolster and pressed it against her eyes, forgetting about the sleeping Bethiah, but it was too late.

A whisper no louder than a child's breath tickled her ear. "I saw it too."

"Saw what?"

"The horse. Mr. Winslow's horse. The one with no ears."

Jane made no answer.

"'Tis an awful sight."

"Yes."

"They say Papa did it."

Again, Jane made no answer.

"Is it true?"

"Of course not."

"How do you know?"

"Because he was here at the time it happened."

"How do you know?"

"Because I lay right here and listened to him snoring."

"You heard him snoring last night?"

"Don't you hear him now?"

"Well, yes."

"So."

"But I didn't hear him last night."

"Well I did. I told you. Now be quiet."

Bethiah fell silent. Across the hall Jane could indeed hear her father snoring, and outside she could hear the millstream fussing over the rocks, and from below-stairs she could hear the tick of the clock. What *could* Winslow's horse hear?

What kind of man *could* cut off the ears of a horse?

Chapter Three

PHINNIE PAINE ARRIVED as promised on the nineteenth. When Jane
heard his horse in the yard she looked out the window in her usual
way only to discover that she'd lost her usual way, that she found herself
looking at him as if he were a stranger and she were taking her first measure. She watched him swing his leg over the horse's rump with becoming grace, hand his reins to the Negro Jot, and stand a minute in the easy
chat of a man comfortable with all creation. She watched him remove his
jacket from his saddle and bravely shrug it on over his sweat-stained shirt,
a nod to civility that Jane didn't require but nonetheless drew him credit.
He'd collected a number of pine needles in his hat brim, but of course he
couldn't have noticed that; when he swept the hat off as he entered the
house the needles floated to the floor.

Jane crossed the room and scooped up the pine needles. When she
lifted her head Phinnie was gazing at her with amusement. "Ah, Jane. What
a fine housekeeper you are." It was an old joke between them, and one Jane
would rather forget, but of course Phinnie couldn't know that. At Phinnie's

second visit he had grown confused over Jane's mention of stepmothers and she'd set out the list for him: her father's first wife, mother to Nate and Jane; the second, barren wife; the third, who'd mothered Bethiah; and Mehitable, the fourth, who mothered the rest. After she'd finished she'd looked at Phinnie's startled eyes and said, "A man must get his house-keeping somehow." Phinnie had tipped back his head and laughed, but remembering it now Jane felt the disservice she had done her stepmothers, especially Bethiah's mother, whom Jane had loved well.

Jane's father brought her back. "Why do you hang about, Jane? Get the man a cider."

Get the man a cider meant that Jane was to get both of the men a cider; she removed two tankards from the cupboard and went to the cellar for the jug. When she returned, her father and Phinnie had settled at the table, her father pulling himself up in the way he always did when seated opposite someone taller. He said, "I make no official speech, Mr. Paine; I never do till a deal's finished; but allow me to say that on this occasion my wife and I are most particularly happy to welcome you to our home."

Phinnie said, "Thank you, sir. Thank you, madam. I've seldom been so eager to arrive at a place or so loath to think how soon I must be gone from it."

"Then we must see that you make hay, sir!" Jane's father barked out a laugh and reached for the new *Gazette* Phinnie had brought him. Jane braced, and sure enough, her father came to a point that disturbed him straightaway.

"Here now! Here! Do you read this chamber-dung of the troops at Boston? If half these tales of beatings and rapes were true there'd not be a soldier with the strength to stand!"

Phinnie said, "'Tis true, sir," which could have meant one thing or the other, but Jane's father seemed to take it as agreement, and needing nothing more, if he needed it at all, talked on in like manner through supper. It was the fault of a small collection of men with the surnames of Otis and

Adams and Molineux for feeding the lower classes tyrannous articles in the paper and rum in the tavern, then sending them out to so abuse the soldiers it would try the patience of Job. And so forth.

After supper Jane's father took Phinnie and his rum and disappeared into his office, where no doubt the details of mill and tannery and house would be laid down. Mehitable and Bethiah herded the children up the stairs to their beds, leaving Jane to the clearing up, but as soon as the family had disappeared from the keeping room Jane sat back down and picked up the *Gazette* her father had left on the table; long ago Jane had learned that this was where she might find the words that had been missing from her father's ledgers.

The first newspaper story she encountered told of another attack on an importer, and as Jane read she found she agreed with her father's opinion on the matter. The Townshend Act had levied new taxes on paper, paint, glass, and tea the previous year, and the old ban on importing British goods had been resurrected in hope of forcing their repeal, but there were still some importers and businessmen who didn't think this the way to proceed, and Jane's father was among them. As for Jane, she could not understand how a man could talk liberty out of one side of his mouth and then brand another man's free choice to import a little tea or cloth as tyranny. And these very men who broke into merchants' shops, threatening tarring and feathering, were the reason the offending king's troops had been sent to Boston in the first place.

But Jane found the next series of stories more troubling.

A Woman at the North End entered a Complaint against a Soldier, and some others for a violent Attempt upon her, but a Rape was prevented, by the timely Appearance of a Number of Persons, for Protection . . .

A Country Butcher, who frequents the Market, having been in discourse with one Riley, a Grenadier of the 14th Regiment, who he said before abused him, thought proper to offer such verbal Resentment as led the Soldier to give him a Blow, which felled the Butcher to the Ground . . .

A Girl at New-Boston, was lately knocked down and abused by Soldiers
for not consenting to their beastly proposals . . .

Were the stories true? Or were they, as her father said, naught but cheap propaganda? Jane went back to read the last few stories again, but somewhere in the middle of them she found herself thinking of Winslow's horse. The same kind of man who would spread such a rumor over a small village was no doubt the same kind who would write lies for the newspaper if it served his purpose, the purpose being the same in each instance: to convince the populace that a terrible evil lurked among them. Having discovered a motive for a man to write a lie in the paper seemed closer to proving that lie, and yet the stories troubled her. Could so many acts so vividly recorded all be false?

Jane set down the paper, cleared and scoured the dishes, and had just swept up the floor when Bethiah returned to the keeping room. They took up their work baskets in expectation of the usual hour of mending, but they'd barely threaded their needles when Jane's father emerged from his office with Phinnie behind him. He said, "Time for bed. Bethiah, come. Jane, you see our guest comfortable." He barked out another laugh and pushed Bethiah up the stairs ahead of him.

PHINNIE SAID, "AH, JANE. What are you fussing at? Come."

Jane left the lamp and crossed halfway to the bed where Phinnie lay atop the coverlet. He'd removed his boots, stockings, and jacket while Jane had fiddled with the smoky lamp; she could see little of him but the liquid shine of his eyes. He patted the bed tick beside him; Jane crossed the rest of the way and sat on its edge, but Phinnie reached up and pulled her down. Jane and Phinnie had lain clandestinely kissing on that bed after the rest of the house had retired before, but nothing beyond that; this time, with his intentions publicly declared, Jane suspected things might go differently.

Phinnie was better at the business of kissing than Joseph Woollen—he didn't cling as if he were drowning; his lips were neither liverish nor cold; he tasted as if he'd drunk a tot of rum, not bathed in it. After a time his hand slipped down to the ribbon tying up the neck of her shift and after a very little more time she could feel his man's part, as solid as the bedpost, through both their clothes; it was there Jane began to think about the consequence to the sin of fornication as she'd been taught it at meeting. If Phinnie got her with child he would have done so under her father's eye and would find himself married in a fortnight, whether he wished it or no, but if she gave birth to a babe before the full nine months of marriage they would be required to stand up at meeting and confess their premature coupling.

All this spun through Jane's mind while her laces were being undone, perhaps in no great compliment to Phinnie, but such was the world she lived in that these matters needed to be considered ahead of time. She might have considered them a little farther ahead of time if she'd thought of them ahead, but as she hadn't . . . And there a new thought occurred to Jane. It would be Phinnie's babe as much as hers, his trip to meeting, his long life with Jane beyond. Had *he* considered these matters ahead? Was he considering them now? Or did his mouth and hands and man's part carry him along without any thought at all? Jane didn't know. There was so much to Phinnie she didn't know. But she had her father's essay on Phinnie's character to reassure her, and she also had her father's dislike of Woollen to add to the sum—to find him in such perfect accord on the matter of Woollen allowed her to double the value of his assessment of Phinnie. She might also add to the sum the fact that Phinnie's hand had left her breast and traveled under her skirt to cause a sensation which certainly helped to explain all those meetinghouse confessions. And so Jane had now arrived at the fateful crossroads; she might follow that sensation down or she might back away from it, but if she wished to back away from it she needed to do it now, while she still kept firm grip on the reins.

Reins. Horse. Winslow.

Jane pushed Phinnie away and sat up. "I should like you to tell me something. You said ''tis true' tonight when my father talked about the soldiers. What did you mean? Do you think the stories in the paper are true, that the soldiers beat and rape the inhabitants?"

Silence. Jane could see nothing but the dark shape of him lying beside her. She poked his arm, and Phinnie rose up on an elbow. "Let me be clear. You're asking me . . . Are you in truth asking me about the behavior of the soldiers in Boston?"

"The ones sent by the king to keep the peace. I want to know if you think the newspaper reports are true, that the soldiers beat and rape the inhabitants."

Phinnie dropped onto his back. "I think all soldiers beat and rape."

"So you don't agree with my father that the newspapers lie?"

"I think all newspapers lie."

"You can't think both."

"Perhaps all ardent suitors lie."

When Jane didn't speak he rose up on his elbow again. "Why do you ask me this, Jane?"

"I want to know what you think."

"Ah! Then I shall tell you. I think we should get married very soon. And I think if talking is to be the thing, then that's the thing we should be talking about. Your father has shared some ideas with me that want discussion, for one."

"When you came through the village did you hear something said of Winslow's horse?"

Silence.

"Did you?"

"I did."

"And did you hear it said my father was behind it?"

Phinnie dropped onto his back again. "Jane. Jane. I know how this talk of Winslow's horse must distress you. For that reason it distresses me too. And for both together I see no gain in continuing the subject."

"But does not the talk of the horse distress you on your own account? Does not the mere suggestion that a man—"

"There are many things that distress me."

"What? What distresses you?"

"Your distress."

Jane looked down and noticed the loose ribbon on her shift. She began to retie it. She said, "My father asked if it were settled between us to be married, and I knew that it was but I didn't know how. I don't recall you asking it of me, or me answering you. 'Tis as if the idea arrived out of the air."

"Like breathing."

"But when did we decide it? How?"

"So this is what troubles you? That you have no day or hour or minute to point to and say, 'Ah, there our love began'? You have no pretty speech to turn to and say—"

"A pretty speech? You think I worry over a pretty speech?"

Phinnie sat up. "Then what is it, Jane? What's all this about 'settled' or 'unsettled'? Nothing in the world is easier to settle. You have only to answer a single question. Do you want to marry me or no?"

The answer arrived as if out of the air. "No."

Chapter Four

PHINNIE PAINE WAS indeed an agreeable man, as Jane's father had described him, so agreeable that Jane had no single past experience of him out of temper to help her anticipate him now. She had intended to be asked something more and was prepared to answer with more—that she felt a couple should know each other something better before they talked of marriage, that she was no longer quite so willing to take the unknown parts of Phinnie on trust as she might have been a month ago. Exactly why that was she didn't know, and that this idea would be new to Phinnie she understood well enough, but she also knew that it must be so.

Jane was prepared to say most of this to Phinnie, but the chance never came. He popped off the bed, pulled on stockings, boots, and coat, and left the room; Jane followed him into the keeping room and was greatly surprised to see him continue through the keeping room and out the door. In no long time she heard his horse snuffling and prancing in the dooryard in its own surprise, and no long time after that she heard it pounding down the cartway toward the King's road.

The rest of the house heard it too. Jane had carried the troublesome oil lamp with her from the front room and set it on the keeping room table; it rested between Jane and the stairs and lit each member of her family as they tumbled down: her father first, her stepmother behind, next Neddy, and then the little girls. At last Bethiah appeared, looking the least startled of all, perhaps because she was still the most asleep. Jane's father said, "What the devil goes on? Did I just hear Paine—?"

"He's gone home to Wellfleet, sir."

"The devil! If he thinks to wiggle out now—"

"'Tis not him wiggling, sir. I told him I didn't wish to marry him."

Behind their father, Bethiah's eyes went round as plums. As if he could feel them, Jane's father whirled around. "Get upstairs. The lot of you."

They went in reverse of how they came, Bethiah first, Mehitable herding the little girls, and Neddy behind, looking over his shoulder as if he never expected to see Jane whole again.

But when Jane's father spoke he was all calm. He said, "Very well. Explain yourself."

Jane did so. When she'd finished, or in fact some good time before she'd finished, her father explained *himself*.

"I couldn't claim the title of caring father if I allowed a foolish case of nerves to destroy my daughter's best chance in life," he said. "You live in a small village, with limited choices before you, and none with the character and resources of a Phinnie Paine. This I am sure you will understand once you have paid better attention to the matter, and once you have done so, this is how you will go forward. Tomorrow you will write Mr. Paine a letter apologizing for your behavior, claiming the onset of some sort of ail, or whatever it is you claim in such cases. At the same time I shall write and explain that on reflection a fall wedding would better suit our circumstance. You see how I bend to your whim in this? You see how I am not the kind of father who would ride roughshod over a daughter's concerns? By the fall you might know all you wish to know of the man. By fall you might know all you wish to know of an entire king's regiment. By fall you might have been to another wedding and seen what poor choice remains. Now, we are clear, are we not? Go to your bed, Jane."

Jane climbed the stairs. At the top she found Bethiah hovering on the landing, attempting to catch the voices below. "Must you take him?" she asked.

Jane said, "Go to your bed, Bethiah."

THE NEXT MORNING AFTER his breakfast Jane's father addressed her again. "I'm off to Nobscusset to see the cooper. I shall expect to see your letter on that table when I return."

Once Jane's father had gone, Jane rose to help Mehitable clear away the dishes, but her stepmother took the plates from her hand. "You'd best get after that letter."

Jane released the plates, but as she did so she took a new, secretive look at her stepmother. Mehitable was a tall, high-colored, well-set woman who might have held her head up in any man's home; instead she spent all her time looking down at a babe, a sleeve, or, as now, a dirty bowl. How was it she had come to marry Jane's father? Jane wondered. Had Mehitable's father fixed on Nathan Clarke the way Jane's father had fixed on Phinnie Paine? *Look up,* Jane thought. *Look at me. Tell me what you know.* Indeed, Mehitable did look up, but only when Bethiah came banging through the door with the milk pail. "Bethiah, take some of that milk to my mother," she said. "She misses her cow."

Jane said, "I'll go."

SHORTLY AFTER MEHITABLE'S MARRIAGE to Jane's father, Mehitable's father drowned. For three years afterward, for reasons that had been half whispered and half spoken aloud, Jane's father and Mehitable's mother had been estranged. A year later the widow had married a lawyer named Eben Freeman, who had boarded with her for some time, a dwelling arrangement that had inspired some but not all of the whispering. Soon after the marriage Freeman had been elected to serve in the legislature, and the couple had gone to stay at Boston while he served out his term. Jane's father had advised Freeman to sell or let the house in Satucket, but Jane's grandmother had argued against it, believing they would return to Satucket to live between sittings of the legislature. In the space of three years, however, Freeman had managed to free himself for only a handful of brief visits home; a lengthy stay had been promised for that spring as soon as the weather cleared; Jane's grandmother had waited through April, May, and into June, but when her husband was forced again to postpone, she had departed for Satucket alone. The situation between the families being such as it was, Jane couldn't have said she knew her grandmother well; indeed, half of what she knew came from rumor and the other half from her father's complaints of what he called his mother-in-law's licentious opinions.

Jane's grandparents lived in a neat, tight house of one and a half stories situated about halfway along the landing road. The early June weather was the weather that Jane liked best out of all the Satucket year—the air was neither hot nor cold, blue had just won out over gray above, the spring mud had dried out below, and on either side of the road new leaves shone whole and clean and bright, not yet dulled by dust or riddled by insects. Jane took the walk slowly and felt the smoke clearing from her lungs as she went; as if sharing the thought, Jane found her grandmother out in her garden instead of indoors.

The past year had widened the frame of silver around her grandmother's face, but the straight back, vivid eyes, and strong jaw hadn't changed. As Jane made note of these things it occurred to her that this woman was much closer than Mehitable to the age Jane's mother would have been had she lived. As to any other coincidental likeness Jane couldn't say—the little she remembered of her mother had long ago gotten mixed up with the death's-head angel that topped her gravestone, complete with painful grimace. But as the older woman folded the younger into a hug that included the milk jar and a fair amount of sandy dirt, Jane seemed to remember that as well.

Jane handed the jug to her grandmother, who peered into it and beamed. "Milk!"

"My mother says you must miss your cow."

"And my hens. And all that should be growing out of the ground." Jane's grandmother carried the milk jug into the house; Jane followed. There too she saw the effect of her grandmother's long absence in the frost of salt on the windows, the thirsty wood, the mildewed plaster, the cobwebs that hadn't yet surrendered to the broom. Jane's grandmother seemed to notice it as Jane did and slashed the air in frustration. "I've been at work on the place since I came and not a minute of it shows." She set the milk on the table and sat down on one side of it, waving at Jane to take a seat on the other. She said, "Now, Jane. Tell me all that goes on."

All that goes on. The list was long, but for a grandmother who was nearly a stranger a shorter list would do. Jane began with Nate's fall, went on to her sister Anne's first stitching, from there to Neddy's good report from his tutor. She considered mentioning Winslow's horse, but already, despite the neglect, her grandmother's house had settled over her with a peculiar kind of sheltering peace—in such a place such words would sound profane. Instead she asked, "How long do you stay at Satucket?"

"Eben joins me as soon as he can; we stay as long as he can."

Jane looked with greater care at her grandmother. Despite all the rumors about her grandparents that had floated around the village, this was the first time Jane had actually thought of them as the human beings behind the rumors, thought of the human feelings that had locked them together despite such rumors. Now that she looked, she could see the claims of husband versus home battling all across her grandmother's features. And indeed, there was something in the house that made Jane reluctant to leave it. She found herself saying, "I was to marry Phinnie Paine, but I may not now."

Jane waited for one of her grandmother's "licentious opinions" but none came. Her father often said his mother-in-law was the only woman of his acquaintance who could speak her mind with her mouth closed, but Jane discovered nothing in her silence either. She decided to continue along. She told her grandmother of her conversation with Phinnie, of Phinnie's riding off, of the letter her father required, agreeing to marriage in the fall.

When Jane finished, her grandmother surprised her by saying, "'Tis no easy thing to go against one's father."

"No."

"Your father does business with Mr. Paine. He may assure you of a fair trade with the man; he may not assure you of a fair marriage."

"You've met Phinnie Paine?"

"A time or two."

"And how did he take you?"

"What little I took I liked well. Which is of course no greater help to you."

No.

THE LOOK JANE RECEIVED from Mehitable as she entered the keeping room told her she'd been overlong at her errand, but she'd still returned long before her father could be expected back from Nobscusset. Bethiah and Hitty were pressing butter into molds at the keeping room table, but with Mehitable's eyes on her back, Jane continued past them to her room. She sat down at the little table by the window, took up her pen, touched it to the ink, held it over her letter book, set it down again. The idea of writing a letter to Phinnie by itself did not distress her; indeed, she felt she owed him more words than her simple *no*; the distress came in attempting to form up the particular additional words. No matter how she tried to work it, every sentence sounded too much like her father's *not now*.

Jane sat, struggling to order her thoughts, but the more she sat the more she began to resent the fact that she'd been forced to such a struggle at all. Her father could marry as many housekeepers as he chose; he could not marry away Jane as he chose. And what of Phinnie? Could he not share some of the blame for her predicament? All these words that would not slide off her pen the way she wished might have slid easily enough off her tongue if he'd but stayed to hear them instead of bolting off in the dead of night and disrupting the household. And she might not have needed to explain anything at all if he'd managed to answer a few simple questions with a little honesty and attention.

The longer Jane sat the greater her resentment grew. She redipped her pen and wrote across the page, *Dearest Brother.*

When the letter was finished she folded it, addressed it, and carried it out to the post table.

WHEN JANE'S FATHER CAME in he caught sight of the letter on the table and smiled. It was the kind of smile that caused Jane to wish for a second that a different letter sat on the table. He picked up the one that did sit there, and Jane watched as the address on the letter blanked out the smile. "Your brother. Again."

"Yes, sir."

"And where is Mr. Paine's?"

"I discovered I had nothing else to say to Mr. Paine just now."

"Nothing else to say."

"Beyond what I said last night."

"Which you understand discharges him from any future obligation to you."

"Yes, sir."

"Which you further understand requires a letter from you to reinstate that obligation."

"I do."

"So you will write him."

"No."

No. The single word sounded strong and clean and neat, as if Jane had just learned a new language of one word and that word contained in it everything she needed to know. She said it again, but with the necessary amendment, "No, sir," and waited in that brief pocket of roaring silence for her father to explode.

He did it well. "I should like to know where you come by such a high opinion of yourself!" he shouted. "You think yourself entitled to my roof, my fire, my food, forever and ever until you grow old? You think you need do nothing to keep yourself? Or do you think your looks will save you, looks that have already begun to turn? Look at that beetling brow! Look at those bony wrists! You'll be a fine match for old Presbury Fuller, who's already pissing his breeches—is that who you think to marry now? Or do you think at all? Well you'd best begin the practice by thinking how you're going to earn your dinner!"

Jane considered telling her father that she was going to earn her dinner by cooking his, but he'd already gone into his office and kicked shut the door.

AT LAST, NATE ANSWERED her letter. He began with the definition of a *qui tam*—"he who sues for the king as well as himself"—a particular kind of lawsuit created to encourage private citizens to inform against their neighbors on behalf of the province. Winslow claimed that in defiance of province law Jane's father had constructed a dam that impeded the flow of the alewives during spawning season; if Winslow won his suit half the judgment would go to the care of the poor in the village and the other half into Winslow's pocket. Nate added the surprising news that explained his intimate knowledge of the case: their father had passed over his local attorney and engaged John Adams for his defense.

Nate had filled a page and a half with the *qui tam*. Enough room remained to have answered Jane's questions about his injuries, but he'd not bothered to do so.

Valley Community Library
739 River Street
Peckville, PA 18452-2313

Chapter Five

J ANE'S FATHER CONTINUED in his benevolence toward Jane for a fortnight. Jane spent that fortnight working for Granny Hall, joining her
in attendance at two births, helping her to apply the more unwieldy poultices and bandages, even being sent on her own to administer emetics and
physicks and any numbers of gargles—the sore throat epidemic continued
strong.

Mehitable spent a good part of that same fortnight in bed with her
sick headache, although she managed to bring herself to her feet for John
Adams, who had traveled the extra day's ride from the court at Barnstable
to meet with Jane's father regarding the lawsuit. At first Jane had been surprised that her father would hire Adams, knowing how the two men's politics differed, but after some additional thought she concluded he did so for
the same reason he'd selected the man as Nate's tutor—according to Jane's
reading of the papers, Adams was now recognized as the foremost lawyer
at Boston. Jane was glad enough that her brother could clerk for such a
respected man, even glad that her father could make use of his services in

the *qui tam,* but she did not look forward to sitting at table between them.

Jane's father had prepared Mehitable with orders for a veal roast at noon and "no children milling about the table," but in fact the children seemed to please Adams as much as the roast. He came in red-faced and shining with sweat, dispensed his letters and papers in a lump to Jane's father, and turned to Mehitable, who stood in attendance with the infant on her shoulder.

"Ah!" he cried. "An angel! I've one of like age at home—my little Susanna—'tis a month since I've seen her, a month since I've been riding the court circuit. Do you suppose . . . dare I ask . . . would I be allowed—?" To Jane's astonishment he took the babe out of Mehitable's arms and cradled it in all its messy damp against his waistcoat.

Jane looked at her father. His own astonishment was evident, and something more, which might have been disdain or distrust or perhaps only doubt over the fate of his *qui tam*; he bore it as long as he could before shouting to Bethiah to collect the babe and herding Adams to table. As Jane served out the preliminary Indian pudding, she waited for her father to bring up the treatment of the importers or some other such subject that daily disturbed him, but it turned out Adams was a new kind of dinner guest. At her father's first bite of pudding, Adams grasped hold of the conversation and didn't give it back until he spied the tart. As Adams gazed joyfully at the last of the winter's apples bubbling in the hot crust, Jane's father leaped in. "May I ask you, sir, do you not decry the sorry reports put about these days in the papers?"

"I am indeed heartily sorry to read such accounts, but a town under occupation must of course result in such nonsense."

"How can you describe the soldiers of your own country as occupiers?" Jane's father cried.

"When my own country denies me my lawful right to have some say in how I'm governed." Adams had not raised his voice but had clipped his words in such a way that even Jane's father was forced to pause before charging after them, and in that pause Adams managed to consume the tart Jane had put on his plate as well as remove his watch from his pocket. "Now then, Mr. Clarke, as I've little time to waste, I suggest we get to our business. Shall we begin with an examination of this impediment to the fishes?"

"I impede no fish, sir! There's the point of the matter."

"My dear sir! I should of course have said let us examine the scene of this *alleged* impediment."

The hard lines that had rucked up Jane's father's mouth a moment before now softened, but just the same, a question Jane had never once before considered rose in her mind: must a lawyer believe his client innocent in order to properly defend him? As soon as the men left, Jane made an excuse of a loose pin and climbed the stairs to look out her chamber window to make a closer study of this foremost lawyer. Adams's well-stuffed waistcoat and breeches had camouflaged the underlying athleticism; he scrambled through the brush, over the riverbank, and up the stream like a ten-year-old boy, but once they'd reached the milldam he pulled a little notebook from his coat pocket and began to write in it in a more lawyerly fashion. The men began to talk, Adams's arms waving about, as if attempting to paint the entire mill valley onto a canvas of air, Jane's father punching at the water, as if to pummel it in a new direction, and there a queer idea entered Jane's head that the scene could be written another way—the two men might be dueling—but over what? They were on the same side in the matter.

THE MEN RETURNED ONLY in time for supper—a cold platter that Mehitable left Jane to serve. This time Adams seemed bent on talking of children and weather and crops and a new recipe for beer, and it amused Jane that her father appeared unable to swerve him. After supper the men went into the office, and when they came out Jane showed Adams to the bed last occupied by Phinnie Paine. At the sight of the bed Jane felt herself blushing and was convinced that Adams took note; she could think of no other reason why he should jog off into such a long compliment over the unremarkable cheese she'd served him at supper.

ADAMS POPPED OUT OF his room the next morning as neatly dressed as a traveling man might hope for; he took a gill of cider and toast and managed a second time to wrest the infant from Mehitable's arms; it appeared for some few minutes that he would ride off with the babe propped on the saddle before him. At the last he trotted off alone, clearly a happier man heading toward his home than away from it.

Jane was on her way to the necessary house to empty Adams's night jar when her father called to her from his office. She set the jar down outside the office door and stepped through; out of the bundle of letters Adams had delivered, Jane's father held one in his hand. "Do you know who this is from?" he asked.

"Phinnie?"

"Phinnie! You think it from Phinnie! Mark me, girl, you've heard the last of Phinnie Paine. This is from my Aunt Gill. You remember my Aunt Gill?"

Jane did. A half-dozen years ago Aunt Gill had arrived in Satucket for what had been planned as an extended visit, but she'd been made so ill by the damp air and the dust in the bed tick that she'd packed up after three days and returned to Boston. Jane remembered her as always holding a handkerchief to her nose and gripping Jane's arm so hard it hurt. She also remembered Mehitable responding to the "dust in the bed tick" remark with a rare burst of feeling.

Jane said, "I remember Aunt Gill, sir."

"I'm glad of it. Because you're to go to town to be nurse to her."

JANE HAD TO ADMIT the scheme was a clever one. Her father had for years received letters from Aunt Gill complaining of her declining health and the incompetent help that attended her; after Phinnie decamped her father had only to write and offer his newly disengaged daughter as nurse to get a winged answer back, offering a shilling a day plus her keep and care. As punishment it was likewise clever, for one day at dinner Jane had allowed a complaint about Granny Hall's old-woman fussing to escape her, and she had more than once expressed her dislike of traveling even as far as Yarmouth. Just thinking of the journey, the nature of the work, and the confinement with a near stranger set the bubble rising in her chest again; but as she stood there, watching her father smile at her in all his cleverness, the bubble began to heat and burn and finally to burst in her. If her father believed that with the threat of the aunt she would choose the suitor, he did not know her.

Jane stood up. She said, "Thank you, Papa. I should like a chance to see something of my brother. And I shall be able to report to you firsthand on the rapes and beatings of the soldiers."

Her father's mouth leveled. She leaned over and kissed its corner. She retrieved Adams's slops, carted them out to the necessary, and dashed them down the shit-hole.

JANE'S FATHER ANNOUNCED THE news at dinner. Neddy at once flew away to the barn and Hitty burst into tears, which made Anne cry too, although she little understood it meant the loss of Jane to her. Bethiah only looked into her mug, but soon after the meal and long before it was necessary she turned uncommonly helpful, pulling the small trunk out from under the eaves, scrubbing out the mold, dragging it down the stairs to dry in the dooryard. Hitty and Anne might walk around hollow-eyed, Neddy might disappear among the cows, but Jane guessed at least one sister wouldn't mourn her departure. An entire bed to herself, the opportunity to escape the kitchen heat and run the choice errands, perhaps the chance to take Jane's place as their father's favored daughter. It was like catching the first glimpse of her shadow.

———

AS FOR JANE'S FATHER, the foul temper she'd been waiting for now assaulted the household with the punch of an awl: his tea was too cold, his cider too new, his lamb undercooked, his beef indistinguishable from the horse dung he'd supposedly twice told Jane to clean off his boots. Jane might have borne all this well enough if it hadn't spilled out at the others—he sent little Anne from the table for clanking the pewter, cuffed Neddy for splashing his beer, shouted at Mehitable that she was as useless as a stopped chimney.

For the first two days Mehitable said and looked her usual nothing, but on the third she came into Jane's room while she was still in her bed, shook her awake, and motioned her to follow. Jane threw a wrap over her shift and groggily trailed her stepmother down the stairs; in growing alarm she continued after her through the keeping room and out the door. It was an hour of the morning that was hardly less night than day, and Jane followed the rise of the ground as much as Mehitable's rapid footsteps; Jane had begun to wonder if her stepmother was completely in her senses when she stopped at the edge of the meadow and turned to Jane.

"There's no need of this, you know. You need only write him. Your father wouldn't send you off if you did, and what you wrote should be your own."

"I don't see how it should."

"You might write him whatever you wish as long as you tell your father what he wishes! And while he waits for Mr. Paine's answer, Aunt Gill must be postponed."

"*If* Mr. Paine answers."

"You're not suited to coyness, Jane. *Once* Mr. Paine answers, you would of course have to write again."

"To say what?"

"Whatever would require another letter! Surely you can't be so thick! You might carry it along for months! A year!"

"And what of Mr. Paine?"

"What of Mr. Paine! What do you care of Mr. Paine? Do you wish to be sent away?"

Jane looked around her. The sky had taken on its first gray hint of day, and the coop, the barn, the house, even the millstream seemed to have drawn in around her. As a child it had seemed such a long walk to the meadow. It had seemed such a long walk only a dark moment ago. She said, "Perhaps I do."

JANE WROTE TO HER brother to inform him of her pending arrival in town, thinking as she did so of the oddity of her letters going in the opposite direction soon. And what letters might she expect in return? Her stepmother would write, surely, but she had little hope of Bethiah or Neddy, although the night before Jane was to depart, Bethiah took an odd turn.

"I don't see why you have to go," she said across the dark.

Jane made no answer.

"Well, I *don't*. I *like* Phinnie Paine."

Well, Phinnie Paine liked Bethiah, or so Jane might assume by the attention he had always paid her jabbering. And he'd once followed Neddy to the barn and stayed there, presumably admiring his creatures with him, till Jane was sent to fetch them for supper. Phinnie had paid no great attention to the little ones, perhaps sensing that if he had they'd have ducked under the table and quivered. But there were all those words again—*assume, presumably, perhaps*. What did Jane really *know* of Phinnie? Well, she knew his eyes, that strange green of a frothless wave, and that nose with the question of a turn before the end, and his mouth, too often amused for her liking. But what was the sum of *those* parts, other than a surface? What else did she know of him? Inconvenient other images began to dart at Jane like minnows—the hands, the mouth, the bedpost. But again, more surface.

Across the hall Jane's father began to snore, and as unwelcome as the sound was, it at least served to divert Jane's thoughts from Phinnie. Despite what Jane had said to Bethiah, she did not know whether her father had lain in bed snoring through the butchering of Winslow's horse or not. Perhaps Mehitable would know if her husband had been lying beside her during the incident. . . . Well, of course Mehitable would know. And no matter what she knew, she would continue to lie beside her husband every night here forward, reminded of it by every snore.

Such it was to be Mehitable, Jane thought.

Such it was to be a wife?

BETHIAH WAS LONG ASLEEP, oblivious to the trouble her three short sentences had caused Jane in her own efforts toward that end, when a shape appeared and hovered over Jane's bedside. The night was a dark one and the figure looked like nothing but a thicker patch of dark until it moved out of the shadow of the door and against the whitewashed wall, revealing the casklike shape of her father. Jane lay still, waiting for him to declare his purpose, but he stayed silent. After a length of time made longer by the dark, his hand came down, not on her head but on the bolster next to it. After another cloudy length of time, he reclaimed his hand and left.

That was the minute Jane's resolve began to flounder. She couldn't remember how it was she'd decided it would be best to go away; perversely, the reasons for staying at home began to grow in number. She counted them off as the downstairs clock ticked away the little Satucket time that remained to her: first was the possibility that this nighttime visitation by her father meant that he too was floundering, that he did not in fact wish his favored daughter gone from him, and only his stubbornness kept him from saying so. Second was the fact that she'd be traveling alone for two days or more, depending on the wind, to a place she didn't know and which thus far had presented little to recommend it. Third was the fact that Aunt Gill had begun to appear to her in her sleep as a huge, beaked creature that grabbed at her with great, scaly pincers. And fourth—she must admit this—fourth was the fact of the reports in the papers.

Jane repeated to herself her father's assessment of the stories as chamber dung; she reminded herself that neither Phinnie nor John Adams nor her brother Nate had in fact confirmed a word of them. None of it helped her. She bumped around in the damp sheets for an hour before finally throwing them off, creeping past her parents' door, and down the stairs. She blew off one of the banked fireplace coals and used it to light a candle; she carried it into her father's office, set it on his desk, and plucked the latest newspaper off the pile in the corner. The stories remained the same—trade restricted, women assaulted, men beaten; Jane had counted on a quiet, private reading exposing their utter silliness but found to her dismay that the trick worked backward, that the stories seemed all the more plausible when read alone in the dark, splashed by the light of a guttering candle.

Jane remembered another time in her father's office, a storm of wind and hail and thunder and lightning. Jane had run into her parents' room and found her mother, or someone's mother, cuddling a screaming babe— Nate perhaps, or perhaps Bethiah. Jane had run down the stairs and into her father's office and crawled under his desk and hung on to his stockings; he'd reached under and scooped her onto his lap, allowed her to stay in the crook of his arm till the storm grew distant.

No. Despite her father's desire to bend her to his will, despite his colossal stubbornness, he would never send his daughter anywhere her safety might be in question.

Jane returned to her bed and slept.

Chapter Six

T HE LAST PREPARATIONS went somehow. In the warmth of June
Bethiah gave Jane her favorite pair of mittens, having been told by
Nate there was no cold like the cold of a Boston winter; Jane's father came
out of his office with four letters that were to be carried to Boston; Mehitable
gave her a sack of bread, cheese, and dried apples for the journey, along with
a request for a letter as soon as possible, reporting her safe arrival.

"You may count on it," Jane's father said, "any news of a disaster at sea
will reach you long before any of Jane's letters," and he went outside to
call for the cart, but as soon as the Negro Jot arrived with it, Jane's father
returned to his office.

The babe began to fuss, so Mehitable could only hug and kiss Jane
around the damp, yeasty smell of the infant. Neddy had disappeared again,
and so the group that followed her out to the cart was made up of only the
three girls. Quiet tears streaked the little girls' faces, but Bethiah scowled
at her, as if she were Wing's dog, about to bite her on the ankles. The only
one who spoke was Jot, as he urged the horse forward.

The gentle warmth of June settled over them, and on another day, in another circumstance, Jane might have better felt its favor—now she felt only the unwelcome tug of it, pulling her toward an unseen future. As they turned onto the landing road and passed her grandmother's house Jane tamped down a wild urge to leap out of the cart and hide in its lee, but then the bay rose ahead, as if coming at her in a huge wave, and she saw the foolishness of hiding anywhere. If her future lay beyond that sea, then best to get herself there and get on with it.

THE DECK OF THE *Betsey* crawled with life, some of the crew at the lines, some heaving up last-minute barrels and crates from the longboat tied to the ship's gunwale; Jot tossed her trunk down onto the sand and Jane followed it. Someone shouted from down the beach and she turned around; the longboat had returned to shore and Ned Crowe and Joseph Woollen were standing by it, waiting. She crossed the sand to the boat, then crossed to the far side of the boat, so it might be Ned Crowe and not Joseph Woollen who handed her in. The men ran the boat out again, leaped aboard, and thrust their backs at the oars. Jane sat in the bow, facing shoreward, scouring the beach in hope of fixing its details, to be recalled at will at a later time. A figure appeared on the bluff: her grandmother standing with her hand lifted, not in a wave but in something flat and still, as if she were making a pledge; Jane lifted her hand in mirror answer.

THROUGHOUT JANE'S LIFE SHE'D not thought one way or the other about the sea—it was there, filling her days with the sound and smell and stickiness that traveled everywhere the air did—but she hadn't thought of it as a thing to love or hate or fear until that day, as she climbed on top of it. The sea had drowned her Grandfather Berry, it was true, but it had also helped to feed her family and carry them trade goods from Boston and England and the West Indies and even China. She tried to remember that as she made her way over the gunwale with the assistance of a few well-placed and misplaced hands and began to think how low the rail that separated her from many fathoms of oblivion. But as she looked down through the water she realized she could see the sand bottom, even a horseshoe crab, some weeds, a shattered piece of whale bone; not so many fathoms, then. No doubt if she were to slip over the side she'd be able to walk to shore, continue up the landing road, down the King's road, up the cartway to her father's house, make her apology, write her letter . . .

There Jane remembered her father's parting words, not even spoken to her, but to Mehitable. She lifted her head and turned her back on the shore. A cry went up from the crew; the sails rose and stiffened; the ground fell away beneath her; she pitched forward and cracked her head on the capstan.

JANE IMAGINED A MARINER might be used to seeing a little blood here and there, but the commotion caused by the red stream running down the side of her face caused almost as much activity as had the preparation for sail. Woollen was first at her, helping her down onto a nearby crate, pulling a yellowed shirttail out of his breeches and poking it at her temple. Cousin Shubael got there next. He was in fact her grandmother's first cousin by marriage and therefore not young or indeed agile by appearance, but he swung along the gunwale as if he were the age of Crowe or Woollen. He replaced Woollen's yellow shirttail with a gray handkerchief and pressed it to the wound.

"Well, lass, you don't make such a fair start to your voyage, do you? Nye! Where's my surgeon, Nye? Nye, get yourself out here where you're needed!"

And there was Harry Nye's sun-blacked face in front of her, square white teeth exposed and grinning. He lifted the shipmaster's handkerchief and clamped it down again; with the other hand he grabbed Jane's elbow, pulled her to her feet, and pushed her down the companionway. A pair of bunks farthest forward had been curtained to separate them from the rest; Nye took her to them, ran back the curtain, and set her down on the right-hand one.

According to town rumor, Harry Nye had left a wife behind in Maine; as he looked at Jane's wound Jane looked at him, hunting for evidence of a black heart, but the gleaming teeth were the best she could make of him. He went away and came back with a needle and thread in one hand, a tin cup reeking of spirit in the other. He handed Jane the cup and she took a sip, but he pushed the cup back at her mouth with a snap of his head indicating what Jane was to do with it. Jane imitated the gesture and drained the cup; Nye grinned, but the next minute he was leaning over her with the needle, and suddenly the white teeth and dark face were too close for her liking. She closed her eyes, and then opened them; she had paid close attention to the stitching together of Jabez Snow's thigh—as best she could she would watch this Harry Nye to see that he followed like procedure. He did, swabbing her temple, pinching up the skin, pulling the thread through, tying, snipping. She counted three of them. Afterward he picked up a piece of linen that she was pleased to see was neither yellow nor gray, tied it around her head, and patted her on the crown.

"Best lie still a bit," he said, and left her.

Jane lay down on the bunk, the outside and inside of her head curiously numb. She looked around her at the double row of bunks, a table and benches, lockers, a pair of swinging lanterns—until her head began to swing with them. She stood up and worked her way backward through the bunks and hand over hand up the companionway.

Once Jane hit the deck and felt the angle under her feet she stumbled again, but the second time was enough to teach her; she righted herself, spread her legs, and waddled across to the railing. She looked to shore— what had once been beach and sedge and road was nothing now but a white and green line pricked by the meetinghouse steeple. The bubble began to rise in her chest, but the breeze pushed it back, smothering her breath, flattening her skirt between her legs. She held up her hand and felt it stream over her palm and between her fingers. She looked down at the water, all dense green now, no crabs or weeds or bones beneath, and discovered that not seeing the bottom was less troubling than seeing it. It took away choices. Only one choice now remained, which of course made it no choice: Boston. Jane turned to face its general direction and there was Nye watching her, grinning. But if she couldn't manage Nye, what else might she not manage at Boston? She turned her back on him.

NIGHTFALL SOBERED HER. THE pair of curtained bunks was left to her, but on the other side of the curtain lay whatever men weren't needed on deck as they slept in shifts, and their bodily noises so nearby kept her too agitated for sleeping. She'd heard her father snore, yes, but she'd never heard this gusting and grunting and thrashing of limbs so close by she might reach through the curtain and touch them. She wondered what noises Phinnie might make in his sleep. She wondered about Joseph Woollen and Harry Nye, and if those were their sounds she was hearing. She slept little.

Jane woke with a headache, but once on deck she discovered her head ached less. She gripped the rail, turned her face into the wind, and let it pull her hair out behind her. So she stood for five hours; by the time the wind blew them into the harbor at Boston, a crust of salt, and perhaps another kind of crust, had formed on her skin. She had survived her first sea voyage. She had survived her first wound. She had survived both Nye and Woollen.

Royal
Exchange Lane

Chapter Seven

THE WATERFRONT WAS packed sky-deep in ships and warehouses and shops; the ground crawled with carts and carriages and more people than Jane had seen in her lifetime. At Satucket she could walk the length and breadth of the village and name every face she encountered; here she might count three she knew, four if she included John Adams, and the odds of finding any one of them among the hordes seemed next to nothing.

Jane's father had arranged with Shubael for the delivery of her trunk but had told her that her Aunt Gill lived at "an inconsiderable distance," and she should have no trouble walking it. Jane had made sure to nod in studied calmness over her father's directions, but she'd felt far from calm, had indeed come close to capitulating at the thought of following them, and it now appeared that had been her father's whole intention. He had, in fact, ordered a chaise for Jane and her trunk to travel in together, but Jane's rush of joy at the sight of the chaise couldn't last—the chaise and the lie came together.

And the chaise caused Jane other problems. The driver stared at her rudely and hummed a tune that she remembered from her uncle Silas as containing some questionable lyrics; he turned left from the wharf instead of straight as her father had dictated, convincing Jane she was on her way to being abducted; the rattle of wheels, the bark of dogs, and all the shouts and countershouts had set her head aching again. But soon enough they were on King Street and again in agreement with her father's directions— she recognized the brick Town House from its description in the papers: the gold dome, with the gold unicorn and lion of the royal crest below it. She marked the other signs as she passed as if she were marking a trail in the forest: the British Coffee House, Mein's Bookstore, the Custom House. A lone sentry stood in the box before the Custom House, the red of his jacket nearly as dazzling as the gold dome on the Town House. Jane stared and the sentry stared back and Jane looked away; thus her first encounter with the wild men she'd read of in the newspapers began and ended.

The driver turned right immediately after the sentry box and just before the sign for the Exchange Tavern; he pulled up in front of a house so tall and flat-topped it would have been laughed at in Satucket. Jane slid to the ground and worked the knocker, but no one answered. The driver didn't seem to care; he heaved Jane's trunk to the ground, jumped back into his seat, and would have ridden off if Jane hadn't grabbed the near rein to hold him. The urge to climb back into the carriage and take her chance with the driver kept her hanging on to the rein until the door behind her opened and a face empty of all expression framed itself in the narrow opening.

Jane gave the woman her name, but before she could answer, a gong-like voice rolled over them from the interior.

"Whatever are you doing, Martha?"

Without livening itself in the least degree the face in the door said, "Your niece has arrived."

The gong answered: "Well get her in and shut the door, then!"

JANE'S AUNT GILL WAS more bent than she remembered, and except for the strange, ringing voice, much weakened; she stood unsteadily at the top of the stairs, clinging to the railings. Jane started up to meet her, but the stairs were too narrow for her to do much but precede the old woman to cushion the fall; Aunt Gill worked her own way down by clinging to the railings with her hands while feeling ahead of her with her feet, which created the impression that she was sliding down the stairs on her behind end. Jane offered her arm at the bottom, but there Aunt Gill must have gotten her first good look at her. She let go of the railing with one hand and clapped it to the side of her face. "What! They've had at you already?"

Jane stood in puzzlement until she remembered: her bandage. She explained how she'd injured herself; it took several tellings and much assurance that she felt no lingering effects before her aunt's hand came down, but she continued to stare in a way that reminded Jane of the driver and the sentry, causing Jane to think something else of their attention. A servant appeared—a man near enough to white so that Jane was surprised to hear him called "Prince"—a slave name. Aunt Gill ordered Prince to take Jane's trunk up the stairs and took Jane's arm, her hand as cold as the millstream.

"We must sit you down and get you tea," Aunt Gill said. "You must be exhausted from your traveling. And all cut up, poor thing!"

Jane hadn't thought she was exhausted, but at that first kind word from her aunt she felt as if all muscle, bone, and sinew in her spine had melted. To sit down, to have tea, seemed the greatest gift she'd ever been offered. At once the old woman's beak and pincers melted.

"Martha!" Aunt Gill called. "Tea, please! In the back parlor away from the commotion. I should warn you, Jane, this 'tea' is more like the dregs of the rain barrel; your father no doubt enjoys the real brew at Satucket."

When Jane made no answer her aunt pulled her to a halt with surprising strength and peered hard at her. "I say, Jane, does your father drink Bohea at home?"

"He does."

Aunt Gill nodded, her mouth in a line that reminded Jane of her father when his smile was most distant. As they executed the right turn out of the hall she pulled back against Jane's arm a second time. "I think we'd best sit in the front parlor after all; we'd not hear them at the back," and they swung in the opposite direction. The front room was stubby and square and cluttered with furniture that seemed to have little to do but to give Aunt Gill something to cling to as she moved around it. Aunt Gill felt her way to a high-backed upholstered chair that faced a summer-cold hearth and dropped herself into it, but she did not release Jane into its companion.

"I ask about your father and his tea for a reason," Aunt Gill said. "I think it best we clear these things up at the beginning. I don't wish you to mistake me—I've looked forward with great pleasure to having you here. So great a pleasure that I've spoken about it around town. It was in that manner that I came to learn something of your father's business. His views. Perhaps I should say his politics. 'Tis apparently well known about town that he sides with the Crown, even trades with importers."

Jane said nothing.

"And speaks free against these persons he would call rebels, or even traitors."

"I don't know what my father does in town. I know he speaks free enough in Satucket."

Aunt Gill had little chin and more nose, which might after all suggest something of a beak. She said, "And do you share your father's view, Jane?"

"I don't know enough of the thing to hold a view, Aunt."

Aunt Gill's face relaxed, allowing comforting half-moons to form below her eyes and chin. "I'm pleased to hear so, Jane. Very pleased. There was a day when you'd not dream of a young woman's offering a political opinion, but now they serve it up with the pudding. I believe you understand me. My sympathies being different from your father's, I'd rather not have rocks thrown at my windows simply because his daughter's come to live here."

There Aunt Gill paused with head cocked, as if waiting for Jane to answer, so Jane said, "I'll take care," but it turned out Aunt Gill had been straining after a new noise from the street. She said, "Look out there, Jane, and tell me what goes on."

Jane got up and moved toward the door, but Aunt Gill said, "No, no, the window! And don't open the sash!"

Jane went to the window and craned left and right; to the right she could see nothing but a number of walkers and carts and carriages crossing the mouth of Royal Exchange Lane as they traveled along King Street, but to the left she saw a British soldier scraping some dung off his boot against the cobbles. She turned back to her aunt. "'Tis naught but a soldier cleaning his boot." The soldier lifted the latch of the next door but one and disappeared inside. "Why, he lives near you!"

"And where did you think they'd keep them? They're quartered all over town, wherever they can squeeze them. You can't empty your night jar without it landing on one of them, and then what a stink they make." Aunt Gill laughed, peering at Jane until she managed a weak laugh with her.

Martha arrived with the tea, and there at last Aunt Gill remembered that Jane was still standing—she waved her into the chair opposite. The "tea" she poured out was the putrid yellow labrador, brewed from the herb of that name, sometimes called "swamp tea," either after the place where the herb was harvested or the actual swamp water it resembled. Still, it comforted Jane, as did the simple bread and butter, and her aunt's good sense in leaving her to eat it in silence.

Aunt Gill also seemed to notice Jane's fatigue—as soon as the dishes were cleared, she said, "A sea voyage is so very trying. No doubt by now you long for your bed as much as this old woman does." She made as if to rise, but fell back; Jane leaped up to help her, and they set off as slowly as they'd entered. At the door Jane spied the first looking glass she'd encountered since she'd left home, and gave a start. No wonder her aunt and the driver and the sentry had stared at her. Her bandage was discolored with old blood and new grime, her hair looked like winter grass after a punish-

ing storm, and she was so short of sleep that the lavender blue of her eyes
appeared to have bled into the skin below. She thought how lucky she was
that Phinnie couldn't see her, until she remembered it didn't matter what
Phinnie thought anymore.

AUNT GILL'S ROOM SAT next to the second-floor landing, and Jane's first
job began right there. Aunt Gill leaned close and squeezed Jane's arm.
"T'was Martha settled me each night before you came," she whispered,
"but I must say to you she did so with a great lack of efficiency."

Jane would have said the word *efficiency* implied no wasted time or
movement, and set about to act accordingly, but this was difficult to do,
as Aunt Gill had a habit of frequently changing her mind. The candle was
moved twice, the bell three times, and the Bible three again. The shutters
were to be pulled to and latched; no, the shutters were to be half pulled but
not latched until Jane finished helping Aunt Gill out of her shoes, stockings, cap, and gown, at which time the shutters were to be latched and
rattled a number of times until Aunt Gill could feel sure the latches had
taken hold. Then came the bed. First the ropes that supported the bed tick
were to be twisted tight; but no—first the bed tick should be punched up,
and two stiff bolsters positioned exactly even to each other at the head of
the bed. But no again! The under sheet was to be smoothed until it looked
like pond ice before the bolsters were ever touched!

At last Jane was able to ease Aunt Gill into the bed, pull up the sheet,
and fold it back two turns . . . one turn . . . two . . . there! And the coverlet
was to be laid across the feet. Or knees. By the time Jane had worked each
thing to her aunt's satisfaction she could think of many words that might
have been applied to the process, but *efficiency* was not among them. By
then her nerves were so frayed that when Aunt Gill touched her cheek and
said, "Well, child, I do believe we'll get on," it seemed a second great gift
that Jane didn't know how to return, beyond applying a last unnecessary
tweak to the bolster.

Jane's room turned out to be a comfortable enough space in the upper half-story, containing a bed, a case of drawers, a table, and a washstand. A small, dormered window faced east, which no doubt kept the room cooler than if it had faced the afternoon sun, but Jane already felt the want of the southwest breeze that stroked her summer nights at Satucket. She stood in front of the tiny panes a while, gazing down at the street; she saw a British soldier go past, perhaps he of the dirty boot, but all other activity seemed to take place at the corner near the Exchange Tavern.

Jane *was* tired, but she would have said it grew more out of the attempt to acclimate to her new life on land than to the sea voyage, as Aunt Gill had claimed. She didn't understand how merely shipping her person from one place to another could make that person feel so different—so awkward and strange. And if she *felt* so different, what might her brother *see* when he came? She might be tired, but she knew she would never sleep unless she made some effort to discover her old self under the unfamiliar travel clothes and the dirt and smoke and stickiness of town. She'd been left a full pitcher and bowl and she stripped to the skin, unwound her bandage, dipped in her hands. The bowl turned pinky brown with the old blood, but as she touched the stitches Harry Nye had left behind she felt nothing but a solid, dry line. She carried the bowl to the window and stepped up to toss it down, then stepped back in a hot fluster. Full dark had not yet dropped down, and outside her window an opposing row of like windows stared back at hers. She turned around, redraped herself in her filthy linen, crossed again to the window, checked the street for passersby, and dashed the water into the gutter. She returned to the jug, refilled her bowl, and scrubbed herself hard. She put on a clean linen shift, sent the next bowl after the first, and sat down to attack her hair. It was stiff and sticky from the salt spray aboard ship; she ripped the comb through it, loosening the odd bit of seaweed and pitch; when she was through, her hair fanned out around her face in twice the usual volume, making her feel as strange as before.

Jane pulled back her bed cover and ran her hand over the sheet; it came away as clean as any sheet at home. She lay down and closed her eyes, hoping to find Satucket behind her darkened lids, but instead she found town still very much nearby in the rattling carts, baying dogs, and inebriated inhabitants collected around the tavern. But after a little more time she discovered it was too noisy and too quiet as well—no mill wheel; no millstream. She'd still not reached any kind of agreement with the subject of sleep when the gonglike voice rang up the stairs and filled her room.

Jane wrapped herself in her shawl and hurried down. The old woman was sitting up in bed, rocking to and fro like a pale white hobbyhorse with a thinning mane. "Did you hear it? Did you hear someone rattling a window below? You must raise Prince and tell him to look it out. He sleeps in the lean-to at the back of the pantry. Oh hurry, Jane! Do."

Jane left her aunt and worked her way down the stairs, listening hard but hearing nothing, straining her eyes against the town-dark—a paler thing than it was in Satucket—with lanterns from the tavern shadowing the street and candles burning in windows at an hour when they would have been long black at home. In the keeping room she found the candles and lit one; she continued to the lean-to door. She called out in the same voice she might have used on their Negro Jot at home: "Prince? Your mistress wants you."

There was no sound from behind the door. She threw something of her father's Jot-voice into her own and tried again. "Prince! Your mistress says get up and check the windows. She's heard a sound." A thump and a rustle answered her.

Jane returned to the keeping room. Prince came out of the back room after her, linen breeches sagging and shirt loose to his knees; no slave Jane knew had ever dared to dress so in her father's household, but perhaps this was no slave; there was something in the candlelit eyes that warned of more knowledge than Jane had been used to seeing in the Negroes at home. She kept well back of him as he made his way to the front room and walked along the windows, using his hands not to test the shutters but to shove his shirt into his breeches. When he'd completed the loop he said, "All sound," and disappeared out of Jane's circle of light into the keeping room. Jane would not have vouched for all being sound on the basis of Prince's examination, but neither could she hear any sounds, either from within or without, except the distant shout of the tavern patrons. She returned the candle to the keeping room table, pinched it out, and felt her way back to the stairs.

But Prince's "All sound" seemed the only thing the old woman needed to hear. She thanked Jane, leaned back against her bolster, and said, "The wind, no doubt. Good night, my dear. I am so glad you've come."

And so it was that Jane spent her first night in town lying awake alone, listening for the absent wind, listening for whatever it might have been that had rattled the shutters below.

Chapter Eight

IN A VERY few days the pattern of Jane's new life was set down. Martha kept the house; Prince kept the yard and performed any heavy work within, as well as most of the errands; Jane kept Aunt Gill. Each morning Jane would help her aunt get up and get dressed, which took a healthy part of the morning, the process extended further by much discussion of how Martha had done it wrong the week or the month or the year before.

Jane would then assist Aunt Gill down to a breakfast Martha had prepared, always a meal so bland as to be tasteless, always eaten with careful pauses between bites to see how it might go down. After breakfast her aunt would announce her intention of sitting and reading the newspaper in the back room, or writing letters in the front room, but more times than not, as soon as Jane had set off to walk her either front or back, she would change her mind, chasing or being chased by every stray sound.

Throughout the day Prince and Martha were called a number of times on their own fool's errands here and there; Jane tried to decipher something in their look that might tell her if this was her aunt's usual behavior or something new caused by Jane's arrival, but she'd never been skilled at reading thoughts in a slave's face, and Martha's blank white one offered little more. She snatched the odd look as it passed between them and understood that whatever Jane was to be in this household, she was not to be one of them. She also understood soon enough that Aunt Gill's alarms were almost always false, and that any reading of the newspaper would be sure to kindle one.

JANE TOOK HER FIRST opportunity to send a note to her brother at his rooms on Cold Lane, informing him of her safe arrival in town. She anticipated an early visit from him, but when it didn't come she remembered something he'd written in one of his letters, reporting on a dinner with his aunt. *I would submit to the Spanish Inquisition before I would submit to another such afternoon!* And indeed, he seemed to have fended off all invitations since then, as the old woman was never again mentioned in his letters.

Jane had found nothing resembling a Spanish Inquisitor in her aunt, but she had found a great difference in nursing the people of Satucket and the so-called nursing she performed for Aunt Gill. Stitching a wound or easing a sore throat or rubbing the first breath out of a newborn babe was work that mattered. What matter front room versus back room, green skirt versus brown, this noise over that one? The specter of wasted day after wasted day dropped down over Jane like a cowl. And it began to look as if the days would be lonely ones as well; her brother did not call.

ONE AFTERNOON, AFTER JANE had brought her aunt above-stairs for her nap and had three times arranged the bolsters, a black urge to press the bolster over her aunt's face and hold it there caught her unaware. It forced her to take a step back. She set the pillow on the floor. "Excuse me, Aunt. I feel . . . unwell." She walked out, down, toward the back door, thinking to step into the yard and breathe the air until the loathsome urge passed, but as she neared the back room she heard an odd scratching noise from within. She pushed open the door and found Prince, attempting to jiggle open her aunt's desk drawer with the aid of a kitchen knife.

Jane said, "Here, now! What are you about?"

Prince turned around. He smiled, the slow, bright smile of an imbecile. He said, "Drawer sticks. Mistress ask me to fix it."

"Without a key?"

Prince opened his hand, and in it lay a small brass key, warmed and smoothed by many handlings. He dropped it into a pewter pot on top of the desk and backed from the room.

Jane stood some time staring at the desk, trying to understand what she'd seen. A servant breaking into a desk drawer with a kitchen knife, or so it had seemed, until the production of the key. Or *a* key. Was the man clever enough, quick enough, to produce some other key just to camouflage his crime? Jane reached into the pot and fished out the key. She fit it to the lock and turned. The drawer slid open an inch and hitched there, but in the narrow space she could see the glint of red, silver, gold. Another tug brought the drawer open far enough for Jane to identify the red as her aunt's sealing wax, the gold as her seal, the silver as two . . . four . . . seven . . . nine . . . ten pounds British sterling.

Jane closed the drawer and stood as she was, thinking. *Had* she almost caught a servant stealing? Had he at one time observed Aunt Gill hiding her key and gone back later to empty out her savings? *Would* her aunt, so nervous over everything, send a slave to mend a drawer that contained ten pounds in silver inside? Jane lifted her hand to drop the key into the pot but instead closed her fingers around it. She climbed the stairs. Aunt Gill was still lying on the bed, but her eyes were open, the bolster Jane had left on the floor now propped behind her head.

"Are you recovered, dear?" she asked.

Jane gave a nod of sorts. She stepped up to the bed and held out the key; her aunt's eyes narrowed, as if focusing on the eye of a needle.

"If you would forgive me intruding in matters of private business, I came upon Prince attempting to fix your desk drawer as you had apparently instructed him. He put the key in the pot as he left, but I thought it a little too handy. I took the great liberty of bringing it to you in hopes that you might find a more secure location for it."

Aunt Gill clawed herself into a more upright position. She reached out and picked up the key. "Yes, yes, a foolish place to keep it, surely. And all my little wealth locked up in that drawer! All that's left me from my father! But where shall I keep it?"

Jane considered and discarded several places before offering up one that Prince would be unlikely to discover. "Your needle case, perhaps?"

"Yes, yes, a fine idea!" Aunt Gill dropped the key back into Jane's palm. "Take it below and secure it, please." She reclined again and closed her eyes.

Jane stood there. The question had not, in fact, been answered. *Had* her aunt instructed Prince to repair the drawer? Or was she just that muddled with sleep or age to have missed the significance of that part of the tale? It seemed crucial that Jane make certain of that instruction, as in it lay the truth of Prince's character. She leaned over and touched the old woman's shoulder. "Aunt. Did you wish for Prince to repair the drawer? If so—"

Aunt Gill opened her eyes. "Yes, how silly. Give him the key and tell him where to put it when he's finished." Which would defeat Jane's purpose altogether. Could the old woman not see? It *was* true, Jane thought; the old grow young again, adopt again the innocence of a child.

Jane went below-stairs, searched out Prince, and gave him the key, but left him no new instruction on its hiding place. She stood by as he worked the drawer smooth, watching as he returned the key to the pewter cup. Later, after he'd gone, she retrieved the key and put it in her aunt's needle case. Her first useful act done.

FROM THAT DAY JANE began to look at her aunt's eccentricities with less innocent eyes. She began to wonder just how much her aunt had known about the creatures she'd taken into her household and trusted with important keys. Jane did not believe in Prince's imbecile smile. She did not believe in Martha's flatness. She began to watch the pair of them and to make better note of the looks they shared that excluded not only Jane but the old woman as well. She began to watch for other things. One day she found Prince wandering out the door when Jane hadn't heard a single instruction for him to do so. Afterward, when Jane asked where he'd been, he answered only, "Errand." A few days later Jane discovered Martha pushing the fresh-baked bread into a sack and setting the day-old on the table. Jane picked up the sack and said, "Whose supper is this, then?" As she expected, Martha said nothing. Jane said, "If that was your old way of doing, you may find a new one as of this minute, or wait here while I speak to your mistress on the subject."

The flat face sharpened. Moving slow enough to keep alive the question of whether she would or wouldn't, Martha removed the fresh bread and exchanged it for the old.

THAT NIGHT AS JANE prepared her aunt for bed she considered telling her something of the loose workings of her household, but as she looked down at the shrunken form beneath the coverlet she could not bring herself to do it. Jane knew well enough from her aunt's letters to her father that a good servant was no easy thing to come upon in town, and in truth, all Jane knew for a fact was that Prince had stepped out, and a loaf of bread had almost been stolen. If Prince and Martha were not utter fools, and Jane did not believe them to be so, they would see that the old woman had a new friend, that the sides had now been evened, that the watch had been set upon them, and that Jane would not tolerate any abuse of her aunt's innocent nature. As if she read Jane's heart, Aunt Gill reached up and touched Jane's cheek. "It eases my mind a good deal to have you here, Jane."

So, not useless then.

AS SOON AS JANE could marshal the time and the will she sat down to write the promised letter to Mehitable, which she expected her father to read, and so constructed it with care. She made a great thing of Aunt Gill's house, describing it in minute color and flattering detail; she spent a long, exaggerated paragraph describing the heartfelt welcome she had received. She struggled most with her description of town, because she could base it on one carriage ride and the view from the window only; she had in fact yet to venture outside. She said nothing in her letter to her stepmother of Martha or Prince, but she wrote a separate letter to Bethiah in which she took full advantage of the aunt's silliness in hope of making her sister smile. She wrote another letter to her brother, reminding him that she was yet awaiting his call.

It was this third letter sitting on the post table that attracted Aunt Gill's notice. "This letter is to your brother?"

Jane nodded.

"I've had the young man to dine, or did you know? I asked him once or twice more, but he was always too engaged in his work for Mr. Adams to spare the time. Are you close to her brother?"

"Indeed so."

"When have you seen him last?"

"Near a year ago now."

"A year ago! Well, then, shall I attempt another invitation to dine?"

"Oh, Aunt—"

The old woman's answering smile almost equaled Jane's own.

BUT STILL NATE DIDN'T come. He declared that he was too pressed with work to take time out of the middle of the day to dine, but that he would be sure to pay a call some evening soon.

JANE READ THE NEWSPAPERS as they arrived, or that is to say she read the radical *Boston Gazette*—it was the only paper to which her aunt subscribed—and she read every word—letters, advertisements, news. It was through the paper that it finally struck her how far she was from Satucket; it was one thing to read of events that could never reach her; it was quite another to read of such events when they took place just down the road.

> *I am informed that next Tuesday Night two plays are to be performed in this Town, the soldiers now being here. I should be much obliged to anyone to inform me what right the Commanding Officers have to give leave to their Men to perform any such entertainment contrary to our laws here? Whether Law to be by the Military or the Civil? I hope the same spirit of purity reign now as did in former times.*

> *On Weds. next Instant at one o'clock will be sold by Public Vendue, at the Bunch of Grapes, in King Street, 5 stout able-bodied Negro Men, that are healthy and strong, Also a Negro Boy about 17 years of age, and 2 Negro Women suitable for Town and Country.*

> *A few days since died a very valuable Negro belonging to Capt. Jacobson; His Death was occasioned by Mortification from several stabs with a Bayonet given him by two Soldiers a short time before, without the least Provocation from the fellow.*

Such was Jane's idea of town life, but it was close to a week before she actually stepped outside Aunt Gill's home to see it for herself. The opportunity came on a day when Martha was deep into the laundry and Prince was in Dorchester after a new kind of purgative Aunt Gill had seen advertised in the newspaper. After Prince had left, the old woman called from above-stairs for Jane. Jane found her in her room at the little table by the bed, pen and ink laid out beside a blank sheet of paper.

"I have but this one sheet of paper, Jane. I don't know how this happened that I let it run so low; I need you to make a purchase for me. Not Mein's bookshop—you must never use Mein's! Tory! You must go to Wharton & Bowes at the southwest corner of King and Main and request my usual order with them. Do you know the place?"

Of course Jane could not know it, but she knew King, and she knew southwest, and despite what she'd read in the papers she was in an itch to get out and see something of the place. Aunt Gill's voice had to follow her out the door.

"King and Main! And keep wide of the soldiers before the Main Guard! And speak to no one but Mr. Knox, the bookseller!"

Jane supposed if she'd been allowed out and about the town her first day there she might have stepped out with greater hesitation; as it was, she leaped so precipitously through the door she almost landed in the gutter, a construction not found in Satucket. She took a deep breath and received her second surprise—this was no Satucket air, but a thing full of too-old food, too-new chamber dung, and too many kitchen fires set too close together.

It being early in the day, the tavern on the corner was almost quiet, but King Street was busy with the usual traffic Jane had come to know from her window. She looked left toward the Custom House as she entered the road, having learned since her first trip past that this was where the king's duty money was stored; as she looked she happened to catch the sentry's eye. She looked away but soon met another eye, and another and another, all looking the wrong kind of question at her. After a time Jane sensed her mistake; in Satucket she looked at everyone as she passed because they were sure to know each other; in Boston if she looked at someone as she passed it could only be taken as either an inappropriate invitation or an unwanted intrusion. The moment Jane became acquainted with her mistake she fixed her gaze hard on the ground, but she found herself unable to keep it there. She wanted to keep an eye out for all the novelties of town. And its dangers. And Phinnie Paine.

Phinnie's business involved barrel staves and shingles, things that came first to the port of Boston and next from there to the other parts of the colony. He was often in town, traveling by ship or horseback, depending on the required stops along the way. Disembarking from the ship Jane had been occupied with other concerns, and while trapped indoors at Aunt Gill's there had been no cause to worry, but now, out in the street, all was changed. He could be anywhere. She heard that singular laugh from across the road; she saw his unique nose coming toward her through the crowd; she spied the long triangle of his back walking away from her down an alley. It made no difference that in actual fact none of them were Phinnie—at each sighting her mind turned into knots, chasing after an acceptable greeting, as if by chance he would even greet her. What could she possibly say? A letter was difficult enough; a conversation was an impossibility.

Jane continued along King Street. Just before the Town House she spied a small crowd gathered around what turned out to be the whipping post; Jane peered between two pairs of shoulders and caught a glimpse of the fleecy black head of a Negro, eyes rolling in either a state of intoxication or swooning. Beyond the whipping post she was forced to pass two sentries at the Main Guard, but she kept her eyes straight ahead as Aunt Gill had directed. She felt free enough to look in the shop windows, however, and although the butcher's window was bursting with more meat than she'd see in a month at Satucket and the goldsmith's wares blinded her eyes it was as if she'd seen nothing—*nothing*—till she stepped through the door at Wharton & Bowes.

So many books lined the walls it seemed the bookshop had been built of them; more filled the tables and even parts of the floor. Jane picked a book off the nearest table and opened it to its title page: *PAMELA: Or Virtue Rewarded. IN a SERIES of FAMILIAR LETTERS from a Beautiful Young DAMSEL to her PARENTS.*

A young man near her age but far too tall and broad for the size of the store emerged from between the shelves. "Good-day to you, Miss. Henry Knox, bookseller. How may I assist you?"

Jane looked at the book in her hand, her curiosity over the beautiful young damsel driving the real purpose of her errand from her mind. She looked at the book again. *A series of familiar letters* . . . "Letter paper. 'Tis to go to the account of Miss Gill of Royal Exchange Lane. Her usual order."

Knox possessed one of those wide, shining faces that would no doubt look happy under tears, but Jane's request made it shine even more broadly. "Ah! You've arrived! The niece! Miss Clarke, is it?"

Jane dipped her head.

Knox disappeared behind the counter and returned with a packet of paper, setting it down in front of Jane. "And you'd like *Pamela* as well?"

"No! Oh, no." Jane set the book back on the table.

"Not *Pamela*? Well, then, what of *Cleomira Supposed Dead,* or *The Nun the Fair Vow Breaker,* or *The Reformed Coquet*?"

"No, no thank you."

"In truth I'm partial to *The Nun.* Such an exotic, scandalous convent! But Pamela! One daren't leave that poor girl alone a minute. Perhaps if you tell me what you've last read I'll know better how to advise you."

Jane's last reading had been a few snips out of the *Gazette.* She said, "Perhaps if you tell me what *you've* last read I'll know better what to think of your judgment."

The happy moon-face glowed. "Ah! Clever you are! In that case I have no qualm in telling you that I'm reading Mr. Locke's *Second Treatise on Government.* 'Men being by nature all free, equal and independent, no man can be put out of his estate and subjected to the political power of another without his own consent.' At the same time I'm undertaking a detailed study of artillery."

He peered at Jane to see if she took his point. She did. And if Aunt Gill told true of her chatting about Jane's father around town, she also guessed why the bookseller felt the need to make it. Something like resentment on her father's behalf began to tickle her tongue; she said, "I'd not have thought the words *consent* and *artillery* would make such compatible reading."

Knox's eyebrows rose in clear surprise, which would have been insulting if the eyes beneath weren't so filled with delight. "Then I must lend my books to you, Miss Clarke."

Jane said, again, "No, thank you. But I'll take a half-dozen sheets of letter paper to my own charge." She looked at the books on the table. *Pamela* cost two shillings—two days' wage. But Knox's infamous *Nun* was only a shilling ten pence, a savings of half a day. She said, "And *The Nun*, please."

JANE DECIDED TO WALK home along the other side of King Street to acquaint herself with the shops there, but as soon as she reached the other side she ran into a pack of boys outside the Brazen Head, catcalling "Importer! Importer! Importer!" She cut wide around the group, making it the rest of the way without disturbance, but coming from the west it forced her to walk within view of the sentry at the Custom House for a block or more. From the distance he looked only straight and neat; closer he looked clean and young. He watched her come; she knew this because it required him to turn his head sideways, and as she reached the corner of Royal Exchange he touched his brim to her in adieu. So he knew who she was now. He knew where she turned. And she now knew he was indeed the soldier of the dirty boot who lived two doors along.

Chapter Nine

J ANE WAS WELL into her third week in town before her brother Nate finally came by. He had always been what their father had called, enraging Nate, "a pretty boy," but now his body had grown more solid, his face more edged, and the moniker no longer suited quite as well. He swept off his hat and kissed her cheek—a new gesture, but one he seemed comfortable enough in making, as if he'd practiced it a time or two before. She watched him as he crossed the room to make his duty to Aunt Gill and could detect nothing but the slightest limp; only as her worry for him lifted did she feel how heavy it had grown. But this new strangeness in him! He seemed to have receded farther from her than the length of the room allowed.

Nate kissed Aunt Gill and turned around. "Well, Jane, I should like to say what a fine thing it is to have my sister here in town, although I'd like to know what our father was thinking to set you loose here just now."

At the word *loose* Jane looked over Nate's shoulder toward her aunt, and Nate grinned. He understood her yet—nothing would be *loose* at Aunt

Gill's. Some of the hollowness that had filled Jane since she'd arrived in town evaporated. She opened her mouth to ask the first of her many questions lying in wait for her brother, but she was too late—the inquisition had begun. How like her father her aunt was, Jane thought—so uneasy over the subject of politics and yet unable to leave it alone, batting at it again and again as a cat might bat a string.

The questions went on and on. What did Nate think of Mr. John Adams? What case did he work on? Had he met any of the other influential people in town—James Otis, perhaps, or John Adams's cousin Sam, or the wealthy John Hancock, the one they called the rebels' milch cow? Nate answered it all, sounding like the lawyer he'd not quite become, so much so that Jane found herself looking at him again and again, losing the brother again and again; the talk went on so long she itched to send her aunt from the room, her aunt whose kindness alone could account for her brother's being there at all. But just as she feared her impatience had begun to show, Aunt Gill called for Martha, pleaded an old woman's fatigue, and asked to be taken to her room. Intentional or no, it was a double gift the old woman left Jane—to have the long-absent brother to herself at last, and to have been excused her nightly duty besides. For the first time, something of Jane's heart went after the old woman as she left the room.

Jane's trouble now lay in the fact that she'd built up such a great store of questions for her brother that they'd dammed up in her throat. She wanted to know of her brother's health, of course; she wanted to know how he liked his rooms on Cold Lane; she wanted to know if he knew the John Adams that she felt she knew—the man who could cradle another man's messy babe in his arms. She wanted to know if there was a lady in his life, and what about the *qui tam,* and whether he'd heard about Winslow's horse. She wanted to know what he knew of Phinnie Paine.

Such were Jane's thoughts, but as well as she knew her brother it shouldn't have surprised her—in truth it didn't surprise her—that his thoughts would still be on the politics of the town.

"Well, Jane, I suppose by now you've been able to observe for yourself what a fine prison these bloody soldiers have us in."

"I've only observed a few at their posts."

"'Tis enough, then. But we'll get them gone."

"So you're a 'we' now?"

"And you're not? Don't tell me you take up our father's view. But why shouldn't you? You eat his food, why not his words? He won't. Hah!"

Jane smiled, not at the poor joke but at the *hah,* a perfect copy of their father's. "You must give our father *some* credit, Nate. After all, he sent you to clerk for a man whose view he must strongly oppose."

"He sent me to clerk for the man he believes the best lawyer in town. He has his plans for me."

"He wants things for you, yes."

"He wants things *from* me."

Jane peered at her brother. How bitter he sounded! But then again, Jane might join him in that bitterness now. She need only tell him what their father had done to her over Phinnie and they'd be together again. But where to begin it? Jane thought back over the recent events and could think of nothing but the horse, which had nothing to do with Phinnie at all. But she said, because she couldn't seem to move it out of the way, "Someone cut off the ears of Winslow's horse."

It was as if Nate hadn't heard. Was Satucket of so little concern to him now? He stood up. "Adams is on the circuit at Maine. I've his work and mine to tend. I must go. Keep away from the soldiers, Jane." He was gone.

JANE'S WORK WITH GRANNY Hall had taught her successful remedies for any number of things that were known to lay the elderly low, but at the end of that third week Jane had yet to find a symptom in her aunt that she could name. She'd witnessed the sporadic unsteadiness in foot and hand, the remarkable sensitivity to noise, an overreaction to the least change in the air from either cold to hot or hot to cold, but nothing that she knew how to treat, like catarrh or fever or boils. Instead Jane spent her days fetching neck cloths and shawls and thicker stockings, helping her aunt to the boiled rice puddings and meat jellies and chicken broth that she claimed were all her digestion could put down.

There were times, like the time with the bolster, when Jane understood that she needed to step away. She didn't like this thing in herself, this absence of the patience to hover unswervingly over the not ill—she disliked having to step into the hall or the yard or her room just to take a breath, but she found such trips necessary in order to continue in the same calm in which she'd begun. On one such side excursion she came upon Prince and Martha at the foot of the back stairs, and as startled as they were at the sight of Jane, Jane was the more so because she found Martha laughing. The face that would not bend or crinkle or contort for Jane was buckled up into *laughter,* and Prince's simpleton mask had dissolved under the residue sparkle of some recent witticism exposed. There in that minute Jane felt again something of a sense of purpose. Who were these two really? Whoever they were they would not show themselves to Jane, and whoever they were, they worked together as a team. But as least with Jane in the house it evened up the sides.

Jane began to make abrupt stops in her work in order to walk around the house, and she began to come upon other things: a too-secretive look, an ill-disguised sneer, an excuse that didn't entirely account for a servant's presence in the back room or on the stairs or out of doors. But as often as Jane stood guard, as hard as she tried to believe there was a higher purpose to her attendance on her aunt, it wasn't enough to wash away the sounds and smells and sights of Satucket. She missed her sisters and brothers. She missed her newly discovered grandmother. She even missed Nate where she had not expected to have to miss him—she had not expected to come to town and receive but a single call.

―――――

SUCH WAS THE STATE of Jane's spirits that one night, as she settled her aunt into her bed, the aunt took up Jane's hand and said, "What is it, Jane? You're unhappy, I know. What might I do to cheer you? Shall we try again and ask your brother to dine?"

"He'll only plead his work."

"Well then, perhaps we must ask them together. Your brother *and* Mr. Adams."

"Mr. Adams is out riding the circuit."

"Then we must ask when he returns."

Jane gazed at her aunt. The old woman had entertained no one since Jane had arrived, and listening to Martha and Prince where she could, Jane had overheard no reference to any such past events or future plans. Such an invitation to John Adams could only be done for her.

"Thank you," she whispered. Indeed, perhaps she was not entirely alone in this town after all.

WHEN AUNT GILL NAPPED, Jane wrote more letters. Aunt Gill's naps weren't long, but neither were Jane's letters, one day full of shawls and meat jellies being much the same as the other, but the writing comforted her, connected her, even though she had yet to receive any letters from home. She wrote Mehitable: *How fare the little ones? Have you slaughtered the calf? How does Neddy at school?* She wrote Bethiah, making much of Aunt Gill's kind invitations to Nate, hoping to make up for the fun she'd poked at the old woman in her last letter. She wrote, surprising herself, *how empty my bed seems . . .*

When Jane had finished all the letters she could possibly be expected to write she began to read *The Nun*, and after a few days of Aunt Gill's naps coming to an end too soon for Jane's liking, she began to bring a candle up to her bed at night so she might continue on. But after the promised scandal and a good deal of ill fortune the book and the nun came to an abrupt end:

She put off her mourning veil and, without anything over her face, she
kneeled down, and the executioner at one blow severed her beautiful
head from her delicate body, being then her seven and twentieth year.
She was generally lamented and honorably buried.

Not only had *The Nun* cost Jane a day and a half's wage, but it had also
cost her something of her respect for Henry Knox. All the same, she kept
close watch on Aunt Gill's pile of letter paper in hope of being sent back to
the shop soon. The first four pages had gone fast, but the pile sat at eight
sheets for days, then went down to six and sat again, then to five. At four
Jane leaped in with her offer to replenish and was surprised when Aunt Gill
made no objection, even though Prince was at home.

Either the thought of the shop full of books or the rekindled alarm
over perhaps running into Phinnie had overexcited Jane. That was the only
thing that might have caused her mistake, or so she believed later on. As
she reached the corner of King Street, the sentry of the dirty boot was just
completing his march to the corner; Jane smiled and dipped her head in
greeting without thinking, just as she might have done to any passerby at
Satucket, and the sentry answered it with a brimming, "Good-day, miss."

That was the whole of it. A *good-day*. Jane hadn't even slowed over it
and had continued into her turn when a young fellow, no longer boy but
not yet man, came charging into the road from across the way.

"Why do you do accosting this lady in such manner? Who do you think
you are, you bloody-backed lobster? Shall I teach you your manners?"

The sentry's grip on his musket tightened. "Take yourself off, boy.
Don't look for trouble here."

"Look for it! You're the thing itself! You stink of it! You stink of a
stable!"

Jane stepped into the road. "If you think this soldier spoke out of turn
you're mistaken," she said, but the harangue went on as if she hadn't spoken. *Bloody-back! Lobster-back! Bloody-backed rascal dog! Son of a bitch dog!*
Damn your blood! So startling were the words and the vehemence behind

them that Jane stood motionless, staring at the creature until the sentry called to her. "Here, miss! Best get along."

Jane took a step and paused again. Across the street a group of other boys had begun to gather; one of them picked up a clump of dirt and shied it at the sentry. Another. A black mud blossom appeared on the sentry's red coat but he didn't move. Jane attempted to back away and stumbled in the gutter, going down onto a wrist and knee. She was already up and batting at the filth on her skirt by the time the boys had crowded around her, now shouting to the passersby who had begun to close around. "He did it! The bloody soldier! He went after her!"

"For heaven's sake," Jane said, "I tripped, is all," but the crowd didn't, or wouldn't, hear. They drew in around Jane, and the boys saw the mess of her and took up the cry, adding to it as it went along. "He went after her! He chased her! He knocked her down!"

After a time a middle-aged man, respectably but carelessly dressed with a face blackened with rage, pushed into the center and captured Jane's arm. "What's your name? Where do you live?"

When Jane didn't answer he shook her arm. "Speak up, girl; I'm all that's getting you safe home."

Jane looked at the thickening crowd around her. She pointed ahead to Royal Exchange Lane.

Chapter Ten

S HE WAS QUITE unharmed. She said so to the gentleman whose name turned out to be Molineux—a name that rang a vague and distant bell—and she said so to Aunt Gill, but the gentleman merely continued to bark out his own litany about the abuses of the soldiers, and the aunt appeared to have positioned Jane at death's door and could not back away from that view. By the time Molineux left, Aunt Gill was trembling so hard she rattled the cups and saucers on the table to which she clung; she would let Jane alone only after Jane promised to give up her trip to the bookshop and rest on her bed till dinnertime, which only made her feel the want of a book more.

At dinner Aunt Gill ordered her own boiled pudding served to Jane and insisted on suffering with the mutton that had been roasting temptingly all morning long. She insisted again that Jane rest in the afternoon, and in truth, by then Jane was so worn down by her aunt's fussing that she happily went up the stairs. She even slipped into a doze, but found any loud cry from the street brought her out of it. She heard similar shouts to those of earlier in the day—or did she? Was it "bloody-backed dog" or "blackened log"? "Lobster" or "stop her"? And if "stop her," stop her from doing what? Going where? And was that a knock at the door or had she now become Aunt Gill? Yes, a knock. And a familiar voice; two. Jane leaped up and flew down the stairs.

Her brother and her grandfather Freeman had just found their way into the front parlor. Jane hadn't seen her grandfather in more than a year, but she had long ago learned to collect his smiles like ripe apples; this one hinted of something out of last winter's store. Even at his best fettle he was more loose angles than fleshed limbs, but the way his coat hung on his shoulders made her think he'd either been ill or worked into a state near to it. He came directly to Jane and dropped a kiss on her brow; he may have been tired, but he didn't miss the faded scar, angling his head for a closer look. He said, "Tell me, please, child, how do you fare?"

Nate's first words tripped over the last of her grandfather's. "How she fares is the same as we all fare with these bloody red coats in our face every time we turn around!"

Jane said, "How did you hear of this, Grandfather?"

"How did we hear!" Nate answered for *him* now. "The whole town hears! And mark me, those who haven't, shall!"

But Jane's grandfather was still looking at Jane. "Are you injured, child?"

"No, sir. I stumbled into the gutter. When the sentry said to get along—"

"The sentry ordered you along!" Nate again.

"He only meant to keep me safe from the crowd. And I would have been safe enough if I hadn't tried to look backward and walk forward. Which I wouldn't have tried to do if the crowd wasn't throwing mud at the poor man. And all because he spoke to me."

"He spoke to you!" Again, Nate.

"He bid me good-day; nothing more. He lives on this street."

"So he takes that as his right to accost you?"

Jane looked at her brother in surprise; his rage now heated the room. "The sentry accosted no one, Nate. 'Twas the boys accosted *him*."

Aunt Gill said, "'Tis not the boys who've invaded our town unasked and unwanted."

Nate turned to his aunt. "At least *you* know who your enemies are, Aunt Gill! But you needn't fear. We'll settle them soon."

Jane looked at her brother again. No matter how much of the man had usurped his form, no matter how many lawyer's poses he'd learned, he reminded her of nothing so much as the boys in the street. The boy-men.

IT WASN'T UNTIL NIGHT, when Jane had finally settled an anxious and clinging Aunt Gill to sleep, that Jane could turn to settling her own mind, but she found it more difficult than she'd imagined; she felt as if she'd dropped right-side up into an upside-down barrel. Even her father's rages over the papers seemed whitewashed compared to the misplaced fury she'd encountered in the street and in her brother; she didn't yet know where to place her grandfather in the scheme. She wished she could have talked to him alone; she wished—how mad it was—she wished she could have talked to her father.

Her father being her last clear thought as her mind shut down for sleep she was unsurprised when his old words came flooding in as soon as her more conscious thoughts had gone. *Otis. Adams. Molineux. Feeding the lower classes tyrannous articles in the paper and rum in the tavern. Sending them out to so abuse the soldiers it would try the patience of Job.*

Molineux? The same Molineux who had picked her out of the gutter and seen her to Aunt Gill's? In Satucket she would have said yes, it would have to be; in crowded Boston she could say only *maybe*.

IT BECAME SOMETHING MORE likely the next day, when Aunt Gill's newspaper arrived along with her mail. The old woman hadn't gotten far in her

reading when she exclaimed and handed the paper to Jane. Jane read, and
with great effort of will restrained any sound of her own.

> Yesterday at the corner of King and Exchange a young woman being
> accosted by a sentry was brought to the ground and only saved from
> further injury to her person by the speedy intercession of some nearby
> concerned inhabitants of the town.

Jane read it through again, discovering a fine rage of her own. Once
Aunt Gill had settled into her nap, Jane picked up the paper and went to the
door, but before opening it she paused, thinking of the trouble she might
cause the sentry if she sought him out in daylight. She waited through a
long afternoon and longer supper until Aunt Gill was settled into her bed
once again before returning to the front room, to sit by the window and
watch, but it must have been another sentry scheduled for duty that afternoon; her dirty-booted friend didn't come.

JANE WAS FORCED TO repeat her watch for another full day and evening
before she spied the sentry passing by the window. She stepped outside; it
was after ten o'clock at night and the sound of her latch lifting and falling
brought him whirling around on his boot heel.

"Lord God, miss! What're you doing about at this hour?"

"Looking to speak to you. I wanted you to know that what got in the
papers—"

"Had naught to do with you. This I knew when you first spoke up in
the street. Now you'd best get in before one of those rabble from the tavern
sees you."

"Is this what it is to live in this town? Neighbor must fear talking to
neighbor?"

The sentry was silent. Against the lesser dark of the sky she saw the
dark shape of his hat come down. "The name's Hugh White. I know

yours. And 'tis glad I am to call you neighbor. Good night, Miss Clarke."

"Good night to you."

JANE'S NEXT ATTEMPT at Wharton & Bowes began better. She set out determined to keep her eyes off anything in a red coat, and in an effort to do that she walked the north side of King Street, which would put her far from the Main Guard and the sentries on duty there. She also set out determined to keep her mind off Phinnie Paine; he had just come from town in May—how likely that he would be back in July? Jane had no idea how often shingles and barrel staves might bring a man to town; they had seemed to bring him often enough to Satucket, but that was another thing. She thought back over his visits to Satucket—the first had been in September, when she had met him in her father's office; but what had come next? Yes, it had been another visit that same month—she remembered being surprised to see him so soon—but she would hardly call it a visit; she'd met him walking north along the millstream on his way to speak with the miller while Jane had been walking south just returning from an errand to the same. She didn't remember how it had happened but somehow he had turned with her, and they had walked together along the stream all the way to the marsh, talking about nothing. About how he liked the look of a fall marsh. About how she disliked what it warned of—the coming cold. He told her if she thought herself warm she could make herself warm and he bade her try it, holding her hands to judge the heat in them. Jane warmed then and she warmed now, remembering—the touching, yes, but also the matching smiles at the joke of it, the feeling of looking in a glass when she looked at him. How enormous a thing it had seemed at the time, and now it only seemed . . . silly.

Jane came out of her musings and discovered that she'd walked straight past her turn to the bookshop. She looked around. On one side of her was the courthouse and on the other side was the print shop of Edes & Gill, publishers of the *Boston Gazette*. The name *Gill* reminded her that her aunt had claimed a distant relation to one of the publishers of the *Gazette,* a relation that Jane's father had understandably never mentioned; staring at the sign Jane discovered a few things she should like to say to this relation. She pushed open the door and went in.

It would be another boy-man who greeted her, of course, his face spotty, his neck too small for his shirt, his fingernails rimmed with ink and frequently in his mouth.

"I should like to speak to Mr. Gill," she said.

"Ain't in."

"Mr. Edes, then."

"Ain't in nether."

"Then I should like to know how to go about correcting something that was printed in the paper."

"Depends what you're correctin'."

"A false account of an episode that occurred at the corner of King and Royal Exchange."

The boy took out a piece of paper and began to write; encouraged, Jane went on. She had been neither accosted nor insulted by the sentry at the Custom House, she said; the boys—she emphasized the word *boys*—had engaged in an unprovoked attack. The sentry and she had exchanged a greeting, nothing more. She had tripped in the gutter, nothing more. The boy asked for Jane's name and address and she gave it with some pride; she left the printer's shop feeling of some use once more.

At Wharton & Bowes Jane discovered that Henry Knox had read all about the altercation in front of the Custom House, but she suspected he'd heard something else that hadn't been in the papers—the identity of the supposed victim. He came at her in a rush and took her hand, which could only remind her, again, of Phinnie, but she took back the hand long before it might have warmed. "Miss Clarke! How glad I am to see you! But may I inquire—I must inquire—how is your health?"

"My health has never been better."

"And your spirits?"

"The same."

Knox peered at her hard, but whatever he saw seemed to satisfy; he moved the subject along.

"And what report do you make to me on *The Nun?*"

"Another end would have left me better disposed toward it."

"You don't find being generally lamented and honorably buried sufficient reward for a beheading?"

"I do not, sir."

"Then you must take another book in exchange. You see I would please you, Miss Clarke."

Did she hear something in that remark? She looked at him and met so clear a gaze she had little trouble reading the thought behind it. A surprise thrill ran through her. A strange town. A strange man. She was only Jane Clarke here, not daughter or sister or intended wife or even neighbor; there was no father to direct her, no family or friend to presume this or that out of any remark she made. But who might this "only Jane Clarke" be? She said, "I wonder what you would recommend, sir, now that you know something of my thoughts on severed heads."

Knox folded his arms and stared, as if making a great study of her. He disappeared among the shelves. He came back with *The Life & Strange Surprising Adventures of Robinson Crusoe of York, Mariner,* a much larger volume than *The Nun.*

Jane turned to the first page, where a subheading informed her that the first chapter would be about Crusoe's desire to go to sea, his father's wise counsel against it, and his decision to leave home anyway. Jane said, "Does he live, or is he too generally lamented and honorably buried?"

"Ah, Miss Clarke, you must trust me there."

"Despite having been given little reason thus far to do so?"

"This is where the trust enters. But it comes with little risk, as I make no extra charge for it."

"Except of my time."

"Yes. That I would charge you. And perhaps more of it one day." If that weren't quite plain enough he added, "And allow me to assure you, Miss Clarke, once you pass through that door you will be most specifically lamented."

Chapter Eleven

WHEN JANE GOT home she found Aunt Gill in the front room asleep where she sat, the rest of the house settled into a rare and utter quiet—no clattering utensils in the kitchen, no shuffling of furniture or chopping or hammering from any of the rooms or the yard beyond. Jane worked her way down the hall to the keeping room; Martha and Prince stood with their backs to the door, but they didn't stand close enough together; in the narrow space between them the light caught and flashed on a silver coin changing hands. Jane tiptoed back as she'd come.

As Jane turned for the stairs to put away her book, she heard something smash against the front windowpane. A bird, she suspected. She walked to the window and caught the second and third mud balls as they struck. She peered out and clearly saw the face of the boy from Edes & Gill; of the other two boys she saw only their heels as they ran away.

Aunt Gill called from behind. "Jane? Jane? What is it? What's the noise?"

"A flock of birds," Jane said.

THAT NIGHT AFTER THE HOUSE had quieted a second time, Jane took herself down the stairs, barefooted and silent, to her aunt's work basket.

She removed the key from the needle case, slid through the hall and into the back room. She fitted the key to the desk lock and opened the drawer. The silver glinted as she counted the coins: two, four, seven, nine, ten. She counted again, not believing, and came again to ten. All there.

WHEN THE NEXT MONDAY'S *Gazette* arrived along with the post, Jane made sure to capture it before her aunt could see it, but she needn't have bothered; there was no correction inside, only more of the same about abuse by the soldiers. But in the collection of letters for her aunt, Jane discovered a lengthy note from her grandfather for Jane, the first part an apology for taking so long to pay Jane the proper attention on her arrival, his excuse being his absence from town on "tedious matters of lesser import." As a lawyer and representative to the legislature Jane imagined the "tedious matters" that required her grandfather's attention were of greater rather than lesser import, and was all the more surprised when the second part of his note contained an invitation for Jane and her aunt to dine. As her grandfather made sure to note that the invitation included her brother, few things could have enticed Jane more. Jane's only worry over the invitation was that as far as she had been able to observe, her aunt seldom if ever left her home. And if Jane's aunt declined the invitation Jane must likewise decline—her duty lay in attending her aunt.

Jane couldn't have been more astonished when Aunt Gill sat down and wrote out an acceptance to Grandfather Freeman's invitation. It caused such a spark of new life in Jane that she found herself unable to contain it; she leaped up from her chair and kissed Aunt Gill's papery cheek, an act that looked to surprise the aunt as much as it did Jane. But as Jane considered it afterward, she was glad for her impetuous act—Jane now knew that the old woman would not be getting any kind of affection from Prince or Martha, and who else was there within those tall and narrow walls to give it to her? Come to that, who else was there for Jane?

———

JANE'S GRANDFATHER LIVED ON Water Street, two blocks south of King. Right up until the minute his chaise arrived to collect them Jane thought Aunt Gill would suffer one or another effect that would prevent her going out, but she called Jane to help her dress at half after eleven, and they were in the chaise only a quarter hour later than they had planned. Jane again expected difficulty from her aunt's nerves once they were under way, but the old woman appeared more at ease out in the middle of all the noise and traffic than she had been inside her own dwelling. She looked left and right with more interest than alarm and only once cried out to Jane, "Look! There! Does that man carry a musket?"

"A stick," Jane said, with credible assurance, considering she hadn't seen the man at all.

The Freeman house was more like the houses Jane was used to in Satucket—wider than it was long and but one and a half stories tall—the only great external oddity was that it was painted white, something Jane had never before seen. Internally it was so sparsely furnished that it gave the look of a temporary abode, and as Jane thought on it, and on her grandmother's as yet unrealized intention of spending most of her time in Satucket, she saw in it something of the woman's strength of purpose. Her father might have called it her stubbornness.

The women were brought into the parlor by a middle-aged servant named Mrs. Poole, whose fire-chapped face seemed to beam wildly at them until Jane realized she was comparing those lively features to Martha's dead ones. Nate had already arrived, and he and Jane's grandfather were deep in conversation, Nate sitting with eyes wide and lips parted as if drinking his grandfather's words as they came. Exactly what her grandfather talked of Jane couldn't say, as he broke off as the women entered the room, but she guessed it to be political by its tone.

Mrs. Poole collected the men and led the way to the table. As they went Jane again took note of empty walls and cupboards, but the meal that had been set out was far from bare: the traditional plain pudding to start, but followed with soup, fish, roast beef, greens, bread, cheese, butter, jam.

Aunt Gill delivered to Jane her second surprise of the day by eating much of everything, so much so that it made Jane look the laggard. Her grandfather was just urging the beef at her a second time when Mrs. Poole ushered in another visitor.

"Mr. Otis," she announced, and Jane stopped chewing. The visitor was perhaps as tall and broad as Henry Knox, but his reputation lengthened and widened him so that Jane was surprised at the ease with which he glided through the door. Even Jane knew of Otis, partly from the invectives her father frequently delivered against him, and partly from the praise her brother heaped on him. It was Otis who had first raised the question of man's natural rights to such things as life and liberty and property, Otis who had written pamphlet after pamphlet denouncing the policies of Parliament, Otis again who had spoken out as moderator at town meeting and representative in the legislature on the tyranny of Britain's taxation without representation.

Jane looked at the visitor as carefully as she might in all politeness, expecting to see either god or devil in him, but she saw neither thing. He greeted her grandfather with a smile as easy and comfortable as an old shoe; he tipped his head to Nate; he gave Aunt Gill an elegant bow; but when he was introduced to Jane his eyes drew down on her like one of the gulls that forever hovered over the herring in the millstream. There were several empty seats at table, but he pulled out the one beside Jane and sat down.

"Would this be the Miss Jane Clarke of the affair at the corner of Exchange and King?" he asked.

"'Tis," Nate answered for her. "But at least it taught her to keep wide of the soldiers."

Jane said, "Or the boys."

"The boys!"

"I'd prefer a 'good-day' to a mud ball. *Or* to a slander in the paper."

The herring gull's eyes fixed harder.

"I should say it stops short of *slander*," Jane's grandfather put in. "An unsolicited greeting by a stranger might well be called 'accosting.' And you were in fact 'brought to the ground' by whatever means it happened, and it would not have happened had you not been so 'accosted.' And we don't in fact know what might have happened if Mr. Molineux hadn't come upon the scene and assisted you home."

Otis, at last, removed his eyes from Jane. "All very well, my friend, but I must side with Miss Clarke here. The soldiers in this town have been treated abominably."

The table went still.

Otis went on. "Admit it, Freeman. Mud throwing and name-calling are one thing, but the courts—any flimsy charge against a soldier upheld, outrageous fines put down—criminal! The law must not be conscripted to serve one particular cause. To lose the law is to lose the fight."

"With respect, sir," Nate said, "I say when a people are under an illegal occupation they must fight with what they've got to hand."

Aunt Gill said, "And what have we got to hand but a few stories in the paper?"

Jane looked at her aunt in surprise. Another *we*.

"We have the people, Aunt," Nate answered her. "Thirty thousand from all the outlying towns, ready to march at a minute's notice, and all it takes to call them is a flaming barrel of pitch on the beacon hill."

"But what use thirty thousand unarmed people?"

"Oh, we have arms," Nate said softly. "We have arms."

Jane said, "So you would pick up these arms and shoot down the patient and forbearing Mr. White, all for bidding me good-day?"

Again, Otis looked at her, and Jane saw in the look something she would not dare to call admiration but might certainly call acknowledgment, perhaps even endorsement. How strange, she thought, that of all in the room, Otis, the voice of the rebellion, should be the only one to feel for the sentry with her. But as Jane looked at the man again she saw something else. She saw he was not at ease with this feeling. She saw the war in him.

"No thinking man can wish for armed insurrection," he said. "The soldiers must be ordered out by official decree, but such decree will only come once their presence is seen to decrease, not increase the peace."

"The king has already agreed to our petition to recall the royal governor as an enemy of the people," Jane's grandfather said.

"He'd better, or we'll hang the governor as traitor," Nate said.

Otis pushed back his chair so abruptly it knocked into Jane's. "I must go," he said. "I cannot stay. I cannot. I must. I *must* go." He dashed into the hall; seconds later they all heard the outer door open and close.

The table fell as silent and still as the mill wheel in an ice storm. Jane looked to her grandfather for some hint of what had just happened, but he was sitting as motionless as the rest, eyes fixed on the hall door, as if willing his friend to reappear. She looked at Nate, but he'd dropped his head and begun jabbing at the fish bones on his plate. It was some time before Jane bothered to notice Aunt Gill. She'd gone white with fatigue, and her hands trembled as she reached for her teacup; no surprise then, that she dropped it on her plate and it shattered. One of the shards must have caught her wrist as it went down, for a bright slash of red sprang up on it. Jane leaped up and went to work on the wound with her napkin, but it was her grandfather who proved more useful, coming around with a large dose of brandy. The pink began to return to her aunt's cheeks, but it was clear to Jane—belatedly clear to Jane—it was time for them to go.

Jane's grandfather called for the carriage. The solicitations and good-byes and thank-yous went back and forth in their usual course, but at last Jane had her aunt secured inside; she'd just put her own foot to the step when someone caught her arm. She backed up and whirled. Her brother tipped his head as close to hers as his hat would allow and spoke at her through a tight jaw.

"I want to know what you think you're doing. I want to know what you're up to with that soldier."

"The soldier!"

"You keep to Paine."

"Paine! You think yourself our father now?"

"*Me* our father! 'Tis you takes his side. But you hear me, Jane. You keep away from that soldier. The lot of them." His hand tightened and released. He strode off.

Jane stood on the street, numbed. Who was this person who had been her brother? What had he become? What was this rage in him? She gripped the side of the carriage and swung herself in, stewing in her own heat, only to find Aunt Gill slumped in the corner, as if she lacked the strength to sit. All Jane's anger washed away under the cold flood of guilt. Jane's selfish desire for an outing and her aunt's unselfish desire to please her had caused the old woman to tax herself past her endurance; indeed, it had been Jane's annoyance at the talk over the sentry that had caused the conversation to grow overheated and overlong, draining her aunt's limited reserve. And what, after all, had any of it to do with Jane? What had she been thinking in even going to the newspaper? What if the correction, along with her name and address, had actually been printed in the paper? What other than mud balls might she have drawn to her aunt's door? How could she have risked such a thing after all her aunt's explicit warnings on the subject, after all her kindness?

The carriage jounced hard on a curb, and Jane put out her arm to cushion the old woman's frail body. The jolt roused Aunt Gill and added another regret to Jane's list, or perhaps this one was to be laid to her grandfather, as there Aunt Gill launched into a nasty rill of gossip so unlike her that Jane could only blame it on the brandy.

"Perhaps you don't know, Jane, that the great rebel Otis's wife is high Tory; she curtain-lectures him like a schoolboy. Whenever he speaks out against the king in her presence she denies him her bed chamber. And perhaps you don't know either, Jane, that Mrs. Otis has secretly arranged an engagement for her daughter to a captain in the British army. Imagine a British captain in the great patriot's family! But I forget! I forget to tell you! How very rich the wife is! *And* beautiful! But you make your bed, you lie in it. Alone!" And there Aunt Gill descended into such an alarming cascade of giggles that Jane began to fear an hysteria.

A long carriage ride later they reached their home. Concerned about her aunt's unsteadiness, Jane called through the door for Prince and Martha, but neither appeared. After an ordeal full of more silliness than unsteadiness, Jane finally secured the old woman in her bed and was able to climb the stairs to her own. She made the usual preparation for sleep, but even as she did so she knew how fruitless the act of closing her eyes would be. She lay between her sheets like a chastised child, staring into the night shadows, repeating every one of her brother's words, burning again over every one, but especially over three of them. *Keep to Paine.* What did he know of it? What right did he have to speak to her of it?

After Jane had worn down over Nate, she thought she might sleep but discovered instead that Otis lurked behind her brother, Otis and all she had learned afresh of him from Aunt Gill. What might Otis's family have thought of his choice of wife? Had Otis married her, despite her Tory views, only because she was rich and beautiful? Or had he only discovered her views after they were married? If the first, he'd earned his suffering. If the second, perhaps he'd earned that too, for not looking past the *sum* to the *parts* before it was too late to do so. Or perhaps the wife had earned it for presenting herself dishonestly. Or the pair together had earned it, just as she and Phinnie Paine would have had to share the blame for their own mismatching.

There Jane came around to her brother again. *Keep to Paine.* And who was he to say? His last great infatuation had been over a runaway indentured servant who'd gone off to Philadelphia in search of a father she'd last seen a decade before when he'd sold her into servitude. What use his advice then?

Chapter Twelve

ON THE TWENTY-FIRST of July Jane read in the *Gazette* that the governor had dissolved the General Court in response to the legislators' efforts to have him removed. On the twenty-second her grandfather sent word that being free of his duties he was off at the week's end for Satucket, and to send with the bearer any letters Jane wished him to convey. Jane had rushed to her pen and ink, but once again had difficulty in beginning. It was one of those irresistible summer days that had persuaded even Aunt Gill to open the window, and a breeze wafted over Jane like a beckoning hand. She could smell the usual town smells of excess humanity, but behind it she could smell the cleaner smell of the sea—diluted and disguised, but still recognizable as the one she had long known. She allowed her mind to waft away with the breeze to Satucket, thinking to bring her letter to better focus, but a bee had wandered in along with the breeze and begun to knock distractingly against the upper part of the glass. She watched the bee for a time, but at length pulled away and went back to her letter.

Trouble awaited her in the first line. Thus far Jane's letters home had been written as if in continuing answer to the original request from Mehitable for news of her safe passage, and the letters had therefore been addressed to Mehitable alone. Now Jane found herself allowing of a question—was it time to include her father's name in her address? She turned again to the window, to watch the bee fumble his way out, and continued to sit staring out at the chimney tops, thinking of bees.

She had been six or seven years old, her own mother dead, Bethiah's mother not yet arrived, the stepmother in between having put Jane at the task of cracking hazelnuts while she went about the week's baking. It was summer—perhaps late summer—and the door had been left open in the hopes of capturing a breeze to offset the oppressive heat of the oven. Jane had grown tired of cracking nuts and was taking a little rest, pushing damp hair off a damp forehead with an even damper hand, gazing out the door with longing, when a bee zigzagged through it and into her father's empty office. Jane had slid off the kitchen bench and raced in after the bee; as seemed to be the habit with all bees, it had gone straight for the window and begun to bump against the pane. Jane took off her shoe and smacked the bee, crushing it impressively, but at the same time putting a good-size crack in the glass.

The operation made enough noise to bring her stepmother running; her stepmother made enough noise to bring her father running; the whole history of the crime was laid bare in front of them: the crack in the glass, the dead bee on the sill, the shoe in Jane's hand.

"What the devil are you smashing up my windows for?" Jane's father cried.

"To keep the bee from stinging you, Papa."

It wasn't the kind of answer that could have saved Jane, and indeed it had not—she was sent out to scrub down the necessary house in place of eating her dinner—but her father never did fix the pane, and years later, so many years that it couldn't possibly have been the first time he had repeated it, Jane overheard him telling the story to his then-lawyer, Mr. Doane: "'To keep the bee from stinging you, Papa!'"

So Jane sat, thinking about the bee and writing nothing, when a second message arrived from her grandfather—he would not be able to leave town after all, due to new matters that had "chained" him again.

ON THE FIRST OF August Jane woke to the clashing of all the town bells. Bells at the off-hour meant *fire*, and Jane had been in town long enough to know the different tolls—the church nearest the blaze would begin and the others take it up as the news went around, but today they set off all at once, nearly indistinguishable one from the other, except for the Anglican church with its royal peal of eight bells, and the sour note at New North. No matter the reason, the tolling of King's Chapel always sounded sad, but for some reason today it didn't; it swelled and rose and sang out in a happy cascade, joining the others from all quarters. But if not for fire, for what then? Jane was at the window, looking at the blank skyline when the china in the cupboard began to rattle, and behind it came the rumble of a queerly repetitive thunder. She looked up at the sky a second time, and saw nothing but clear blue to the horizon. She dressed in a hurry—Aunt Gill's voice was now ringing out as well—and rushed her aunt into her clothes and down the stairs, the old woman for once as eager as Jane to get below. They arrived in the front hall just as Prince was coming in from the street with the news.

"'Tis the town sending off the governor."

Aunt Gill gripped Prince's arm. "He's gone?"

"Set sail on the *Rippon*. Or would do if he had the wind. Ship sits dead in the harbor." He slipped out the door again.

THROUGHOUT THE DAY THE cannon and bells crashed on, and Jane couldn't help summoning some feeling for the unpopular governor, forced to lie offshore and listen to the merriment caused by his departure, until Prince came back again, grinning his imbecile grin at Jane, reporting that the *Rippon* carried with her thirty-six thousand ounces of Custom House silver, custom paid by the inhabitants of the town. Prince continued to go in and out, reporting to his mistress: townsfolk now lined the shore, jeering at the still becalmed *Rippon,* a great pile of wood was being assembled on Fort Hill for a bonfire, drink was going around and firearms were being discharged into the air, the one no doubt in relation to the other. Jane wished her aunt would order Prince to stay at home and tend to his chores, but he continued to come and go and report, to no good effect for Aunt Gill. Any joy she might have felt over the town being rid of its tormenter seemed overridden by the strain all the noise took on her nerves. She sat white and still in the front room, undistracted by the newspaper or any conversation Jane struggled to offer. Jane brought her some tea but had to hold it to her aunt's lips in order for her to get any of it down.

AUNT GILL DID AS poorly by her supper. As dark came down, a wide fiery band of yellow painted the sky above the roofline—the bonfire on Fort Hill. So brilliant was the effect of the flames that it would have been visible all the way across town; it would have been visible across the harbor aboard the *Rippon;* and it was certainly visible to Aunt Gill. That was when Jane learned that Aunt Gill didn't do well with fire, either—she turned pale and flushed in turns; she wanted to be taken up to her bed, but then asked to be brought down again in case the fire escaped the hill and she got burned up in her bedclothes. Only when Jane insisted the fire had subsided would she agree to go back up again, but long after Jane thought her aunt settled for the night she heard steps on the stairs, and went into the hallway to find Martha coming down them. Jane hadn't heard Martha go up and was startled to see her. Jane was also startled to see Martha carrying a thick, leather case, the kind her father used to hold his most important papers.

"Is there some trouble?" Jane asked.

At first it appeared Martha would pass by without speaking. Jane said sharply, "Martha! I ask if there is trouble here."

Martha lifted her eyes and fixed them on Jane's ear. "She told me. Secure her papers in the cellar."

"She told *you*?"

Martha pushed past Jane and continued down the stairs. Jane continued up them. Her aunt appeared to be asleep, but this could now give Jane no comfort—what kind of instruction could a sleeping woman have given Martha? Jane looked down at what she could see of the shrunken form, nothing but a gentle rill beneath the coverlet, but the cloth rose and fell too rapidly for any kind of peaceful dreams. Jane touched her aunt's shoulder. "Aunt. Do you sleep?"

Silence.

Jane nudged the shoulder harder. "Aunt."

The old woman started up. "What? What is it? The fire!"

"No, no fire. I only wish to ask you . . . I must ask you, did you instruct Martha to secrete some papers for you?"

"What's happened? What happened to my papers?"

"Did you ask Martha to take them to the cellar?"

"T'won't burn in the cellar."

"We shan't burn, Aunt."

She grasped Jane's hand. "You're keeping watch?"

"I am."

"I may trust you in this?"

"You may. In all things."

"Will you stay with me till I sleep?"

Jane sat down on the edge of the bed and stayed there until her aunt's grip on her hand loosened. She stood up but leaned down again to make sure the old woman had remained undisturbed—the illumination from the window just tipped the sagging, papery eyelids and the now-peaceful smile of a trusting child. Jane leaned down and kissed her aunt's forehead as she would, indeed, have kissed a child. She went below to hunt out Martha.

Martha slept in a small room off the kitchen, but Martha was in neither that room nor the kitchen. Neither was she in the cellar; Jane climbed down to make sure and poked about among the cider jugs and firkins of butter and pots of cream and milk, baskets of potatoes and onions. She could find no leather case. She examined the dirt floor but could see no place where the hard-packed surface had been disturbed. As she came up the stairs Martha was just coming through the door.

Jane said, "What did you do with my aunt's papers?"

The inevitable pause, so drawn out that Jane's hand itched to slap the dead face into life. "Sister's cellar's better," Martha said at last and turned away to slide a pot of beans into the oven.

Jane climbed the stairs again, tiptoed into her aunt's room again. She was sure, or almost so, that she could see the glint of open eyes. She said, "Aunt."

The old woman rose up. "What? We must go! The fire's here!"

"No, not fire. I thought you should know. Martha says she's put your papers in her sister's cellar."

"Her sister's cellar! Oh, clever girl. Her sister's house is nearer the water. Thank you, my dear, for troubling to tell me of it. I shan't sleep, of course, but perhaps I'll rest easier." She closed her eyes.

Jane climbed the stairs to her own chamber, but if there was no escape for the governor at sea, there was none for her, either. Her room glowed through the night long after the bells had quieted, and as hard as she'd argued against it to Aunt Gill, Jane fully expected to hear the bells strike up again any minute, to warn of a nearby house ignited by flying cinders. In the end Jane gave up on sleep, went to the window, and stood watching the light-fingers play over the night sky like the aurora borealis. She breathed in and smelled it: the smoke; the ash; the hatred.

JANE HAD BEEN IN TOWN well over a month when she received her first letters from home. Her stepmother had addressed her letter to *My Dearest Daughter* and signed it *Your Most Affectionate Mother;* there was nothing more in the words than the customary epistolary form, but it struck Jane queerly, never having received such words from her stepmother before. She read on, hovering over reports of each child's health, the health of the creatures, the Satucket weather. And then: *I wake each morning in the false ease of believing you still among us, of listening for your determined tread upon the stairs, remembering at last how empty the day shall be because you are gone from it.*

Jane set the letter down, stunned. She thought, again, of the early morning in the meadow, of following Mehitable through the dark, listening to her anxious argument for Jane's remaining at home. Jane had assumed her stepmother had wanted Jane at home because of her heavy contribution to the running of the household—she would also, always, want any breach healed that might disrupt her husband's humor—but rereading Mehitable's last sentence, stopping on the word *empty,* brought Jane to think again. *Was* it possible that her stepmother might miss her? Jane was too far away and too lonely to be able to decide it one way or the other, but one thing Jane needn't have pondered over long—her father's name was not included beside his wife's signature, nor did he send his regards to her within the content of the letter.

Jane remembered another day—a late April day of the sort uncommon in Satucket that carries both the memory of winter and the promise of summer. The branches had looked bare from the distance, but as Jane drew closer she could spot new leaves on the oaks and shadblow and cherry, fat buds on the lilacs. Jane's father had sent her with a letter for the tanner, but Jane had grown distracted as she drew near the millstream—the herring— and the herring men—were at their most frantic and entertaining. She'd watched so long, mesmerized by the music of the water and the dance of the nets, that she'd forgotten about the letter altogether. Her father's words when he'd called her to the office had faded from her memory long ago, but the look on his face lingered yet. To see such disgust and even dislike in a parent's eyes, to see the thought flash as if written in script across his features that he wished her gone from his sight . . . Well, now she was gone from it. Perhaps forever.

Jane answered Mehitable's letter at once, making greater effort with it than she had done heretofore. She began as she had begun before, with *Honored Mother,* but although the words looked different to Jane, she suspected they would look no different to Mehitable. She thanked her stepmother for the sentiments in her last letter, and inquired after her doings and health in a line unto itself, before inquiring in general after the rest of the children, hoping that might be noticed as something beyond the usual form. She made no mention of her father.

Bethiah had also written—a letter of surprising gloom with an undercurrent of anger in it—blaming Jane for going off as if it had been an elopement, hinting at a father in constant temper and a stepmother in her bed more often than she was out of it. At its close she wrote: *I read horrible things in the papers. Papa says 'tis none of it true but I hear other talk in the village. Our brother never writes. I may count only on you. You must tell me all that happens there. I wish you would come home. Your Affectionate Sister, Bethiah.*

So it was to Bethiah that Jane wrote her longest letter. She wrote of the fracas on King Street and her anger over its abuse in the paper. She wrote a fuller version of Nate's visit than she'd included in the letter to Mehitable, more of the distressing nature of the evening at her grandfather's. She admitted to the fear she'd tried so hard to disguise at the governor's send-off. *As the town rages our brother rages,* she wrote, *but I can't help but think his rage comes from something other than the soldiers—he rants so against our father.*

When Jane finally set down her pen she was shocked to discover she'd filled three pages of her letter book with Bethiah's letter. As she read it over she saw that she could never send such a letter to such a child. But *was* Bethiah a child? The fourteen-year-old sister Jane had left behind would never have troubled with a newspaper, and here she was reading it and asking for more news of town. Could she have indeed grown up so far so fast?

Perhaps she had only needed Jane's absence to find the space to do so. Or perhaps Jane was the only one who had changed, so in need of someone to share this new experience that she would advance Bethiah's understanding to meet it.

Whichever the case, it little mattered. Bethiah wanted to know. Jane wanted to tell. She copied out and signed the letter.

Chapter Thirteen

IN THE *BOSTON GAZETTE* of August fourteenth Jane read:

> *At a meeting of the Merchants at Faneuil Hall, August 11, 1769, voted,*
> *that the names of the following persons be inserted in the Publick papers*
> *as importers contrary to the Agreement of the Merchants, viz: Richard*
> *Clarke and Co., Thomas Hutchinson junior and Elisha Hutchinson,*
> *John Mein . . .*

The first name belonged to the cousin with whom her father did business; the next two belonged to the sons of the acting governor; the fourth belonged to the publisher of the *Chronicle*. Jane didn't know the cousin, and certainly her father was safe at Satucket, but the governor's sons, the newspaper publisher, to name these men was another thing altogether. How bold, thought Jane. How foolish.

THAT SAME DAY AUNT Gill sent Jane to Wharton & Bowes again for letter paper. At the corner she risked a quick look at the sentry, but the soldier who stood in the box was a stranger to her—someone older and darker. She continued along King Street, noticing that it lay queerly empty; when she got to Wharton & Bowes she found the shop closed. A languor she wasn't ready to call disappointment dropped over her; she stood in the street before the shop, all purpose washed out of her, until the door opened, and Knox came out with his hat under his arm. "Miss Clarke! How delightful to see you, but I'm sorry to say we're closed. I'd be happy to assist you later, but just now I'm off to the festivities."

"Festivities?"

"Why, Miss Clarke! 'Tis the fourteenth of August—the fourth anniversary of the union of our noble Sons of Liberty and their glorious protest of the stamp tax. They assemble at the Liberty Tree to mark the occasion. Pray, do come with me."

A sudden thrill ran through Jane. To step out into the town, to see something of it besides Royal Exchange Lane and King Street and the few shops that lined them—the idea pushed aside duty and caution together. She would see this place and this festivity; she would follow her own desire for the first time since she'd arrived in Boston. "Very well," she said.

"Delighted!" Knox cried, and indeed he was, or Jane had never stood under a moonbeam. His high spirits drew her along; she forgot about Aunt Gill and began to look forward to her first real enjoyment in two months. Two months? More like three—her last moment of joy in Satucket certainly must have occurred a good long time before her miserable departure. She scoured her memory to recall the last bright day but could call up only dark ones. Well, then, she decided, it was time to begin the count over, and she would begin it today. Today, she would be joyful.

Someone bumped into Jane, sending a second thrill through her, this time of mild alarm, but at once Knox took her hand, pulled it through his elbow, and snugged her securely to his side. Jane felt the muscles in his arm expanding and contracting under her hand as he steered her clear of

manure, carts, and the numerous small boys who inevitably ran everywhere without looking. There was no doubt that this man, of all men,
could keep her safe amid the strife and clutter that was Boston. She relaxed
against him.

They now walked so close that Jane discovered she could recognize
Henry Knox's smell: books, ink, tobacco, the beginnings of the day's sweat.
Phinnie Paine always smelled of horse and sweat when he arrived, but
after he'd been with her father a time he smelled more of rum and tobacco.
Under those surface smells there had always been the real Phinnie-smell,
of course, a thing no other smell could quite wash away—part soap, part
leather, part something else that was like but not exactly like the smell of
fresh-cut salt hay. The fact that Jane couldn't better describe how Phinnie
smelled troubled her until a more troubling thought struck her: if Phinnie were indeed in town, might he be tempted to attend the celebration?
Another thing she didn't know.

Jane made an effort to turn her attention back to Knox—he had now
decided to educate her on the history of the day. Four years before, in protest over the new stamp tax, an effigy of stamp agent Andrew Oliver had
been hanged on the Liberty Tree, carted in a long funeral procession to
the steps of the Governor's Council, and burned in a bonfire kindled by
Oliver's own household furniture. The next day Oliver resigned his com-
mission as stamp agent; no soul being brave enough to take his place, the
false funeral had indeed signaled the death of the stamp tax in Boston.

"But the day marks more than the death of the stamp tax," Knox went
on. "The day marks the birth of the Sons of Liberty."

"And who are these Sons?"

"Men from the high and the low. Men from all the factions in town,
brought together and forged into a powerful weapon against tyranny.
Men you know. Men you don't. Men whose names cannot be committed
to paper for fear of their safety."

Jane considered this and decided she didn't like it—these men might
engage in any actions they desired and never be held accountable for

them—but there was a new fire in Knox that reminded her uncomfortably of Nate and kept her silent.

They had by now covered five blocks along the High Street, and as they walked Jane noticed that Wharton & Bowes wasn't the only shop that had closed in order to observe the celebration. When they reached the intersection of Essex and Frog Lane and she spied the crowd around the Liberty Tree, Jane understood where all the shopkeepers and shoppers had gone. The tree was hung with flags; below it stood a large knot of men and any number of barrels and casks of beer and cider; spreading outward in a tightly packed circle stood what surely had to be most of the inhabitants of the town—women, children, servants, tradesmen, gentlemen, all mixed in together. Jane thought she spied the tall figure of Otis but couldn't be sure; she looked for her brother and might have seen his pale hair under one of the hundreds of tricorns standing next to another diminutive figure that might well have been John Adams; she was three times convinced of Phinnie Paine and three times disabused of the conviction.

Henry Knox seemed content to hang about at the perimeter of the crowd, but whether because he wasn't notable enough to take his place at the core, or because Jane had made him late for his party, or because he wished to protect Jane from the crush, Jane couldn't determine. Standing at the outskirts as they were, they missed something of the speeches, and Jane, at least, couldn't identify any of the speakers, but the toasts rang out loud enough to be heard at Satucket.

"To the king!"

"To the queen and the royal family!"

"To America and her brave Sons of Liberty!"

"To the virtuous, loyal, and spirited House of Representatives!"

"To American manufactures!"

"May the fourteenth of August be the annual jubilee of Americans till time shall be no more!"

The sun bore down; the toasts ran on; Knox joined in with every huzzah from the crowd. Jane tried to imagine Phinnie Paine in such a free expression of his feelings but could no more picture it than she could picture him sitting in the Liberty Tree among the flags. After a time the speechifiers and the casks ran dry together, and the crowd began to drift away. Knox pointed to the group of men mounting their horses or climbing into carriages. "There they go. The brave Sons."

Jane had grown hot on the walk and even hotter standing in the sun; she'd also recognized several of the boys who had been pestering the sentry on King Street. She said, "You call it brave for a man to stand under a tree and make a speech that excites small boys to make his trouble for him?"

Knox looked down at her in surprise. "I call it brave when any one of them could be shipped off to England and tried for treason."

Jane snorted. "As if our king would trouble with this lot!"

"The treason list has already been drawn. I believe you'll find a number of your acquaintances and even one distant relation on it. John Adams, Sam Adams, James Otis, Mssrs. Edes and Gill of the *Boston Gazette*—"

Jane stared at him. "They would ship these men to England and try them for treason?"

"In full knowledge that no jury in America should convict them. Perhaps in full knowledge that no *English* jury should convict them, for they will be tried without a jury in England. Do you know the punishment for treason, Miss Clarke? To be hanged by the neck and disemboweled while yet alive. I don't know who you would put on your list of brave men, but anyone who faces that and dares speak out at a meeting such as this would appear at the head of mine." He was looking down on Jane, but he did not look the same—his little speech had changed him. Or perhaps it had changed Jane. Until that moment she had seen his size and strength and his good-natured ease—now she saw his conviction. Now, perhaps, she saw something better of her brother Nate's conviction. Perhaps these were more than boy-men at play.

Knox still held Jane's gaze. She could not pull away. Here lay all her objection to Phinnie, she thought—his lack of conviction—or so it must be, for it was not the physical strength of Knox that held her but the thing that was held inside *him*, hard and bright at the back of his eyes.

In the end it was Knox who drew away. "We'd best get back." He took her elbow, wheeling her back the way they'd come. Slowly, Jane came out of herself and began to look about at the crowd, now surging with them in the opposite direction. The mass parted and she thought she saw her brother ahead; the gap closed and she decided no; it parted again and she was sure.

"Nate!" she called.

The man kept on. Like Knox, he was gripping a young woman by the elbow, attempting to shepherd her through the crowd. Jane shook free of Knox and took a pair of skips ahead of him. "Nate!"

The man turned around. Yes, Nate. He bent to speak to the woman. He turned again. He stood and waited for them to catch him up. "Jane."

"This is Mr. Knox," Jane said. "My brother, Mr. Clarke."

Nate said, "Hello, Mr. Knox."

Knox said, "Clarke! Delightful to see you again. Fine show, was it not?"

Nate made no answer. He was busy looking at the woman beside him, as was Jane. She was white-skinned and dark-eyed, her hair the blue-black color of a crow's wing; she wore the edgy thinness that came from either illness or nerves. She tipped her head down and left it there, leaving Jane little to examine further but the scarlike part of her hair. There Nate seemed to remember Jane. "Please allow me to introduce Miss Linnet," he said. "My sister, Miss Clarke. And Mr. Knox."

Miss Linnet raised her head. She gave a quarter smile and tugged almost indiscernibly on Nate's arm. If Nate gave any resistance it was indiscernible to Jane; if he had recovered from his outburst over the soldier that too was indiscernible. Nate and Miss Linnet moved on.

————

THAT EVENING, AS AUNT Gill was going through her boiled rice a grain at a time, Jane heard a cry out on King Street that might have shaken the lion and unicorn on top of the Town House to the ground. Prince was again nowhere to be seen; Martha was shifting a heavy kettle; it was left to Jane to go to the parlor window to survey the scene. When she saw what appeared to be a parade going by on King Street she ignored Aunt Gill's yelping from behind and stepped out the door. She recognized them at once: the Sons of Liberty, passing in a great procession of carriages, huzzahed through the street by a cheering crowd, the usual swarm of boy-men running alongside. The last carriage in the line carried Otis, and the frenzy rose there to its highest pitch before it died.

THAT NIGHT JANE BEGAN a new letter to Bethiah, including the events of earlier in the day, spending a fair amount of paper and ink on Miss Linnet, finishing with the parade. She concluded: *Having seen something more of town today you might expect me to have more in the way of description, but one bit of it is like the other—shops, houses, taverns, crowds, noise. Always noise. Why is it we only listen to those who shout the loudest? Oh, how I miss the stillness, the quiet of Satucket!*

Chapter Fourteen

A UNT GILL RETURNED Grandfather Freeman's dinner invitation by inviting not only Jane's grandfather to dine but the Adamses and Otises as well. When Martha heard the news the first crack in her features appeared. "You wish . . . you wish . . . the lot . . . that lot? To dine?"

"Yes, Martha, the lot. To dine. How little work I've given you since Jane's come to ease your load. 'Tis time to end this reclusive life. We shall have them all to dine, and any others that Jane should like to have along. What say you, Jane?"

"Might we have my brother as well?" There Jane hesitated, pondering Miss Linnet. She could not say she'd warmed to this Miss Linnet—she could not forgive that tug on her brother's arm, as if to draw him away from her, as if to hoard him from his own family. But she would not be her father. Let him choose as he would. "And might we include my brother's friend, Miss Linnet?"

"Of course we might have your brother and his friend. Any other?"

Henry Knox, thought Jane. She should like to have Henry Knox to dine. She should like to listen to him conversing with her brother. Or should she?

Martha decided it for her. "You're at nine, Mistress, already overfull at table."

"Why, yes, yes we are," Aunt Gill said. "We must have some other of your friends another time."

AS IT HAPPENED, MISS Linnet did not come, but the remaining eight did indeed fill the table, although one took up the most of it. Jane would have admitted to some curiosity about the infamous Mrs. Otis, but she hadn't troubled herself pondering much on the wife of Adams; once the women arrived however, she found her eyes darting back and forth equally between the pair. Perhaps Mrs. Otis's face and form could claim the beauty, but Mrs. Adams claimed the life, and by the time they'd been at table a half hour Jane gave Mrs. Adams all the liking as well.

Mrs. Otis preceded all into the dining room, swirling the only pro-scribed silk in the room. At once Martha began setting down dishes, and soon the kind of feast Jane hadn't seen at her aunt's table since she'd come to town covered the cloth: onion soup, oysters, striped bass, roast goose, peas, boiled cabbage, and four pies—two meat and two fruit.

Otis said, "Miss Gill, I must accuse you of traitorous sympathies. Clearly 'tis the king you're accustomed to serve."

Aunt Gill pinked.

Mrs. Otis said, "May I remind you, sir, you're not at one of your cock parties above the tavern? You may leave off your talk of kings and parlia-ments here."

Aunt Gill said, "I do hope all subjects might be allowed at my table as long as the general rules of civility are observed."

Mrs. Otis said, "Ah, but my husband is ignorant of the rules of civility, Miss Gill."

"Come, Mr. Otis," Mrs. Adams tried. "Let us prove the case for your civility. I think that the handsomest bass I've seen all season. Would you not agree?"

Otis smiled. "I might top your compliment, madam, and add that I should like to vomit it."

"And there you have all my husband's civility," Mrs. Otis said.

"Hold! Hold!" Otis cried. "You cut too soon! Such would be the finest compliment one might pay one's host in ancient Rome—to vomit a meal to make room for more of it."

"I assure you, sir, no one here is the least interested in Rome."

A hush fell, into which Jane said, "I'm afraid I must confess a great interest in Rome."

Otis turned his eyes to her, the hurt and sorrow and loneliness so honestly exposed making her fear what her own eyes might show. "I have a fine book about Rome I'd be glad to lend you, Miss Clarke," he said. "Their walls. You must make note of the walls. They march across a continent. You see how the walls explain so many things?"

"Of course she doesn't," Mrs. Otis said.

The table fell silent again, all eyes turning from the couple to the food. Compliments on the meal rose up from time to time, but no one seemed disappointed when the talk ran out along with the food and Mrs. Otis rose, announcing it was time for them to go.

Otis stood without argument. He bowed to each in turn. "'Tis my honor, Miss Gill, to have been included in this evening. Mrs. Adams, it is ever a delight. Mr. Adams, Mr. Freeman, my young friend; we shall take our brandy another time." At Jane he paused. "Miss Clarke, my kindred spirit." He followed his wife from the room, leaving behind a silence as deep and gloomy as a cellar hole.

John Adams and Jane's grandfather made their efforts to resurrect the talk, but each failed in his turn; one by one the guests rose to go—the Adamses first, soon followed by Jane's grandfather. Nate stayed behind long enough to settle Aunt Gill into her parlor chair, which pleased Jane, not only because of her aunt's evident fatigue, but because it gave Jane and her brother a chance to speak alone, to perhaps repair what had gone before. She walked with Nate to the door.

Jane said, "I'm sorry Miss Linnet was unable to come."

Nate opened the door. "I must get on."

Jane said, "You and Mrs. Otis in like rush! Must I suspect something there?"

It worked. Nate smiled. "'Tis you and Otis are the 'kindred spirits.' Perhaps 'tis *you* plans to push her out of the way."

"I should like to push her out of something."

Nate laughed, the old laugh, but even as he did so he stepped out the door. No, thought Jane. Not today. She followed him through. "I'll walk with you a ways."

Nate made no objection, and Jane fell in by his side. He even continued the joke along. "In truth, Jane, if you push out Mrs. Otis, perhaps I shall scoop her up—I shouldn't have to beg father for every halfpenny, then."

"But what of Miss Linnet? Is she so easily cast aside?"

Nate gave Jane a sharp look.

Jane said, "I only mean to ask if your acquaintance is long."

"Not long."

"And then of course I must wonder next if Father would approve."

Nate stopped and turned on her. "*You* would ask if Father would approve?"

Jane blinked. "Only to spare you what I suffer."

Nate studied her. "And who do you suffer over, Jane? Father tells me you spurn Mr. Paine, but not who for. It can't be Knox—you can only have met Knox since you came to town. Not Woollen!"

"Not anyone. 'Tis the principle of the thing."

"The principle of the thing! Ah, Jane. You'll come over to us yet."

They moved ahead, the silence proving more comfortable than the words. After a short distance Jane tried again. "What news have you of our father's *qui tam*?"

"'Tis well in hand."

"I wonder too what you think of what else goes on."

Nate paused. "If you mean the horse I think it beneath a worm."

"Beneath our father, then?"

Nate said nothing.

"He did speak to the deacon about Winslow's blaspheming. 'Tis generally acknowledged he left the dam in ill repair. But the mill! Who could believe it of the mill? And the horse! Surely—"

Jane stopped there; they had reached the corner of King Street; Nate had looked left and spied the sentry. "Here now!" he cried. "Why is that man gaping at you so?"

"Perhaps because I'm the only person in all the town who will greet him with civility."

"Greet him with civility! Did I not tell you to keep away from him? You get on home."

Nate strode across the street. Jane stayed as she was. An urge to scoop up her own handful of mud from the gutter and plant it in the center of her brother's back tickled at her fingers. *You get on home.* Instead she watched in disbelief as Nate walked up to the sentry and tapped the heel of his hand against the soldier's chest—once, twice, hard enough to cause the soldier to stagger backward. Jane couldn't hear what her brother said to the man, but it caused him to redden from collar to brow. Sure that he would strike out at her brother she took a step forward, but the sentry didn't move.

THAT NIGHT THE SENTRY'S red face and hot gaze appeared against Jane's eyelids as she prepared for sleep—no surprise then that sleep didn't come. She got out of bed and looked out the window at the narrow, crowded buildings cleansed by moon-wash. She looked up at the sky, all but the familiar triangle formed by the three brightest stars either bleached out by the moon or blocked out by the roofline. She thought of her brother and wondered if he slept, or if he looked out on another street nearby, still raging at the sentry. Or did he stand at his window and think of Miss Linnet?

She thought of Otis and his wife and whether on that particular night they slept together or apart; she thought of Henry Knox and the feel of his arm and the look on his face when he talked of the traitors' disemboweling; she thought of Phinnie Paine and the night on the bed when she'd felt him livening against her; she thought—inexplicably—of Harry Nye.

At the thought of Nye Jane pulled herself away from the window, picked up her shawl, and headed below-stairs after . . . something. Knox's *Crusoe*. Martha's maple butter. Aunt Gill's brandy. At the landing she looked in at Aunt Gill to make sure she slept sound, but the moon had bleached her skin as it had bleached the stars, almost to the gray of death, and Jane felt the old bubble rise up in her chest. She crept closer until she could hear the throaty breathing and turned for the door in relief, but there she turned back again. Aunt Gill was unused to company; Jane had seen the ill effect on her twice now and must remember what she'd seen. She must stand on watch for it; she must stand on watch against Prince and Martha and the advantage they might take—perhaps already took; she must take better care of this old woman in her charge. That much resolved, Jane turned to go again but found herself lingering yet at the door. The urge to touch that gray cheek, to smooth the thinned hair on the pillow, to pull the disordered sheet over the exposed shoulder was so strong it took her unaware. How had such strong affection grown up in her? Was it the effect of the night, the effect of her carnal thoughts, the longing to connect by the flesh to any human being at all, even if the flesh was old and worn?

Jane left the room and climbed up, not down, the stairs. Whatever craving had drawn Jane below had left her. She returned to her room and settled herself at her table with her writing tools. She opened her letter book and began a letter to Bethiah which she didn't owe. When she was through she copied it over and lifted the pen to sign her name, but found herself writing one more line: *I wonder if you hear or see anything of Phinnie Paine.*

Chapter Fifteen

ON JANE'S NEXT TRIP to Wharton & Bowes she saw a new kind of ghost. A couple came walking her way arm in arm, deeply engaged in the kind of animated chat that spoke of a first or second outing. By no stretch could the man in the limp waistcoat be Phinnie, but the woman was Jane—the winter-grass hair, the posture so conscious of the man's eyes, the suggestion of new possibilities about the mouth countered by the pucker of doubt between the brows. Jane could read the girl's thoughts as if she were reading the Wharton & Bowes sign: Could it be right to feel so *happy* just because she was being touched by this man? So Jane must have looked on her first walk with Phinnie along the millstream.

The couple passed by, oblivious to Jane; she heard none of their words, but that didn't matter—no doubt she remembered only half of what had been spoken on that first walk with Phinnie Paine. The feeling had been all, and out of that feeling had grown the boldness to contemplate leaving what she knew for what she didn't know, to contemplate marriage to Phinnie Paine. Where *had* such audacity come from? No doubt some of it had spilled over from Phinnie's abundance, but not all. Not all. And now where had it gone?

When Jane walked into Wharton & Bowes, Henry Knox was much engaged with one of the British officers and she slipped unnoticed between the shelves. She was surprised to hear Knox and the officer going back and forth in utter politeness, even perhaps liking; she doubted Knox could give off so hearty a laugh out of pretense alone. Jane poked among the books until she must have made a noise loud enough to be heard— Knox came bounding into her aisle and cried, "Miss Clarke! When did you come in?"

The officer came up behind. He was near forty, with a pocked face that she almost didn't notice because of the perception in the eyes; as if in proof of it he gave her the kind of close-mouthed smile that promised either more or less, depending on her whim. Knox said, "Miss Clarke, may I present Captain Preston to you. You will observe, Captain, that I present you and yet keep you behind. I know the way you have with the young women in this town."

"I protest, sir. As would my wife. How do you do, Miss Clarke?" Preston bowed.

Jane made her return.

Preston said, "I suspect 'tis Mr. Knox you must beware of, Miss Clarke—I note a certain light in his eye that's new in your presence. But what have you there? Ah! *The Nun!*"

Knox reached over and removed the book from her hands. "She disliked it. I offered *Crusoe* in exchange."

"Ah, *Crusoe*. And do you find him a better trade?"

"I prefer to reserve judgment till the end."

"A most sensible course, Miss Clarke. Knox, you must bring her to our play-reading. Now I must be off. My pleasure, Miss Clarke. And I do hope to see you on Tuesday."

The soldier departed. As Jane looked after him something of her wonder must have shown, for Knox said, "Do you see? You look after him just as all the girls do, pocked face and all! I would know what it is in him that draws you so."

"My intense curiosity at encountering a gentleman in a red coat, having been told by the papers that no such creature lived."

"So you would call him a gentleman? Well let me shock you by telling you I would call him one too. And I shall miss his company once he departs this town, but depart it he must do, along with all his other red-coated friends, gentlemen or no." Knox peered at Jane for a time. "I wonder, Miss Clarke, if it would also shock you were I to take up the captain's suggestion and invite you to the play-reading Tuesday next?"

"Such a thing must be decided by my aunt, as I attend her in the evenings."

"Well then, what would you say if some evening soon I paid a call and begged for your release?"

Jane's first thought was of her father, and what he would say to the rebel Henry Knox paying a call on his daughter. Her second thought was that her father was at home at Satucket and she was away at Boston, and she could do as she liked. Her third thought was the same one over again, only lightened by something like wonder. She could do as she liked.

"I'm sure my aunt would be pleased to receive a call from so ardent a patriot," she answered. She thought it a clever reply, so clever it reminded her of Phinnie, which immediately made it less clever by half, if not all.

AS JANE APPROACHED HER own corner, she found Hugh White again at the box and a pair of young boys, no older than six or seven, accosting him with the same old words: *bloody-back, lobster-back, bloody bitch,* round and round. Jane didn't know what it was that set her loose—perhaps the memory of her brother abusing the poor man, perhaps the ages of the boys and the sense that it would go on generation upon generation without end, just like the Winslow-Clarke feud. She picked up her step and charged toward the boys, clapping her hands. "Get along now! The pair of you! Get home! Go!"

The boys ran. From all the way across the street Jane could see the sentry's smile; it was a thing one never saw on a sentry's face, and that real- ization enraged her as well. She crossed the street to him and said loudly, "Good-day to you, Mr. White."

The sentry said, "Good-day to you, Miss Clarke," still in his grin, but Jane had no smile in her. She walked on.

IT WAS NOT A THING she could talk of to Aunt Gill, nor did she feel like bringing it out when Knox came to call, but neither did she feel like listen- ing to the two of them talk over a rumor of a cache of arms being stored in Faneuil Hall. Aunt Gill seemed to enjoy the talk, however—she stayed up a good deal later than her usual bedtime, her eyes fever-bright, her shawl twice cast aside. When she finally announced her desire to go above-stairs, Knox and Jane rose together, but Aunt Gill waved them back to their chairs. "Stay as you are, please, stay as you are. An old person's bedtime is not a young person's bedtime; Martha may take me up this once. I trust, Jane, you're fully capable of entertaining Mr. Knox alone?"

Jane looked at her aunt in surprise. It was one thing for a father to leave a daughter alone with a declared future husband; it was another for an aunt to leave a niece alone with a near stranger.

But Knox continued on without seeming to notice anything out of the ordinary, intent on his plan. "Before I say good evening, Miss Gill, I won- der if I might ask permission to take Miss Clarke to a play-reading Tuesday next."

"A play? You would take my niece to a play?"

"A play-*reading*, Miss Gill. Not a play performed."

"Oh! Very well. I can see no harm. Martha may wait on me now and then." But there she peered at Knox as if thinking it all over again. "Although I do rest easier with my niece under my roof during the dark hours, Mr. Knox. If you would humor an old woman and hurry her home?"

Knox promised to hurry her home as soon as the play-reading ended, and Aunt Gill in turn promised all the refreshment he should like, waiting for them in the parlor on their return. As Martha led her to the door Aunt Gill stopped and turned. "Are you acquainted with Mr. Otis, Mr. Knox?"

"We've met from time to time."

"I wonder what you would say of these rumors of his mental decline."

Knox hesitated.

"Yes, yes. A delicate subject. And were you not so polite you might tell me not one's business besides. Good night, then."

But after Aunt Gill and Martha had climbed the stairs, Knox seemed compelled to answer the question for Jane. "He has not—" he began. "Of late he has not exactly been—" He fell silent, all his happy glow gone, leaving Jane struggling to think how she might help the conversation to its feet again.

Jane said, "I move along nicely with Mr. Crusoe," and for a second time heard in her voice the shadow of Phinnie Paine, turning the subject from the difficult to the facile. In fact Jane had much she might have said about Mr. Otis, much she wanted to know of him, and in the process she might have learned something new of Henry Knox as well. But Knox took up the subject of Crusoe happily enough, going on to describe all the other books and poems and plays that he had waiting in the wings for Jane, as if safe in the assumption that their acquaintance would be long.

Chapter Sixteen

THE FOLLOWING MONDAY an article appeared in John Mein's loyalist newspaper, the *Chronicle*, printing the cargo manifests of a number of noted patriots which proved them to have been importing goods from England throughout the embargo. Two letters from the customs commissioners appeared in the same paper, accusing Otis of being a traitor to the Crown. Jane wouldn't have seen such a paper in Aunt Gill's house if it hadn't been brought there by her Grandfather Freeman; he carried both *Gazette* and *Chronicle* under his arm, as well as letters he'd collected at the wharf for Jane, and on Aunt Gill's inquiring of the *Chronicle's* latest tricks her grandfather opened the paper and read to her aloud. Jane's first thought on hearing the stories was that her grandfather wished to know his enemies the same as her father did, and she found a queer kind of comfort in the thought. Her second thought was not so much a thought as a warning, albeit a silent one, to the publisher of the *Chronicle*.

Once Jane's grandfather left, Jane turned to her letters. Bethiah had written in a near-frenzy, wanting more of everything, especially Mrs. Otis and Mrs. Adams. *You tell me nothing of the looks of things! And how can you talk of the stillness and quiet of Satucket? Do you forget the sea? The wind? The gulls? Do you forget your father lives here?* Finally, at the end, she wrote: *You ask of Phinnie. He's come but once. He spoke to Papa and left. He wouldn't dine.*

Jane cracked the seal on Mehitable's letter with clumsy fingers. On the first side of the page she read through an account of all the usual illnesses suffered during the summer dog days, of the firing of the tanner's apprentice, of the early returns of the whale men. She included no personal thoughts this time, which puzzled and disappointed Jane, until she turned the paper over and saw the addition at the bottom in her father's undisciplined hand: *I hear from Aunt that you are all she hoped and she has no wish to give you over, which is no surprise to a father who would say the same were your duty done to him as it should. Paine has been here over business and would not speak of you but to say you were a great surprise to him. I made query of what might happen if a letter from you came to him, to which he answered he reads all letters with his name writ across the back, which you may take to mean you have not quite done for yourself yet, either in his eyes or mine.*

Jane's father had not signed his name, which allowed for the exclusion of the customary endearment, not that Jane had expected one. Jane folded the letter and sat thinking of sea, wind, gulls.

THAT NIGHT JANE HEARD the roar of a crowd out on King Street again. She and Prince arrived on the stoop together, just as the cart came by, a creature cowering like a half-plucked bird in the back, lit in part by a lantern he'd been forced to hold and in part by the illuminated windows along the way. Prince dashed down the lane and into the street; Jane went as close to the corner as she dared until she could see the patches of black tar that gleamed through the man's involuntary coat of feathers. As Jane watched, the windows of the only house without a light received a shower of stones through the glass. When Prince returned she asked, "Is it Mein?"

"Couldn't find Mein. Tarred a custom informer instead."

Whose poor luck it had been to choose that hour to go abroad, thought Jane.

THE NEXT MORNING AUNT Gill kept to her bed, complaining of the sweats and an uneasy stomach. She refused any breakfast. Jane made up some of Granny Hall's "gripe water," but her aunt refused that as well. Jane spent a longer than usual amount of time through the morning chasing after various noises; at noon her aunt asked for the newspaper to be brought to her; Jane offered to read to her, but the old woman shooed her away. By supper she seemed somewhat revived and took some broth, but the next morning she again declined to rise. At noon Jane asked if she'd like to get up and take her broth in the chair by the window, but she declined that as well. That night was the play-reading, but Jane couldn't think of going while her aunt was ill; she asked her aunt's permission to send Prince with her regrets, but there Aunt Gill roused.

"No, no, no. You shall not be denied your pleasure on account of any pain of mine. Here, child, help me to the chair."

The chair was gained. The broth was brought. And when Knox came to collect Jane, Aunt Gill was dressed and sitting in the parlor to greet him.

THE NIGHT WAS AS fine as August made them. Their host, John Rowe, lived on Water Street, not far from Jane's grandfather, and Jane would have much enjoyed the walk if she weren't so concerned about her aunt; when Knox inquired how Jane fared with his friend Crusoe it therefore took her some time to reorder her thoughts. She'd finished the book and had pondered long on a man who could leave all his family and lived for years alone, returning at the very end to the old life he had once known, marrying and settling into it with no apparent difficulty. Could she ever return to Satucket with so little fuss? Could she ever return to Satucket at all? Would she ever marry? Or would she end as the nun ended? Or would she marry a man like Crusoe, who could spend an entire page describing a turtle egg and but one sentence describing the wife? Jane decided to mention her thoughts about the unfairness of Crusoe's word allotments to Knox, but to her dismay, instead of fixing on the subject of the writing, he fixed on the subject of the wife.

"There are some wives who require but a sentence," he said. "There are some who require a book. You, Miss Clarke, would require volumes." And he looked at Jane with a meaning she could not mistake.

So it was that Jane walked into Rowe's house with the very beetling on her brow that her father had once criticized, lifted her eyes, and met Phinnie Paine's.

He was leaning against a wall holding a cup of punch and speaking with a British officer, looking so at home that it made Jane feel all the more out of place. She'd brought a silk gown from Satucket, but Aunt Gill had almost toppled at the sight of the imported cloth, so Jane had made a last-minute change to a fine lawn, thinking herself done up well enough until she looked around and saw the fancy shoes and embroidered bags and jewels glinting at every neckline. Very well, but there was no need for her to worsen her effect; she smoothed out her brow, dropped her shoulders, and lifted her head. She looked at Phinnie again, but his attention had returned to the soldier beside him. Jane's instinct told her to cross the room, speak with him, and be done with it, but Knox had taken her arm and begun to guide her in another direction, introducing her first to Mr. and Mrs. Rowe and then to any number of people whose names Jane left behind with their faces, until they reached a Mr. Shaw, who stood alone.

When Knox introduced Jane, Shaw frowned at once. "Miss Clarke of Satucket. I know a Mr. Nathan Clarke of Satucket. What would be your association with this man?"

"He's my father."

"Is he now? Well pray allow me to inform you that he's no friend of mine."

Or mine, Jane might have said. Or, she might equally have said, *then you, sir, are no friend of mine.* She stood and considered the strangeness of it, that either remark might come as easily off her tongue, and chose a third thing instead. "Then I imagine neither of us shall object if I move on." She stepped away, leaving Knox to take a small leap to catch her up. She did spare a minute to wonder if Shaw were a particular friend of Knox's, but she didn't greatly care.

Jane looked around the room and found that their circling had brought them in range of Phinnie Paine, that he'd likely overheard her exchange with Shaw. She couldn't *know* he'd heard it—it was entirely possible that his mouth had adopted that familiar, amused cant over someone else's joke and he only looked her way by accident—but she decided it was time to cross the floor to him and get it finished. She took three steps; Phinnie took only one before someone hailed him from the other side of the room; he slanted off in the new direction. *Coward,* Jane thought.

In due time the parties were directed to the chairs and a gentleman with a florid face and lusty voice began to read: *Now fair Hippolyta, our nuptial hour draws on apace.* Jane shuddered. More wives. She allowed her eyes to drift off and discovered Phinnie's shadowed profile a number of seats to her right. She looked away. Back. She caught the flash of a jewel against a naked throat beside him. Did the woman next to him lean toward him so extravagantly out of lazy posture or was she attempting to work up an intimacy? Or did she already know what Phinnie's hand felt like under her skirt?

Jane looked down at her own hands and flushed. It was odd to think of it, but her hands had touched Phinnie before he had ever touched her. She'd gone out to the barn to rescue him from Neddy; he'd been sitting in the hay with the boy, and he swiped the stuff from his breeches when he rose, but some straw still clung to the back of his shirt. After Neddy ran off Jane took Phinnie by the sleeve, turned him around and brushed him off, thinking as she did so: *This is how a man's back feels,* and there Phinnie turned a second time and swallowed her up. That was how it had seemed—that he had swallowed her up—and she'd learned the feel of a man's mouth on the same day that she'd learned about the back. Woollen, she'd decided that day, could no longer count.

The people in the seats around Jane began to applaud; she looked up; the play had ended. Knox took her elbow and helped her to her feet, but Phinnie had come up out of his seat too and was moving toward her with the kind of stride that implied some purpose. He lost some of his size as he approached the looming Knox, but against Knox's smooth, round features his appeared more finished, as if Knox's sculptor had left off in a rush. Phinnie bowed deeply before Jane—nothing like the quick dip of the head Jane had gotten used to in Satucket, but she responded with her usual country version and let him think of her as he liked. Jane's thought was that a person should be of one place or another, and his place should show on him as brightly as a well-shined pair of shoe buckles or a clever pair of eyes or a fresh-bleached shirt.

Phinnie said, "Miss Clarke."

Jane said, "Good evening, Mr. Paine. May I present Mr. Knox?"

Phinnie smiled. "You might do if Mr. Knox and I weren't already sufficiently acquainted. How do you fare, Knox?"

"Exceeding well, Mr. Paine. *Exceeding* well. I've not seen you about of late."

"I've been at New York."

"New York! And what news have you from New York?"

"None whatever." Phinnie turned to Jane. "And how long do you expect to be in town, Miss Clarke?"

Miss Clarke. Jane listened but could hear nothing of the old *Jane* in it. But what had been the question? How long? And where lay the answer to that?

Knox said, "If I may cast a vote for Miss Clarke remaining in town a long while yet—"

"Ah, but a vote does you no good," Phinnie said. "Dictatorship rules here."

And what did *that* mean? Was Jane the dictator? Her father? Or did Phinnie play at politics with that remark, like all the rest of the men around her? And if so, did he mean the Sons of Liberty dictated, or the royal governor? The British officer to Phinnie's left apparently took it to mean the latter. He swung around.

"Good evening, Colonel," Phinnie said. "May I present to you Miss Clarke? Miss Clarke, you may wish to remember this name—Colonel Dalrymple, the man in charge of keeping the peace in your streets." The colonel made his bow to Jane. Jane looked at Phinnie but still could not determine if he spoke to flatter or goad. But what did it matter? Already he was moving on. "If you would excuse me," he said, "I've had a long day and must here say good night." He bowed again to Jane. Jane didn't trouble with a second Satucket curtsey, as he'd already turned his back.

The night continued on. There was more talk—hours of it. The delights of the play had to be discussed, and the newfound beauty of the nonimported homespun, and the health of everyone's relations. Jane was seldom required to join in with more than the usual smile or the usual small answer, but she answered and smiled until her lips had stretched so tight she could scarcely get them over her teeth.

Finally they were paying their duty to the Rowes and making their exit. Astonishingly, Knox still possessed life enough to chat at her all the way home, but Jane's answers were short and dull and dropped like stones. At Aunt Gill's door Knox said, "Well, Miss Clarke, here we are, and here, I believe, I'd best say good night. I wish I felt sure of giving you some pleasure this evening, but I'm in some doubt of it."

"No! Oh, no! I enjoyed myself immensely. Or rather I should have; 'tis no fault of yours that I did not."

"Now there's a compliment I shall carry to my death. Pray then, where lay the fault?"

Jane made no answer.

Knox's large voice dropped a key. "Do I understand you and Mr. Paine were acquainted at Satucket?"

"Mr. Paine and I were acquainted, yes." And in the words Jane heard the whole of it summed up, ended. One did not contemplate marriage to an acquaintance. She turned to Knox. "My father once attempted to push us together," she said. "I must therefore take care when we meet not to frighten Mr. Paine excessively. I find it . . . wearing."

Knox peered at her. "Indeed. Yes."

Jane moved the subject. "I observed the other day that you and my brother were acquainted?"

"Acquainted, yes, but not well enough. I hope to remedy the situation as soon as I'm able."

"And have you had occasion to meet my father on any of his visits to town?"

"I have not. Although I have heard tell of him."

"No doubt you dislike his politics."

"No more than he must dislike mine. Which evens us nicely, wouldn't you say?"

She might. Some others might not. A wild desire to tell Knox about Winslow's horse bubbled up in her, to ask him what he thought of a man who could do such a thing—perhaps in town such acts were common—but as fast as the desire had risen it sank. She said, "I fear I'm greatly fatigued. I must beg to say good night here."

"Well, then, we shall say good night here." He took her by the shoulders and ran his thumbs over the bare skin just below her collarbone, causing her flesh to ripple. He touched his lips to her temple, where the scar had faded to a small, white line. It was no Woollen. It was no Phinnie. It was . . . Jane had no idea what it was, but whatever it was, it was not the night for it. She slid from under his hands and ducked inside.

THE NEXT WEEK JANE discovered an embroidered bag in a shop not far from the mantua maker's and gave long thought to making it her month's purchase. But at her next trip to Wharton & Bowes she also found a novel called *Clarissa,* whose frontispiece promised to include "The most Important Concerns of Private Life, and particularly shewing the Distresses that may attend the Misconduct Both of Parents and Children, In Relation to Marriage." She chose *Clarissa.*

But when she handed it to Knox with more of her aunt's letter paper he frowned. "Oh, no, Jane, I think not *Clarissa.* Allow me to find you something more to your liking." He began to come around the counter, but Jane only pushed the book back, snapping her coins onto the counter. Why did no one credit her with the wit to make a decision for herself?

"*Clarissa,*" she said.

It took her some portion of the walk home before she realized that she had turned from *Miss Clarke* to *Jane.*

CLARISSA'S PARENTS—AND BROTHER—wished her to marry a particular man, which Clarissa refused to do. In the meantime another man began a pursuit of her—a rake who had some sort of business dealings with her family—and for reasons not made clear to Jane, Clarissa felt called upon to correspond with this man in order to keep her family from ruin. Jane disliked Clarissa at once, which made her irrationally annoyed with Knox for knowing she would. Just the same, as with *The Nun,* she brought a candle above-stairs with her that night so she might continue to read.

Chapter Seventeen

THE STORIES IN THE PAPER grew worse—more stabbings, beatings, attacks on women. Having been at the center of an episode and seen how it had gotten twisted and turned, Jane knew better than to believe all she read, and yet she continued to read it, all of it, as if reading what wasn't true would somehow magically flip the mirror and show her what was. One day as she was reading a particular account of a single soldier who had apparently chased and beaten seven boys all at once, she found an old thought of her father's rise up as if it were one of her own: *if all this were true, there wouldn't be a British soldier with the strength to stand.*

Jane turned from the newspaper to *Clarissa* but fared little better there. Clarissa had been disowned by her family, kidnapped by the rake, and forcibly married, but she continued to defend her virtue against his advances unto her untimely death. The rake was to be despised as a matter of course, but Jane found herself unable to admire Clarissa's virtue as she should. In fact, once it became clear that Clarissa appeared content to waste away, Jane decided she disliked her intensely.

———

ON THE FOURTH OF September an item appeared in the paper:

> *Advertisement: Whereas I have full evidence that The Commissioners*
> *of Customs, have frequently and lately Represented me by name as*
> *inimical to the rights of the Crown, and disaffected to his Majesty, to*
> *whom I Annually, swear and am determined at all events to bear true*
> *and faithful allegiance, for all which general as well as personal abuse*
> *and insults, satisfaction has been personally demanded, due warning*
> *given, but no sufficient answers obtained.*
> *I therefore humbly desire the Lords Commissioners of his Majesty's*
> *Treasury, and his principle Secretaries of State, and all the other who it*
> *may concern, to pay no regard to any of the abusive misrepresentations*
> *of me on my country.*
>
> *James Otis.*

THAT NIGHT HENRY KNOX took Jane to a concert of strings, and Phinnie Paine being absent, she was better able to attend than she'd been able to attend at the play. She was able to attend Henry better too, Phinnie having been purged from her mind, but perhaps she also thought some of the detestable Clarissa. On the walk back to Aunt Gill's Jane was thinking of nothing but Henry's physical self and how close it was, how easily she might touch his hair or cheek or chest, when he reached out and clamped his arm around her shoulders.

"Look!" he said, pointing at the sky.

A brilliant comet with a long, sparking tail careened across the heavens in a lazy arc, as if determined to hold itself above until all below had seen. Jane took in her breath and forgot to let it go until not even the afterimage remained.

"'Tis a sign," Henry said. "'Tis for us a sign. Did you not see how it hung over us as if to say—"

Jane reached up and touched her fingers to his lips, not yet ready for something as earthly as speech. She looked up at the forever-diminished stars, exhaled, and slipped her arm through Henry's. They walked the rest of the way to Aunt Gill's in silence.

No doubt Henry expected that Jane would invite him inside, and certainly Aunt Gill expected it, considering the repast she had promised, but for once the world outside Aunt Gill's door seemed too sane, too peaceful, too *hers* for Jane to give it over to the aunt so soon. And indeed, Henry seemed in no great hurry to go in. She felt his fingers caressing her neck, his lips on her temple. The door opened.

Henry started. "I say!"

Jane pulled back to see Prince, a dark shape against the weak light, but certainly Prince just the same, looking equally startled. He slipped past them and hurried down the lane without words. It was late for a servant to be abroad, especially for a servant in such haste.

Jane said, "I must go in," and left Henry at the door.

Aunt Gill was asleep in the front room. Jane listened but heard no sound anywhere in the house. She picked up the old woman's work basket, searched out the needle case, and found the key. She made her way to the back room, looking for but not seeing anything of Martha. She turned the key in the desk lock and opened the drawer. The coins, all ten of them, were still there.

JANE AND HER AUNT were still at their supper the next night when someone began to abuse the knocker with violence. Prince made speed to the door and returned with a strange Negro behind. He greatly surprised Jane by stepping up to her and handing her a note written in her grandfather's hand. *Jane—If you please—come—at once—to Otis's on School Street—he's received a grievous wound. You may trust George who carries this to see you safe there and back. E. Freeman.*

Jane handed the note to her aunt. The old woman made to rise but tangled with her chair and sat back down. Jane took a step toward her, but she pushed against the air with both hands. "Go, child. For heaven's sake, go." She plucked her shawl off her shoulders and held it out to Jane. Jane wrapped the shawl around her and followed the Negro out the door.

The man walked fast, just ahead of her, nearly breaking into a jog; Jane hauled up her skirt so she could trot alongside. They traversed King and crossed onto Corn Hill, turned again onto School, and paused at the largest house on the street; the Negro led Jane up the steps and inside. The width of the hall, the mirrors, the paintings, the finely turned banister, all confirmed the outer promise of elegance. Jane climbed the stairs behind the Negro and entered a room that she couldn't have described later beyond the curtained bed and the man that lay on it.

Every lamp and candle in the room had been lit and drawn near the bed to better illuminate the patient; Otis's head was wrapped in a towel, and the towel, the shirt, the bolster, and the coverlet were all awash in the ruddy tide that still seeped from his wound; multicolored scrapes and bruises covered all that remained visible of his face, neck, and chest. He rolled his head back and forth against the bolster, his eyes closed, his mouth wide, shouting nothing that made any sense to Jane. Crows. Cows?

Jane's grandfather and a young stranger stood nearby, their shirt-sleeves blood-smeared. A servant girl hovered just behind, her own apron clean. Jane's grandfather nodded to Jane, and she stepped up to the bed. "Mr. Otis, 'tis Jane Clarke. You must lie still now; I've come to check your wound."

Otis opened his eyes. "Miss Clarke?"

"Indeed, sir. Now you must keep as still as you can and let me see the damage done."

"Damage done."

As she pulled the towel back from the wound her bile rose; Otis's scalp had been cleaved so deep she could see the white of the bone. She turned to her grandfather. "Is there no doctor who can come?"

"The regular man could not be found. I've sent George to try to shake out someone else. But my wife tells me you've engaged in some nursing at Satucket—?"

"Alongside Granny Hall. Nothing like this, not on my own."

"Can you do naught?"

"I might clean and bandage, but the bleeding—"

"Can you not stitch it closed?"

Could she? She'd paid close attention as Granny Hall had stitched up Jabez Snow; for that, she had paid close attention when she'd been stitched up by Harry Nye; she believed she *could* stitch it closed. "But what's wrong inside—"

"For the love of God, Jane, do what you can."

Jane commandeered the girl's apron and sent her for needle and thread, and remembering both Snow and Nye, the brandy. She applied the last first, and generously, which went a long way to easing the rest in—through all the pricking and tugging Otis moaned and spoke unintelligible words but kept still enough under her grandfather's and the young stranger's hands for Jane to get the job done. As she worked the stranger began to talk.

"He was at the British Coffee House. They said he went after satisfaction from the customs commissioner, Robinson, for calling him traitor in the papers. They said he asked Robinson to step outside, and the man made as if to come, then whirled around and caught Otis by the nose. Otis lifted his cane to fend him off but Robinson got his in first. The room was full of officers—navy—army—no friend of Otis's to be seen—till I came along. When I walked in Otis was being held by the arms while Robinson beat him with the cane. Held! While they beat him! I pushed my way into it and took Otis's part—also a crack on the arm that looks to have broken the bone." Jane took a quick look at the young man; indeed, his arm hung wrong.

"Gridley," Freeman said with feeling. "You're a noble man. We'll see to that arm as soon as the doctor comes."

The stranger named Gridley went on. "The lights were knocked out;

I could see naught; but I heard the officers shouting—*kill him, kill him*—it took all Otis's strength and mine to batter our way free of them, but not before his head got carved near in two. I managed to get him home—there was no one in the house but the Negro and the servant girl; I sent the Negro for the doctor, and for you, Mr. Freeman—"

And Jane's grandfather had sent for Jane. "Why, Jane," he said now. "You've done a fine job there."

Jane had indeed managed to pull the gap together and bandage it, but there was more to be done. She went with the girl to the kitchen and mixed up a tincture of honey and camphor to treat the other wounds. She sent the girl for clean linens for both patient and bed, and with the men's help was able to shift Otis's large body and replace the soiled sheets and clothes. Otis began to moan and speak as if in tongues of people and places Jane didn't know. He didn't know who Jane was. He thought her his wife, Ruth, or someone named Louisa who had apparently done him an injury in his youth. He called, in turns, for his father and his king, as if not sure which was which anymore. Jane allowed him a sip of brandy at a time, and after a fair amount of it had gone down he passed into something like sleep, if not the thing itself.

The Negro George returned with the doctor, who found little more to do for Otis, but he set and bound Gridley's arm right there at Otis's kitchen table, Gridley telling the story again much as it had come from him the first time, sounding only worse in the repetition. The doctor seemed especially incensed by the grabbing of the nose, which appeared to be an act of such insult that it carried nearly the weight of the beating with the cane. What happened after the lanterns broke was no clearer in Gridley's second telling, but he repeated with exactitude the cries of "Kill him! Kill him!" that had come from the officers of the king.

THE NEXT MORNING JANE brewed up a tea of yarrow, catnip, mint, and sage to treat Otis's fever and received permission from Aunt Gill to carry it around. At the corner outside the tavern she recognized Colonel Dalrymple, the officer Phinnie Paine had introduced her to, and slowed. He was speaking low to another red-coated officer, "Between us, sir, Mr. Robinson beat the other most excessively."

Dalrymple's remark may have been the first Jane heard on the street but not the last. *Otis was very rascally treated . . .'Tis a man's right to ask for satisfaction and to be answered like a gentleman . . . An attempted assassination is what it was!* And twice the same rumor blew by on the breeze—that the customs commissioners had gathered after the brawl to pass and receive congratulations all around.

In the front hall at Otis's Jane found her grandfather and Adams, deep in conversation. Jane's grandfather's angular face would carry the wear of life more plainly than Adams's plump one, but between them the pair looked as carved up as a postdinner fowl.

"We'll get naught against the military," Jane's grandfather was saying.

"A civil action, then," Adams answered. "Breaking the king's peace." He saw Jane and broke off. "Ah, Miss Clarke. Perhaps you might help us as to the nature of Mr. Otis's scalp wound. 'Tis being said a cane—"

"'Twas no cane did that. He was cut to the bone."

"They found five bludgeons and an empty scabbard on the floor."

"The scabbard. A sword. I might have laid two fingers in the wound."

The men stood silent.

Jane said, "How does he fare?"

"Fevered now."

"And the state of his mind?"

The two men exchanged a look.

Jane climbed the stairs to Otis's room and heard him before she saw him. She thought that perhaps by now his wife had been fetched back to town, but it was only the servant girl sitting by the bed, looking almost as wild-eyed as her charge. "He calls out. He calls out nonsense. He thinks me his sister now!"

Jane went to the bed and picked up the cup on the table next to it. It was half-full of brandy. She filled the cup the rest of the way with the tea and held it to Otis's lips. When her hand was at a distance he didn't seem to see it, but as she drew closer he saw the hand and followed it to her arm, from there on up to her face. He said, "You."

"Yes, sir. I've a good brew here to heal you." She held the cup closer; he covered the hand that held it with his own. She could feel the weakness and didn't dare release the cup to him, so he drank with their hands combined, his eyes fixed on her. He said again, "You."

She put her hand against his forehead and felt the heat. He said, "'Tis a great bird—I think a gryphon—he claws at me. He darts about trying to blind me. I should greatly appreciate it, miss, if you would chase him off."

"Do you see?" said the girl. "He's nonsensical."

Jane said, "'Tis not a great bird, sir, 'tis a great wound in your scalp. If you drink some more you might sleep and that will heal you best."

Otis drank in obedience and closed his eyes, but even the task of dropping his lids drew a wince, and looking down at him something of Nate's fine, hot rage burned into Jane at last.

Five bludgeons. A sword.

BY AFTERNOON THE MOB had formed. Henry Knox came to call that evening and described it in more detail than Jane would have liked, considering Aunt Gill's pallor. The crowd had found the civilian who had broken Gridley's arm and carted him to Faneuil Hall to receive his charge, but because they'd been unable to vent their rage against Robinson or the officers at the scene, they took out their disappointment on the *Chronicle*'s John Mein, by painting his bookshop and newspaper office with chamber dung. Jane looked for the sense in this act and found none, but she also found it troubled her less than it might have done a week before.

———

BY THE NEXT DAY Otis's fever had dissipated, the wound appeared clean, and he was better ordered in his senses. He touched Jane's hand. "I'm told I owe you my sincerest thanks."

"'Twas nothing."

"Then you count the contents of this poor skull as nothing."

"I didn't mean—"

She felt, again, like the herring in the millstream; it was perhaps fitting that John Adams should arrive to release her.

As she left the room she heard the pair talking of the civil charges they planned to file against Robinson, and to hear Otis's strength and sense returning gave her greater ease than she'd felt in three days. Jane's grandfather appeared as Jane was leaving, and his relief over her report of the patient's progress took a year of wear off his features too.

Jane said, "You leave now for Satucket?"

Jane's grandfather looked up the stairs. "Soon."

EACH DAY JANE ASKED and was given permission to visit Otis, and she did so for more days than reason could account for. After the first few days Otis needed little if any nursing and it never could be said he lacked for company, but the nature of his company did not sit well with Jane. To most of Otis's guests he was the cause, not the man; even in her grandfather Jane saw a dual motive in his attentions. Many times when Jane visited a third man was also present—Samuel Adams—they clumped together and spoke in hushed tones in the hall. Samuel Adams had a large head, bulging eyes, and arms that were too short for his form. Jane would not have called herself a person who judged another by his looks, but she took an instant dislike to the man. He made no direct inquiry of Otis's health, only asking over and over, "When will he be back? *Will* he be back? Well? Well?"

Jane's other objection to Otis's list of visitors was that it was short by one—the wife didn't come. How bitter or disappointed could the woman be to leave her husband lying in such a state alone? It was perhaps the lack of the wife that prompted Jane to continue her visits. She never stayed long—she checked his wound and his general health and shared in a brief, quiet, almost apologetic conversation over nothing, but always somewhere in it she could see the struggle in him that went beyond the condition of his wounds. When Jane returned to her aunt's she suspected her own distress showed, for Aunt Gill always called her into the front room, sent for tea, and allowed her to talk over her visit; that one small gesture warmed Jane's heart almost as much as the invitations to her brother had done.

Jane continued her visits until Otis's wife finally returned from the country, and there she left off.

KNOX TOOK JANE to a fine dinner at John Hancock's, where the hall was lit with so many candles it turned the room to daylight. Knox paid her the usual attention, but Jane returned it poorly—she was too busy looking around at the officers in attendance and wondering. *Whose bludgeons? Whose sword?* When Colonel Dalrymple came up to greet them Jane could barely make her neck bend, even in its country curtsey. If Dalrymple had indeed been at the Coffee House and seen Otis beaten so excessively, why hadn't he intervened?

Perhaps it was Jane's new anger that heated her. Or perhaps it was her fear of dying like Clarissa, untouched, unopened. Or perhaps it was the specter of Aunt Gill sitting in solitude each evening, waiting on Jane's return. When Knox walked her home and leaned down to drop his usual kiss on her temple, Jane turned just so, lifted just so, and took his mouth flush on her own.

Chapter Eighteen

SEPTEMBER WORE ALONG. Every day in town there came news of another altercation of some kind between the inhabitants and the soldiers, but Jane could no longer think each account a lie; she could only think of Otis lying on his bed with a ravine cut into his scalp and bruises rising like plums all over his face, neck, and arms. She chased no more boys away from the sentry; she no longer nodded to Hugh White when she passed—Hugh White, who had done nothing to Otis or to anyone. She longed to see her brother, longed to discover if this new rage in her would allow them to see each other as of old; she sent around a note, but he didn't come.

If the attack on Otis could make Jane feel so, it could hardly surprise her that the state of affairs in town should become too much for Aunt Gill. She began keeping to her house again, refusing Jane's grandfather's invitations, starting up at the odd noise much as she'd done when Jane first arrived, even objecting to any invitations for Jane that took her from home.

So Jane stayed home, not because she feared for her safety in the streets, but because more and more she found herself unwilling to leave her aunt alone. The old woman's concern for Jane was no doubt part of this surge of feeling, but a part of it had to do with the way Prince disappeared and reappeared at will, and the sidelong glances she continually intercepted from Martha. Who watched whom? What might those two get up to if she were gone? Jane imagined small thefts going on daily behind her aunt's back; she imagined a great one planned for that time when she would be out of the house and Aunt Gill asleep, alone. She imagined her aunt waking to a bludgeon or a sword. But underneath those fears lay a simpler reason for Jane to stay at home, formed out of all the bricks that had been piling up all along the way—her affection for her aunt. Aunt Gill might not have taken the place of the family Jane had left at Satucket, but she had at least begun to fill up the empty spaces that letters could not, that a distracted and distant brother could not.

As Jane stayed at home more, Henry Knox came to call more, an arrangement that seemed to please Aunt Gill as much as it did Jane, although the aunt took care not to hover too long below-stairs. They fell into something of a routine—Aunt Gill would make her inquiry after Henry's health and receive his in turn; she would next inquire after the health of his family and, always, of Otis; she would ask what books he'd sold that day in his store; Henry always answered the last with a heavy list full of philosophers and political pamphleteers that sooner or later sent Aunt Gill calling for Martha to assist her up the stairs.

Jane and Henry would then continue on with the subjects of books for a time. Jane had confessed her aversion to *Clarissa* and vindicated Henry's judgment with the kind of grace that should have come to her with ease and nonsensically did not. The only excuse she could make for herself was that it was one thing to strive to discover everything about someone to whom she was about to be married; it was quite another to be herself discovered by someone to whom she was not. And she *was* discovered. Henry knew to bring plays by Dryden and Shakespeare and odes by Pope—he even knew which bits to read aloud to her and which to not. Some nights Jane found herself looking at him through her father's eyes—or Clarissa's—but her father was in Satucket, and Clarissa was in a vapid bit of fiction. Most nights, at the end of the night, Jane gave over easily enough to the comfort of his arms; long ago she had stopped comparing him to either a Woollen or a Paine.

AT THE END OF SEPTEMBER a lull dropped down, broken in October by John Adams filing suit against John Mein for unpaid bills, forcing the closing of the *Chronicle*. The *Gazette* had only just stopped trumpeting that bit of news when thick clouds muffled the sun and Prince reported a rumor around the docks of a great storm at sea. The next morning it began to blow hard from the southeast; Jane looked out the window and saw objects whirling by so fast as to be unrecognizable; by noon the rain was sheeting down so thickly she could not see out the windows at all; it might have been eight o'clock in the evening for all the light the sky held. Jane, Prince, and Martha ran about hooking shutters, moving delicate objects away from the windows, stopping up the sills and thresholds with old flannels and toweling. Judging by the sound it made—louder than the wind and rain—something of considerable size crashed against the house, but not even Prince dared open the door to look outside.

At one o'clock Prince said, "'Tis high water, now." Jane looked at Aunt Gill, but she seemed to be taking the storm with unnatural calm. An hour or two after Prince's announcement regarding the tide, the wind veered to the northwest, but if it lessened in strength Jane couldn't detect it. The household retired early, like rabbits into their burrows, but Jane doubted anyone slept. She lay listening to the wind beating against the shutters, to the rain scouring the roof, thinking of Satucket and what the storm might have done as it crossed so fragile and low-lying a spit of land; her father's house sat high on a hill, but her grandparents' sat too near the landing for Jane to feel easy. The night crept on.

By morning the rain had turned to a sputter and the heart of the wind had grown soft. Martha checked the cellar and found it dry; Jane and Martha sopped up what water had managed to creep in around the doors and sills; Prince went out to repair two loose shutters. Jane stepped out into the street to look at the debris that had blown and washed into it—sodden newspapers, a man's hat, dirty straw, more leaves and branches than she had imagined remained in so deforested a town—and there Jane remembered her grandparents' other house, their house in town, the house that sat at the end of Water Street, too appropriately named.

She went back inside and found Aunt Gill, out of all the things she might be doing, sorting the thread in her work basket. Jane said, "I worry over my grandfather, so near the harbor. I wonder if you might spare me while I call around."

Aunt Gill looked up. "Of course, of course. If he's flooded out he must come and stay here." She gripped Jane's hand. "I insist on it, you tell him. He must come and stay here." Jane squeezed her aunt's hand in return.

THE AIR REMAINED HEAVY, but the sky had lightened from pewter to silver. Half King Street was silted over with mud and littered worse than Exchange, with branches, boards, shingles, broken shutters, old papers, leaves, straw, and manure fetched up in doorways and corners all along the way. Shopkeepers and residents armed with rakes, shovels, brooms, hammers, nails, and shingles worked at clearing away and replacing what had been lost; Jane could not help but think of the new business the storm meant for Phinnie. She picked her way down Quaker Lane and onto Water Street; she'd covered the greater part of the distance when she came upon the wrack line formed by the swollen tide, seaweed and driftwood and rope and the detritus of shattered boats deposited in a wavering line across the width of the road. She looked ahead and spied several masts askew, a wharf in shambles. A solitary man was struggling to right an overturned cart; a brace of off-duty soldiers passed by but made no effort to lend a hand. She heard one of them laugh, the other take it up and carry it until they drew abreast of Jane.

The nearest soldier doffed his hat. "Good-day, miss."

Jane moved on without reply. Soon she found herself standing beside her grandfather's house before she quite recognized it—she'd been looking for the old elm, but it had been sheared by the wind, half its height and most of its leaves now spread along the ground. In addition to the damage to the elm, the vegetation on each side of the door had been stripped, a pair of shutters ripped off, and eight panes of glass smashed.

Jane knocked, but no one answered. She pushed and it opened; she walked in. The floor was covered with mud and wet; she hallooed and heard an echo from beyond. She found Mrs. Poole in the pantry, her grandfather just coming up the ladder from the cellar, wet to the knees and carrying a pair of dripping sacks. Jane hurried forward and helped Mrs. Poole relieve him of the sacks as he dropped again below. With few words they set up a working chain, Jane's grandfather remaining in the cellar and handing up the stores, Jane depositing them on the pantry floor, Mrs. Poole sorting them into three categories: good, gone, salvageable. When a neighbor and his son stopped by, Jane sent the boy to her aunt with a note: By her aunt's leave, she would stop the night and help her grandfather and Mrs. Poole clean up from the storm. While the son went off on his errand the neighbor stood in the pantry and reported on conditions elsewhere: all the wharves had overflowed and three of the smaller ones had been torn to pieces, warehouses full of sugar and salt and any number of other valuable goods were lost, cellars all along the waterfront were flooded; he would measure the damage at seven thousand pounds.

The son returned with a scratched note from Aunt Gill: *Of course you must stay while he needs you, but you must bring him here tomorrow to dine.*

When the cellar had been emptied of all that was worthy of the labor, Jane's grandfather went outside to board up the broken panes and do what he could with the shutters. Mrs. Poole and Jane rummaged up a cold meal of bread, cheese, mince pie, and applesauce, which tasted as fine to Jane as the feast at Aunt Gill's. After the meal Mrs. Poole returned to her salvage and Jane attacked the floors. Supper was more bread and cheese and a good deal more cider than Jane had drunk in some time, which no doubt accounted for the fine sleep she experienced. Or perhaps it was the room, which reminded her of her room at home, simply fitted out with a maize-colored homespun coverlet, earthenware pitcher and bowl, battered case of drawers, and a small window that looked over the remains of the decapitated elm to the sea beyond.

JANE WOKE TO THE SOUNDS of hammers and saws and carts and workmen calling to one another all up and down the waterfront. She went belowstairs to find her grandfather just finishing his breakfast, but he lingered while Jane dispatched her own. As they had talked the storm through the night before, this morning's conversation took up Mein and the closing of the *Chronicle*; her grandfather's glee was poorly contained, giving rise to more of it in Jane than she'd thought she owned. She blamed the *Chronicle* in good part for what had befallen Otis, and should have liked to have had the chance to say so to her brother, to share such a thing with him, to share anything with him. Surely, she thought, the storm would bring him to call.

Jane's thoughts were brought back to the room with a sound from behind; thinking again of her brother she turned and discovered her grandmother banging a large satchel through the door.

Jane's grandfather stood up, knocking back his chair. "What the devil!"

Jane's grandmother dropped the satchel on the floor. "Now those are the words I've waited five months to hear."

"Don't tell me you traveled through this storm!"

"Well, 'twas calm as milk when I got aboard."

"You didn't . . . You mean to say you came by *sea*?"

"I should like to know how else I was to get here. Jane, how glad I am to see you! And at least *you* appear glad enough to see me." She came around the table and kissed Jane on the forehead. She continued on and grasped her husband's face between her hands. She said, "You look like death."

Jane's grandfather said, "You look . . . you look—"

Indeed, this was not the grandmother Jane had left behind at Satucket. Her hair had been beaten loose and caught back up in a careless, leaking knot, her shawl was frayed—or torn—at one end, her skirt was watermarked with salt and stained with mud and something else that could have been either blood or wine. She said, "How might you expect me to look after being blown almost to Canada?"

"But you were to wait—"

"And just how long did you think me to wait? I walked to the landing day after day, looking out for the ship you were never on. I sat in my house and watched the carts go by in preparation for the next sail, and one day I said 'enough.' I scratched a note for my daughter, packed my bag, and climbed aboard."

Jane's grandfather said, "If you knew how many times I planned to come. *Tried* to come. The political situation has been such—"

"The political situation can go hang. At least for a day. You will grant your wife that, sir?"

Jane's grandfather stood motionless for breath, and then he began to grin, a foolish-looking thing for so dignified a man; but in it Jane saw at once that her grandparents would not be coming to Aunt Gill's to dine.

Jane made her own departure as soon as grace allowed. Once outside she discovered another world than the one she'd left the day before—the sun shone unfiltered through a brilliant blue sky as if the heavens had been washed clean and the tub of dirty water that had washed them had been dumped below. The cart across the way had been righted and moved off, but the foul taste of the episode lingered behind; a glazier and shopkeeper called back and forth the names of the damaged shops and warehouses looted by the soldiers in the early hours after the storm. Where Jane might once have doubted the truth of such rumors, she now found that with little struggle she could swallow it whole.

Chapter Nineteen

THE FINAL EVENT of October came fast on the heels of a premature winter chill. Jane had risen that morning and gone to the window, as it had become her habit to do, and discovered an icy glaze on the gutter below. She pressed her fingers to the glass and felt them go numb; she looked over the rooftops and saw a thick slash of gray that surely held rain—no matter the cold it was far too early for snow. Perhaps it was the thought of snow, of winter in town, that put Jane out of sorts; all she knew for certain was that she turned from the window and found everything wrong: the nearness of the bed to the wall as she pulled up the coverlet, the pitch of the stairs as she worked her way down, even the color of Prince's skin—it should have been the Negro Jot filling the wood box. Throughout the day the images of Satucket persisted, some real, some fancied: Mehitable with her head bent over the babe, the little girls winding wool, Neddy at his books, Bethiah being called into their father's office and given some direction for the miller or the tanner—Bethiah, now the favored one.

The day dragged on like a toothache, and Aunt Gill helped none.

She was cold from the minute she rose, and no amount of wraps could get her warm; she wanted the fire built up no matter how it flamed and bolsters piled around her feet to ward off the draft from the door. In the end Jane bundled her early to bed and returned below-stairs to read her latest gift from Henry—a poem by the slave Phillis Wheatley—but she couldn't attend; the thought of the long winter ahead hung over her like the weighted sky that still refused to unleash what it held.

Such was Jane's state when the knock sounded at the door. It would be Henry, and Jane knew herself poorly set up for his good cheer. She set Wheatley's slim volume down, closed her eyes, and attempted to breathe herself into life; she heard the voice in the hall and her eyes flew open. She leaped to her feet. Martha called into the front room, "A Mr. Paine to see you," and with only that much warning Phinnie stepped through the door.

They stood in silence.

Aunt Gill called from above, "Jane! Jane!"

Jane said, "Excuse me a minute, please." She pushed past Phinnie, into the hall, up the stairs to her aunt's room.

The old woman sat upright in the bed, clutching an empty candlestick, but all Jane's impatience with her aunt had evaporated on her way up the stairs; that minute to gather herself before addressing Phinnie was worth any number of annoying, unreasoned fears.

"Who's here?" Aunt Gill cried. "Who is it? 'Tis not Mr. Knox! 'Tis not his voice I hear!"

"No, Aunt. 'Tis Mr. Paine, a friend from Satucket. No one to fear."

"From Satucket? A friend of your father's?"

"A friend of mine, Aunt Gill. No one the Sons would object to. Your reputation is clear." She leaned over and removed the candlestick from her aunt's hand. She resettled the bolster, and her aunt lay back.

"'Tis terribly cold."

Jane drew the coverlet up high and tucked it tight around the old woman's thin shoulders. She leaned over, dropped a kiss onto her aunt's forehead, and drew herself up, or in, or out, she wasn't sure. On her way down the stairs she recalled Phinnie Paine at the play-reading, talking to the soldier, talking about dictators, and realized she had no idea if what she'd said to her aunt about the Sons was true.

He stood in the parlor, hat still in hand. He whipped around as Jane came in. He looked changed since the play—more cautious about the eyes, more grim about the jaw. He made no bow to Jane, either country or town. He said, "I apologize for so late a call; I have news from Satucket I thought you would want to hear."

Whatever calm Jane had managed to collect on her way down the stairs abandoned her. Her father, she thought. She had long feared his nature too excitable for his health. Or Mehitable, so often ill. And the babe not yet out of that dangerous first year.

But Phinnie had continued. "I thought you should like to know that Mr. Adams has won his case."

So disjointed was Jane's mind that she thought first of Mein—that Phinnie should come from Satucket to tell her about Mein—and no doubt her confusion showed.

Phinnie said, "The *qui tam?*"

"Oh! Yes."

"'Tis good news for your father, then."

"Indeed."

"I knew you to be worried over it. I thought you should like to hear."

"Yes. Thank you."

They fell silent again until Jane realized they stood yet, just inside the door. She said, "Would you care to sit down?"

Phinnie looked around, spotted the pair of chairs near the fire, crossed to the distant one, and sat down. Jane sat down opposite him and stood again. "May I get you some cider?"

"No. No, thank you."

Jane sat down again. "Have you other news of home?"

"Your family is well. As I trust you are."

"I am. And you?"

He made a crescent-shaped move with his head—neither up nor down. He said, "I was surprised to see you at the play."

"And I you."

"You are well acquainted with Mr. Knox, then."

As it was not a question, Jane made no answer. After a time Phinnie's mouth did what Phinnie's mouth did. "Perhaps you're not so well acquainted with Mr. Shaw."

"You know the man?"

"Well enough."

Again, an answer that could be taken two ways. Jane said, "Did you enjoy the play?"

"I couldn't follow beyond the first line."

"Well, you must read it for yourself then."

His eye traveled to the table where Jane had set down Wheatley. "Get myself a copy from Mr. Knox?"

"If you patronize that shop. Or were you a customer of Mein's?"

"I have patronized Mr. Knox from time to time. Perhaps not as often as you."

Ah, thought Jane. So this was to be the game. Well, she would not play it. She stood up. "Should you like a cider?"

Phinnie's mouth twitched. "No thank you. Again."

Jane flushed, sat down. Phinnie did not move or speak. But then, it was not his turn. She searched about for something presentable among her thoughts. "I'm indeed happy to see my father vindicated at last."

"Or to see Mr. Adams vindicated."

"So you think my father guilty yet?"

"I don't speak of your father's guilt or innocence; I speak only of the splendid argument of his lawyer, which I happened to witness, being at Barnstable at the time."

"And I don't ask what you speak of at all, I ask what you think. Knowing my father as you do, do you think him capable of cutting off a horse's ears?"

She heard her mistake before she saw it in Phinnie's lifted brows. He said, "So we've turned fish to horses now?"

It was the usual Phinnie-answer, clever and to the purpose, or at least to Phinnie's purpose, which was to turn away her question once again.

Jane stood up. She said, "Thank you for delivering the news of my father's verdict."

Phinnie stood too. He dipped his head, executed a smart turnabout, turned around again. He pointed at the Wheatley book on the table. "Before I go, I wonder if you would satisfy my curiosity on a small point. Do you take that note as a compliment, considering it contains so great a slur upon your sex as a whole?"

Jane whirled around. The note Henry had sent with the book lay exposed where she'd left it on the table. Henry had copied out one of Pope's shorter poems—"On a Certain Lady at Court," and written across the top "For a Certain Lady from Satucket."

> *I know a thing that's most uncommon;*
> *(Envy, be silent and attend!)*
> *I know a reasonable woman,*
> *Handsome and witty, yet a friend.*

She whirled again. That Phinnie should dare to read her personal note, that he of *sum over parts* should question how a man should pay a compliment!

He said, "It has been my personal observation that reasonable women are no rarer than reasonable men. It has been my further observation that if man or woman should lose his reason for a time it is always possible to regain it again."

He exited the room, banging his hat against his thigh.

———

IT TOOK JANE SEVERAL days to recover from Phinnie's visit. She went back over it and around it and under it again and again. What impulse could possibly have driven him to come? To ease her concern over the case did not hold water beyond the point where he had mentioned Adams's name. And who was he accusing of losing his or her reason? Henry? Phinnie? Jane? She had not understood Phinnie in Satucket, and she did not understand him in town. She was tired out with Phinnie. Tired *of* Phinnie.

And Jane was tired of all that went on around town. As the days wore on, her grandmother's words pressed often on her ears: *The political situation can go hang.* Jane stopped reading about politics in the paper and sought out other stories: *A child born at Freetown was at the time of his birth uncle to ninety-nine persons . . . Fahrenheit's thermometer records today is the coldest of the year so far . . . Mr. Winslow of Duxbury has died aged 101 years, husband to sixteen wives and father to none.*

Jane saw and heard nothing of her grandparents for a fortnight, but at the end of that fortnight she and her aunt received an invitation to dine. Jane prepared to decline the invitation in deference to her aunt, who in addition to her usual poor nerves was nursing an abscessed tooth. Jane could at least treat the tooth with a powder of cloves, but for the nerves she could only continue her attendance at home; she was greatly surprised when her aunt urged her to go to her grandparents' alone.

Otis and Nate had been invited to dine as well; Otis came; Nate did not. Jane, and soon enough her grandparents, or so she suspected, might have wished the reverse. Otis sat down and leaped up and sat down and rambled from topic to topic throughout dinner, beginning with criticism of the food and moving on to criticism of his friends, until at last he landed upon the subject of the king.

"I have one wish, one hearty wish," Otis declared. "That King George might rule forever the father of all mankind."

Jane's grandfather set down his knife. "My dear sir—"

Otis leaped up again. "This country is in ruin!" he cried. "I wish myself never born!" He dashed for the door.

Jane's grandmother got up and returned with the cider jug. Jane looked at her grandfather and saw with some shock that tears stood in his eyes, but no doubt his wife saw it too; as she passed his chair she dropped a gentle hand on his arm.

That night Jane sent a note around to her brother; she had missed him at dinner and hoped he was well. She sat and pondered on the powers of a Miss Linnet for a time but soon discovered that thoughts of her grandmother had pushed Miss Linnet aside. It had been such a quiet thing—that hand dropping down and along her husband's arm—and yet it spoke so loud.

AS JANE HAD PREDICTED, Aunt Gill grew worse with the cold. She glued herself to the fire, wrapped in a blanket now as well as her shawls, and started at every snap of a log. She leaned on Jane more and more heavily as she walked and seemed unable to hold a conversational thought through to the end. She ate little. Once, as Jane accompanied Henry to the door at the end of an evening, she found her aunt standing at the midpoint of the stairs as if lost, and she started so violently when she spied Jane that she nearly fell the length of them to the floor. Jane's concern grew.

BELATEDLY, NATE SENT an answer to Jane's note: he had regretted missing the dinner at his grandparents' but had been kept to his bed with a stomach complaint. That afternoon, as Jane wrote a long letter to her sister in which she was once again unable to offer up any other news of their brother than a stomach complaint, Jane decided something for herself: *she* would make the call. She left her sister's letter on the post table, checked on her napping aunt, and went to the kitchen after Martha.

"If Aunt wakes before I return, please tell her I'm gone on a visit to my brother and will be back soon." As Martha gave the expected blank stare Jane's gaze fell to the seed cakes that had just been removed from the oven, a childhood favorite of her brother's. "And I'm sure my aunt wouldn't mind if I took a few cakes along." Before Martha could speak, if she even intended to, Jane had wrapped up a half-dozen cakes and made for the door.

It was late to be setting out—the sun's winter rays had already weakened—but Jane told herself she would not be gone long. She did not look at the sentry as she passed, and either the cold or the hour seemed to have kept the boy-men at home; the worst Jane encountered were two pigs got loose from their pen. She dodged the pigs and proceeded without further disturbance to Nate's rooms above the wig maker's on Cold Lane. A set of stairs in a questionable state of repair hung from the side of the building, and Jane climbed up with care. She knocked on the door. She waited. In time, it opened.

Her brother said, "Jane!"

Jane said, "I came by to see that you'd recovered from your ail."

"My ail! Yes, yes. Indeed so."

Jane handed her package across. "Then these won't set wrong?"

Nate peeled back the wrapping. "Seed cake! What a good sister you are!" He hesitated. He said, "Come, you must sit down."

Jane looked around the room. The furniture had been knocked about some, as was the way with any furniture in rented rooms, but Nate appeared to have taken surprising pains to make the place neat and clean. He waved her toward a comfortable-looking chair by a good fire, and the very look of it made Jane say before she sat, as if in reminder to herself, "I can stay but a minute." Her brother took the chair alongside and stretched out his legs, soles to the fire, as their father was wont to do. It prompted her to ask, "Have you news of home?"

"A letter from our mother which says the usual naught. I hear more from Mr. Adams."

"What should you hear from Mr. Adams of Satucket? The case is done."

"That case. Winslow sues again over the horse."

So quickly, thought Jane. So quickly could a sentence rub out all the joy from a room.

Silence fell, the kind of silence that had until then been a stranger to any room that held the two. Jane cast her eyes about in search of a more pleasing topic, but she hadn't gotten far when Nate stood up.

"Sister, I am sorry to say I have plans that take me out this evening, but I should like to walk you home before I go."

Jane rose. "'Tis no need. The cold keeps the troublemakers home."

To her surprise Nate didn't argue the point. He stepped to the door and held it open. She kissed his cheek and stepped through; the door closed. She was halfway down the stairs when she heard raised voices from behind the door. Her brother's she knew well enough; of Miss Linnet's she wasn't entirely sure.

As abbreviated as her visit was, it was nearer to dark than Jane should have liked when she started home. More pigs roamed about now, and a collection of chickens; sties and coops must have been blown down all over town. She passed another group of off-duty soldiers and took care to cross the street and walk wide around, not out of fear but out of distaste. How altered her thoughts had become! As she turned into Royal Exchange she looked ahead and saw Prince disappearing into Dock Square at the other end of the lane, letters in hand. But when she entered her aunt's hall she found her single missive to her sister still sitting on the post table. This, then, was how the servant would take his revenge.

Chapter Twenty

IN JANUARY BETHIAH wrote: *Yesterday when Papa yelled for his toast I gave it first to Hitty, who had been quietly waiting, and when he said did I not hear him call for toast I said I did not know it was the rule that we must only listen to those who shout the loudest, as you once wrote me, and oh how Papa raged! Prepare yourself—I shall be sent to Aunt Gill's soon!*

Jane wrote into her letter book: *My Dearest Sister, Come to Aunt Gill's! Come! Come!* And then crossed it out with thick black lines.

THROUGH JANUARY AND FEBRUARY fights began to erupt outside the Royal Exchange Tavern. Jane could hear the noise from within a closed house, as could Aunt Gill, which aggravated Jane's task of keeping her warm, calm, well. One night after her aunt was safe in bed, Jane heard a peculiar howl and leaned out her window to try to discover what could have made such a sound; she saw, or believed she saw, a pair of men disguised as Mohawk Indians bursting out the tavern door.

When Henry came the next night Jane asked him. "I saw two men disguised as Indians at the tavern. Why should anyone disguise himself so?"

"Best ask Sam Adams. He's the one sends them out."

"But why?"

"To stir up the crowd."

When Jane looked her confusion he went on. "When Otis was full of his old fire there was no need of these charades. But now Adams must work at it another way."

"Work at *what*?"

"At keeping the feeling up. These things must be fed or they die."

Jane thought of the two faces, darkened with lampblack and sprouting feathers, which she'd seen from her window. They could have belonged to anyone. There was no reason to think one of them her brother. None.

ON A BITTER, WIND-BLASTED afternoon in February, Jane and her aunt were sitting pressed to the fire when they heard shots in King Street; at the sound of guns being discharged the old woman crumpled in her seat like a pile of ash. Prince dashed out to discover the news and returned banging his arms against his chest to release the cold.

"A great lot of boys were attacking the importer Ebenezer Richardson. They knocked out all the windows in his house. He took out his musket and fired. A boy was killed."

Already the bells had begun to toll. Aunt Gill sent Prince out again and again, and on each of his returns the news grew worse: the boy was but eleven years old; a mob was attacking the house; Richardson was fighting back with a sword; Richardson was secured; a noose had been brought and a signpost selected; William Molineux was working at calming the crowd. In the end Prince reported the lynching abandoned, but Richardson was beaten and hauled through the streets to Faneuil Hall.

MORE FOUL WEATHER CAME down on Boston like hell descending—thunder, lightning, snow—a sure sign from God of his displeasure over the boy's death, or so the *Gazette* reported. On the next Monday a huge funeral procession led by five hundred schoolboys assembled at the Liberty Tree and marched through town. Prince estimated two thousand mourners and thirty carriages trailing behind for a distance of over half a mile.

No one had seen or heard of such a spectacle in all the town's history, and it must have shaken every inhabitant, but none could have been more distressed than Aunt Gill. The morning after the funeral she would not rise; she ate only as much as Jane spooned into her; she cried out three times through the night and the next morning again refused to rise. Jane tried any number of things to rouse her—promise of a blazing fire below, a rereading of the Wheatley poem she had much admired, new wool stockings—but nothing stirred her until more shots were heard on King Street.

Prince was again dispatched, and as soon as he was gone Aunt Gill ordered Jane to help her into her clothes. They had just gained the front room when Prince returned.

"'Tis Otis, full mad, shooting up the Town House windows." Prince laughed. He had made to turn for the door again, but Jane reached out and caught his elbow hard enough to pull him around.

"Who do you mean? Which Otis?"

"The Otis they talk of. The one they call the Honorable James, the Esquire. Tying him up and carting him off now."

Jane released him. She called to Martha to sit with the old woman, pulled her cloak off the peg, and went out into the blow.

An ocean wind ripping up the mill valley floor had never been as cold as the funnel of vaporous ice pushing against Jane as she rounded the corner into King Street. Her chest burned as she breathed, and her eyes watered so that at first she doubted what she saw. The cart sat in front of the Town House; Otis sat in the cart, bound to a chair. The crowd stood around the cart, but at a distance, as if the man were poxed; four men took their places on either side of the cart; the driver gee-ed at the team. The cart moved out. As it drew near Jane she took a step into the street, but Otis never lifted his eyes; he sat staring at his boots, his head snapping back and forth on his neck every time the wheels hit a jog in the road.

HENRY KNOX ARRIVED THAT night with his already liquid eyes made more so by the rum that rose off him like a vapor; he kissed Aunt Gill and offered to take her up to her bed, an offer she gigglingly declined. Once Jane had got her aunt settled and returned to the parlor, Henry picked Jane up and carried her to Aunt Gill's high-backed, thickly upholstered chair, tumbled backward into it, and pulled Jane with him into his lap. Jane had only just recovered from this first surprise when he shocked her again by tucking his face into her neck and erupting into tears. He wept as all men did—in silent gulps and grimaces meant to keep back something that had already left the barn. He didn't cry long, but just where it ended wasn't entirely clear; one minute she had a wet face in her neck and a heaving chest against hers; the next minute she had a hot mouth pressed into the crevice just above the lacing on her bodice and the breathing had taken another turn. Jane took him by the ears and prised his face out of her chest, but he seemed to think she only meant to direct him to her mouth.

It was a kiss full of rum and wanting and spent salt tears, and Jane stayed inside it because of one of those things and perhaps a second of her own. But when she felt his hand rucking up her skirt, she pushed against his massive chest and slid off his lap to the ground. She discovered her bodice was somehow unlaced; she turned her back, fastened it up, and fed out her petticoats till they fell back to the floor. She turned around again and realized she needn't have bothered with the turning around—Henry's head had fallen back against the chair, and his eyes had closed.

Jane said, "Henry, 'tis time for you to go home."

He opened his eyes. He said, "'Tis a British sword did this to him."

"Perhaps," Jane said. "Or perhaps it was the boy who was killed. Or perhaps the times we live in."

"Do you mean to say we shall all go mad with him?"

"I don't know. But you must go home."

Henry heaved himself to his feet, all the towering, rosy, gleaming physical health of him once again in something like command. He took up Jane's hands and pressed the backs to his eyes. "You must know—surely you must know—but I must tell you now—"

Jane said, "Now, Henry, you must go home."

WHEN THE KNOCKER SOUNDED early the next morning, Jane expected to find a sheepish Henry on the other side of the door and beat Prince to answer it, hoping to keep any discussion of the previous night out of range of her aunt's ears; instead she found her pale and heavy-eyed brother. She took him into the parlor and brought him a cider, which he drank down. He said, "I have news of Otis."

"I know it."

"'Tis as if they murdered him. They beat out his mind, and the whole heart went too. And they clap one another on the back and go freely all over the town. If there were murder in me—"

"There's already been one too many murders done."

"The more reason."

"It was no soldier killed that boy."

"It was one of their kind."

Jane let it be. After a time she said, "What news of the case?"

"Case?"

"Winslow's horse."

"Winslow's horse! I'd not be likely to know."

"But Mr. Adams—"

"Mr. Adams declined the case. Did I not say so?"

"No! But . . . why decline? Did he tell you his reason?"

Again, Nate made no answer. After a time he looked at Jane anew. "When Father was here he went on about Paine, again. About how you disobeyed him over Paine."

"Father was here?"

Nate looked his surprise. "A fortnight past. Did he not stop and see you?"

"No."

"Hah! Who would think I should turn up the favorite! I must say, Phinnie Paine seems a fine enough fellow, but I'm not about to argue him to you. 'Tis Knox, then? There you'll get your argument—from Father—though I'd like to know what worse he could do to you. I'll do what I can, but it might hinder more than help, you know. At the least I could create a diversion, provide someone worse for him to take his fit over." He fell silent. Miss Linnet, thought Jane, thinking of the raised voices she'd left behind in Nate's rooms. But Jane couldn't think about Miss Linnet for long. Her father, who had sent her into this roiling, raging madness, had himself traveled all the way to town and not even troubled to see how she fared.

When Jane looked again at her brother she saw that he was looking at her with the kind of fellow feeling she'd almost forgotten he owned. He said, "I told Father what happened to you at the hand of that sentry."

"'Twas nothing happened to me by that sentry's hand! How many times must you hear me say it? I tripped and—"

"I showed him the piece in the paper. He'd seen it, of course, and had been going on in his usual rant about the paper being full of lies. I picked up that paper and showed him. I said 'twas his daughter was accosted and what did he think now?"

"He wouldn't believe it."

Nate looked at her.

"Well, he *shouldn't* believe it."

Nate said, "He's been to town three times now. Has he once called on you?"

No.

HER FATHER, THREE TIMES in town and not once come to call. Her father, being told she'd been accosted by a sentry and *still* not come to call. As soon as dinner was over and Aunt Gill at her nap, Jane took over an errand to the butcher's from Martha just so she could walk her mind into quiet, but the butcher's was not far enough away for such an undertaking. She kept on, making her turns at random, until she came out of her fumes to discover herself on Hutchinson Street, before Gray's ropewalks; Jane had never seen the making of rope before and paused. Thick cables, many hundreds of feet of them, hung in the air, with walkways constructed on each side; men lined the walkways, using long wooden sticks to twist the cables into rope.

Jane made to continue, but as she returned her eyes to the road she discovered a soldier standing in the way before her, staring at the rope-workers; he took a step toward them, paused. Jane had heard from her grandfather of a growing problem in town—the underpaid soldiers hunting for extra jobs and taking up the work that the inhabitants felt was their own. The ropewalks were, no doubt, a popular place for such job searching, and indeed, one of the ropeworkers now called out to the soldier in the road, "Are you looking for work, man?"

The soldier brightened. "Faith, I am!"

"Then you may clean my shithouse!"

The line of men on the ropewalks collapsed into laughter. The soldier's face suffused till it matched his coat; he took three long strides and pulled the nearest ropeworker off the walk and onto the ground. The ropeworker was strong; in no little time he had the soldier down and landed a blow to his face; a pair of soldiers passing by leaped in. Foolish, foolish men! How many ropeworkers were there at hand? Even as Jane thought it they began to pile off the walks and into the melee, pummel-ing the soldiers with fists, sticks, even tar pots; the noise of it drew more soldiers, and soon the street ahead was filled with grunting, swearing, grappling men.

And Jane? Foolish, foolish, woman! She stood like a stuck pig through the whole, and was still standing there when the defeated soldiers scram-bled to their feet and ran, swarming past her on either side. She caught a shoulder in the cheek and a boot in the ankle and only kept her feet because one of the soldiers caught her elbow and dragged her along. Another sol-dier caught her up and shoved her into a third; that soldier took her and shook her till her head snapped back, his mad, blind, raging eyes inches from hers; she drew back and kicked as hard and as high as she could; he let go; she ran. She started to run for home but was too rattled to remember all the turns she had taken to get there; at last she spied a familiar corner—the corner of Water Street—her grandparents' corner. She began to shake. She turned down.

JANE'S GRANDMOTHER PUT CAMPHOR poultices on Jane's swelling cheek and ankle; she swabbed the scratches on her arms with balsam. She took up the brandy bottle and poured it into a steaming cup of what smelled like but couldn't possibly have been real tea; Jane's fingers still shook as she gripped the cup, but she took as long a swallow as the heat allowed. It *tasted* real. She took another.

Jane's grandmother had been talking since Jane had burst in—hard, clipped words that Jane hadn't managed to sort out till now. "'Tis what happens when you quarter two poorly paid regiments in amongst the inhabitants. The winter's been a hard one; the soldiers need wood and a meal the same as anyone. They take any work, and I don't mind saying they've been known to work harder than some. Such it is all over town."

"I should have walked on. I should have walked on."

"'Tis over now."

Jane set down her empty cup and looked at her grandmother. "Is it?"

Jane's grandmother sat abruptly in the chair across from Jane. "No."

BY EVENING JANE'S EYE had begun its journey to black, her ankle had swelled, the scratches of strangers' nails had made vivid red streaks along both arms. Aunt Gill's horror at the sight of her was soon overcome by her horror at the tale; not that Jane had been handled so but that she'd dared to walk about that part of town alone, dared to walk about the *ropewalks* alone. She clutched Jane's arms, if not digging new trails in Jane's flesh then sufficiently aggravating the ones that were already there till they felt new, and extracted promise after promise that Jane would never do so foolish a thing again.

Henry Knox called late, on his first hearing of the news, after an exhausted Aunt Gill had retired. He exclaimed at the sight of her, "Good God! This isn't to be borne!" but from there he turned into another Aunt Gill. "What are you thinking, wandering about the ropewalks? Do you have the least idea—"

Jane held out her arm, her ankle. "I do."

"I can't fathom it! In truth, I cannot! You're not without your wits, Jane."

"Nor are you. At *this* visit."

Henry took her meaning at once, if not her intention to divert him, and swung into a fine apology for his liquored call, but he seemed to have no recollection of its details, a fact Jane found suspect, since in no long time he'd found his way there again. Soon a breast escaped its lacing and a petticoat rose to the thigh; Jane stopped him there, but even as she stopped him she couldn't think *why* she did so. Suppose it ended in a swollen belly? Henry would do by her as he should. Henry would keep her safe. And she must marry somebody, after all.

———

THAT NIGHT JANE OPENED her letter book and wrote, *Honored Father, This day I was caught up in a melee at Gray's ropewalks and mauled by the soldiers—I write you this so that when you read of such an occurrence in your newspaper you may count on its being true.*

Jane set down her pen and sat back, looking at the black words on the white paper—the words of a child. She scratched them through.

Chapter Twenty-one

THE NIGHT AFTER the incident at the ropewalk it began to snow; during the next day and that next night over a foot of the stuff fell. On Monday the sun came out just long enough to melt the top layer in preparation for that night's chill; on the evening of the fifth of March King Street was glazed all over with moonlit ice and snow.

Henry Knox had prevailed upon Aunt Gill to be allowed to take Jane to another play-reading, this one to be held at his store, convincing the old woman that Jane would be at no risk as long as she remained under his substantial wing. Indeed, Jane clung hard enough to that wing, her ankle in some doubt, the frozen drippings from the eaves having thoroughly iced the edges of the road; they walked arm in arm to the store. There were no soldiers in attendance—such was the changed mood in town since the ropewalk—and the evening began dull and stayed so. Henry locked up the store and escorted Jane into the street soon after eight o'clock, arm in arm again, the brilliant moon helping them pick their way along. Soon ahead of them the sentry appeared—Hugh White again—and a pack of boys shouting the usual names. *Bloody lobster! Son of a whore-bitch! Flea-bit dog!*

At the word *whore* Jane reflexively clutched harder at Henry's arm, but White took it as he'd taken all the rest. When another boy stepped into the street and began shouting something about a Captain Goldfinch—that he was mean, that he never paid what he owed—Jane hardly turned. That the insult to his captain would pull White off his post where the insult to his mother would not, Jane could never have foretold.

White left the box and came up to the boy in the street. "Let me see your face!"

The boy stepped up to the sentry, chin in air; White brought his musket around and smashed it into the side of the boy's head.

Jane saw it, *heard* it, and didn't believe. She looked at the staggering, crying boy and still didn't believe. A crowd began to form around the boy, and soon enough they turned their attention to the sentry—the usual names, the usual missiles began to fly, only this time made of ice, not mud. When the first one cracked against White's boot like a lead ball, he fixed his bayonet, lowered his musket. Henry dropped Jane's arm and hurried toward the sentry. "Here, now do you wish to die? I promise you, fire and you shall!"

"Damn them!" White shouted. "If they molest me I'll fire!"

Henry turned to the boys. "Get on home! Get on! Stop molesting the sentry!"

No one moved. Jane noticed there were more of them now and that they weren't all boys, weren't even boy-men; some of the men she recognized from the affray at the ropewalks. Too many of the men. From somewhere nearby a church bell began to ring, the call for fire; another bell took it up and another. More men began to appear out of the alleys, some carrying buckets, some clubs. They swarmed around the sentry; he looked wildly left and right; he screamed, "Call out the Main Guard!"

The Main Guard was barracked no great distance down King Street. In no time a column of grenadiers, the tallest of the king's soldiers, marched into view, their high bearskin hats making them taller still. Jane recognized Captain Preston marching beside the column; she recognized one of the soldiers who had been knocked to the ground at the ropewalks. A boy stepped into the road in front of the column, and one of the lead soldiers shouted at him, "Stand out of our way!" The boy didn't move. A bayonet gleamed—all the bayonets gleamed—like ice under the moon, but the column parted calmly around the boy and continued on.

In the meantime Henry had been working hard on the crowd, urging them to go home, but no one paid him any mind. When he saw Preston he crossed the road and caught hold of his sleeve. "For God's sake, Captain, take care of your men! If they fire, you die!"

Preston shook him off. "I am sensible of it, sir!" The grenadiers marched on to the sentry box; Preston ordered White to fall in with the line and attempted to swing it around, to march it back as it had come, but the crowd had pressed in too tight; it would have taken the bayonets to make room to move.

The press of the crowd had also separated Jane from Henry. She looked for him as Preston gave up on marching and fanned out his men in a semicircle, backs to the Custom House, bayonets to the crowd. Hugh White had taken up a position nearest Jane; he saw her and called out, "Miss Clarke! For God's sake, go home or you'll be killed!"

Jane would have liked to go home—she would have very much liked it—but she had better chance of getting to Satucket than she did of getting through the crowd that blocked the entrance to Royal Exchange Lane. She pulled back as near as she could to the tavern wall and watched in horror as Preston's pleas to disperse the crowd were met by curses, chunks of ice, even rocks now. Bodies in the back pushed against bodies in the front to see what went on; the press against the soldiers grew. Jane was so close she could see Hugh White trembling, but whether from rage or fear she couldn't know.

A cry went up from the street: "Damn you, you sons of bitches, fire! You can't kill us all!" The cry was taken up through the crowd. *Fire! Why do you not fire? Fire and be damned!* So close were the two sides that Jane could hear the smack of sticks and clubs against musket barrels, but by now the two sides had become less well defined. A townsman in a dark-colored cloak slipped out of the crowd and behind the soldiers' line; he began to pace up and down behind the soldiers, calling to them, "Fire! Fire! Be the consequence what it will!" Jane looked back and found Preston standing in front of his men, his mouth fixed in a hard line. A club sailed over the crowd and out into the moonlight, catching one of the soldiers dead on; he went down on his hindquarters, the musket clattering to the ground. He struggled up in visible rage. "Damn you, fire!" he shouted to his fellow soldiers and discharged his musket. Jane looked again at Preston, still standing between his men and the mob. She thought, *If they fire, he dies,* but unbelievably, the soldiers held. Someone from the crowd swung a club, and it glanced off Preston; if it had found its mark his head would have been a match for Otis's. He stepped back and the cry rang out loud from behind the soldiers: "Fire by God, I'll stand by you!"

And there the soldiers fired. It came in no concerted volley but in random bursts—a muzzle-flare here, another there, the flash of powder bright against the red coats, the sound bouncing off the stone in the street and the brick in the walls. The bodies began to fall. There followed the kind of silence that comes with disbelief, with horrified wonder; the next sound Jane heard was the *click-click-click* of the soldiers' muskets as they were loaded and cocked all around.

The crowd heard the sound too. It drew back. Preston heard it and ran along the line of men, knocking up their guns. "Stop firing!" he shouted. "Do not fire!"

That fast, it ended. Preston ordered his soldiers to fall in and began to march them back down King Street; the crowd saw the soldiers moving off and stepped in to see to their dead and wounded. Jane found Henry leaning over the body of a big mulatto, but he stood up and left the body to lie, pulling Jane back under his arm. She could feel his heart thrumming, thrumming, thrumming. Or was it her own? "For the love of God," he said. "Come. I must get you home."

Too late. Henry was too late. And besides, lying there in the street was, at last, something Jane could do. She twisted free of Henry; someone called to him from the outskirts of the crowd; he slipped out of her field of vision, and she thought of him no more. She moved swiftly to the nearest motionless form lying in the snow; she leaned over and felt for life—none. She straightened and moved to the next, this one struggling to sit up, and Jane helped him, steadied him, until two men came forward to lead him off. The next victim had suffered a head wound that bled freely, which meant life; Jane took her teeth to the lining of her cloak and ripped out enough cloth to compress it against the gash; after a time more men came and carried that victim off as well. Next she found a weeping boy, apparently unharmed but too frightened to move, and Jane knelt and comforted him until a young woman came and took him away. Next she found her brother.

Jane dropped onto her knees in the hard-packed snow. Nate was sitting up, propped on the one side by an old woman clutching his jacket and on the other by a young boy gripping his elbow. His queue was untied, his jacket half off his shoulders, his stockings torn, as if all the rage inside him had finally blown outward, but where was the evidence of the soldiers' rage that had blown him to the ground? Jane saw no blood or wound. "Are you all right?"

"Right."

"What hurts you?"

"Right. Bloody right."

Jane stepped closer to the old woman, signaling to her that she had taken the patient into her care now; the old woman drifted away into the remains of the crowd. Closer now, Jane could see the tear in the shoulder of her brother's coat; she peeled it back and saw the discoloration on the shirt, dark on light; blood. The wound.

She said, "Your shoulder? It hurts?"

"Right."

"What else? What else hurts? Can you stand?"

In answer Nate scuffled his heels across the snow, and without speaking Jane and the boy lifted; Nate was not steady on his feet, and the iced-over street helped none. The boy, however, helped greatly—he took his half of the weight and more and followed Jane's directions well: "This way. Left. Back, now. Here. Turn." They walked, swaying, teetering, past the tavern, up to Aunt Gill's door. The boy freed a hand to rap on the wood hard. Jane heard steps within and the door opened to Prince, with Martha standing behind. Prince would have been out to discover the trouble, of course. Prince would have come home and told. Prince, who might have helped and had instead run home to gossip for his mistress. Jane felt the beginnings of the old rage form, but before she could feed it into flame Prince came around and took the boy's place, leading Nate through the keeping room to the small bedroom beyond, the room nearest the central fire. Jane removed her brother's jacket and shirt, in fear of the worst, but in truth she was relieved at the site of the wound. The flesh had been penetrated, yes, but the bleeding had already stopped, or close to; she called to Martha for water and cloth and her juniper tincture to clean the wound.

"You right," Nate said as Jane swabbed his skin.

"I'm fine," Jane answered.

"Bloody right," Nate said. The words were half nonsensical, but Jane didn't—wouldn't—fear for his mind. "Brandy, please," she said to anyone, and Martha returned so quickly with a mug and leaned over the bed with such attention that Jane wondered why she hadn't forgiven her a little stolen bread, a private laugh, a smirk with Prince before now. Jane slipped a hand behind her brother's neck and raised his head. She held the cup to his lips, and he drank it down.

So intent was Jane on her brother that she heard no knock at the door, none of the usual shuffling required for the admittance of the visitor, and Henry Knox appeared beside her as if dropped from the ceiling. "Good heavens, Jane. I've been combing every shadow in search of you. Are you unharmed?"

"I am. My brother has received a wound to the shoulder only."

"Dear God. Dear God. I was so in fear of the very thing that happened; I could not prevent it; I tried and I could do naught. And then to have lost you again—"

Jane began a search for words to soothe him but gave it up before she'd gone very far. Henry, her big, strong Henry, who above all the men she might have expected to keep her safe from harm, had instead carried her into danger and left her there, left her to Hugh White to worry over.

Aunt Gill said from behind, "Perhaps we should leave the boy to rest," and all but Jane left the room. She sat down in a chair that someone had brought her and watched over her brother, from time to time pulling back the sheet to make sure the wound had not seeped through. The second time she did it she noticed her hand trembled; she poured herself her own tot of brandy and drank it down as Harry Nye had taught her to do. It steadied her hand but it also loosened her head; when Nate spoke again she heard it as he meant it, as he'd no doubt meant it before. Not *right*. *White*. Hugh White.

"Hugh White. Bloody White. Looked at me. Aimed at me. Shot me down." Nate, the boy, looked at Jane, and—unbelievably—grinned. "And he'll hang for it too."

JOHN ADAMS BROUGHT THE first news the next morning when he came by to check on his clerk. As little as Jane knew Adams she recognized the look of a mind in calculation of the future even as he spoke of the recent past. He had arrived late at the scene, and seeing all in hand, hurried home to his pregnant wife to ease the alarm the bells would surely have brought on. Being Adams, the rest of the news had come to him.

"The big mulatto Attucks is dead, as are two others. Two more look to be mortally wounded. There are six others with lesser injuries, this lad to be counted among them. Preston and his grenadiers have been arrested and confined to gaol; all the town's crying for their necks in ropes. The remaining soldiers have been ordered out of the town to Castle Island."

And so the "horrid massacre," as it was already being called, had accomplished that thing which two years of petitions and protests had failed to do.

Jane's grandparents came. Jane's grandmother went straight to her grandson, but Jane's grandfather and Adams stepped into the front parlor for a word. Before they'd finished, two young men arrived, whose names Jane recognized from Nate's letters from school, with Henry Knox close behind. The young men joined those in the sickroom but Henry joined the men in the parlor, and Jane could hear his voice rise and fall in equal part with the others.

Late in the day, after the other visitors had gone, Jane heard a woman's voice at the door.

"I've come to see Mr. Clarke."

"Who is it come to call?" That from Martha.

"Miss Linnet."

Jane stepped into the hall. Miss Linnet approached her and clutched her arm, all her feeling in her eyes, her fingers, her entire knotted form. "Miss Clarke, I must see him."

Jane led the way to her brother's room. The woman went to the bed and leaned down. "My Nate, oh, my Nate." She pushed back his hair, cupped his head. Whatever they might have been arguing about that day as Jane had listened on the stairs, it appeared to be of little matter now. Indeed, what *could* matter now? All Jane's resentment of Miss Linnet's hoarding of her brother drained out of her. She left the pair alone.

THAT NIGHT THE FEVER set in; by dawn Nate was in a delirium. He carried on about White. Hugh White. Bloody White. He called it attempted murder, over and over again, but Jane could not believe him, that the patient sentry had singled Nate out of the crowd and all because of a few words that had passed between them on the street so many months before. She tried to remember the shooting exactly as she'd seen it—soldiers on guard in a semicircle, bayonets addressing the crowd, the club sailing through the air and knocking the soldier down, the soldier calling for his brother soldiers to fire, others from the crowd calling for fire, but still the soldiers held, until the final cry had come from behind the line. Hugh White had been at the end of the line near Jane, and indeed his musket must have gone off, but Jane's eyes had been fixed on the other end of the line, first on Preston and then on the man in the dark cloak. Jane could not have said if Hugh White had fired on her brother or not, but she could remember his impressive restraint day after day, his concern for her safety even at the moment of his own greatest danger. Only after Jane had recalled all of that did she recall the other thing: White bringing his musket into the side of a young boy's head for so little a thing as an accusation over an unpaid bill, and a bill not even his own.

Chapter Twenty-two

JANE'S GRANDPARENTS, JOHN Adams, Henry Knox, and Miss Linnet came to visit Nate each of the next few days; if Jane's grandfather or Adams or Henry happened to arrive together they always retired to the front room and spoke in low tones, sometimes for half an hour, sometimes for more. At first, occupied with her brother, Jane paid them little mind, but by the third day she found herself anxious to know what went on. By making her way in and out she discovered that a group of radicals from the town had gone around collecting depositions from all the witnesses to the scene; Henry had given one, along with ninety-five other inhabitants of the town. It appeared no one had thought of Jane.

Jane also learned that John Adams had been asked to defend Preston and the soldiers.

"You consider this?" Jane's grandfather asked.

"I must. All others have refused. A proper defense is the last thing a man should be wanting in this country."

"But you can't call them innocent," Henry said.

"Their guilt or innocence is not my concern. That will be the work of the trial."

In quick succession Jane's thoughts flew to the *qui tam*, Winslow's horse, and, for the first time in days, to Phinnie Paine.

Henry remained in the front room after the others had left, waiting on Jane. He held a rolled-up paper in his hand, which he unwrapped for Jane: an engraving by Mr. Paul Revere depicting "The Bloody Massacre." The soldiers stood on one side of the street in perfect formation, bayonets fixed, guns drawn and blazing; the inhabitants stood cowering a good distance away, their dead lying awash in flaming crimson in the street below. Jane looked from the print to Henry. "But it wasn't so."

"Well, he makes his point."

Jane handed back the print. "You were asked to make out one of those depositions?"

"I was."

"To what purpose? Do they intend to put them in the newspaper?"

"By order of the town the depositions are not to be published before the trial, for fear of influencing the jury."

Jane pointed at Revere's engraving. "But all the town may see this."

Henry made no answer.

Jane moved on. "Mr. John Adams's defense of the soldiers must displease his cousin Samuel."

"Not at all. All parties insist complete fairness must be observed."

And they might as well, thought Jane, for all the hope the soldiers had of it in such a town. But why should she care, with her brother lying bloodied by one of them in the next room?

Henry stepped close and pulled Jane into him. He dropped his mouth to her collarbone. "Jane. My Jane. If I had allowed anything to happen to you—"

Again Jane's first impulse was to hush away his guilt; again her second was to leave it lie, but for a different reason this time. As hard as Henry had worked to prevent the so-called massacre, he didn't seem overly distressed about it now. In fact, he seemed quite cheerful. Jane pushed herself free.

NATE'S CONTINUED DELIRIUM HAD a poor effect on Aunt Gill. Her own speech became nonsensical at times, mixing up soldiers with rebels and visitors with strangers. One day, on leaving the guests in the front room, Jane found her aunt again standing alone in the middle of the stairs; another time she found her standing in the middle of Jane's room, thinking it her own. The aunt and the brother together began to wear Jane down; she was short with Henry and no doubt with others too.

Finally the night came when Nate's sweat drenched the sheets, and in the morning his fever was gone. When Jane entered the room, he lay in a deep sleep, and she stood gazing down on him in exhausted relief. The unconscious Nate seemed so much more her brother than the awake one, the eyelashes still against his skin, the pale hair quiet on the pillow, the mouth relaxed into its old gentle curve. But *was* this the brother she thought she remembered? When had his lashes not been on wide alert around his eyes? When had his hair not blown about his face as he ran? In truth, how often *had* he smiled? But the sleeping Nate soothed her and healed him, and Jane would disturb him for no one—not Mr. Adams, Miss Linnet, or Phinnie Paine.

He'd come on hearing the news of Nate, to see how he fared, or so he said, but his eyes worked over Jane, as if checking for her wounds. He would find no wounds, but he would find someone more worn down than he'd seen last; this might have disturbed Jane more if she hadn't noted the changes in Phinnie too—the tensed shoulders, the tight mouth, the line across the brow. As she looked at him he seemed to shift into someone she no longer knew, which was of course impossible, since she'd never known Phinnie at all.

"Your brother's wound," Phinnie said. "Is it . . . will it—" He seemed unable to finish either the thought or the sentence, which was another thing new.

"His fever is gone," she said. "I have excellent hopes of him. He sleeps now, his first fair sleep; I shouldn't like to wake him."

"No! Good God, no."

After a time Jane said, "I was there with Mr. Knox. I saw the whole."

Phinnie took a step forward. Back. "You were there! With Knox!"

"I was." She looked away and was displeased that she did so. She looked quickly back, but Phinnie's head was now bent, studying a pamphlet Jane only now noticed he held in his hand, flipping it restlessly from page to page. "I knew Knox to be there. I read his deposition in here. I never dreamed he was such a fool as to pull you along."

Jane held out her hand for the pamphlet and Phinnie handed it across—the depositions that were not to have appeared in the newspapers ahead of the trial were printed out, page after page of them, in a small booklet. Jane looked up. "Where did you get such a thing?"

"'Tis all about town."

Jane began to read.

Daniel Calef of lawful age testifies and says that on the evening of the fifth current, hearing the bells ring which he took for fire, run out and came into King Street, seeing a number of people about one hundred he went up to the Custom House where was posted about a dozen soldiers with their officer. This deponent heard said officer order the soldiers to fire, and upon the officer's ordering the soldiers to fire the second time, this deponent ran off about thirty feet distant, when turning about, he saw one Caldwell fall, and likewise a mulatto man.

I, Samuel Condon, of lawful age, testify and say, that on the night of the fifth instant March I stood near the door of the Royal Exchange Tavern, apprehending danger as the soldiers stood with their muskets and bayonets in a charged or presented position; during this interim I saw no violence offered the soldiers; in a few minutes a musket was fired by the soldier who stood next the corner, and so in succession till the whole was discharged. I went up to the head of the lane where I saw the people

*carrying off one dead person, two more laying lifeless on the ground
about two muskets length of the said soldiers, inhumanly murdered by
them, the blood then running from them in abundance; a person asked
the soldier who fired first the reason for his doing, the soldier answered,
"Damn your blood's, you boogers, I would kill a thousand of you!"*

*Joseph Hooten, jun., of lawful age testifies and says that between
nine and ten o'clock came into King Street and saw about eight or ten
soldiers drawn up in the Custom House, and an officer, which he since
understands was Captain Preston, between the soldiers and the Custom
House. In about five minutes after the deponent first stood there, he
heard the officer give the word "fire"; they not being firing, he again
said, "Fire," which they still disobeying, he said with a much higher
voice, "Damn you, fire, be the consequence what it will!" Soon after this
one of the guns went off—in a few seconds another and so on.*

*I, Henry Knox, of lawful age, testify and say, between nine and ten
o'clock, P.M., the fifth instant, I saw the sentry at the Custom House
charging his musket, and a number of young persons crossing from
Royal Exchange to Quaker Lane; seeing him load, I stopped and asked
him what he meant and the sentry said if they touched him, he would
fire. Immediately on this I saw a detachment of about eight or nine men
and a corporal, headed by Captain Preston. I took Captain Preston by
the coat and told him for God's sake to take his men back again. When
I was talking with Captain Preston, the soldiers of his detachment
had attacked the people with their bayonets. There was not the least
provocation given to Captain Preston or his party, the backs of the
people being towards them.*

Jane stopped reading. She handed the pamphlet back to Phinnie. She
went into the front room and knelt before the fire, jabbing the grayed logs
into flame.

Phinnie came up behind her and touched his fingers to her shoulder. "That you should have seen such things—"

Jane shrugged out from under Phinnie's hand, stood up, turned around. "If you mean such things as I read about in that pamphlet, I saw no such things."

"Thank God for that, then. I feared you would have seen the whole bloody mess."

"I saw the 'whole bloody mess,' as you call it. I also saw a mob throwing rocks and ice and calling foul names. Waving sticks and clubs. The soldiers only came because the sentry was endangered, and whoever wrote up those depositions is the same lot who's written every lie in the paper."

Phinnie's eyes widened, but not long afterward his mouth twitched in something that he would once have let loose in a smile. Was he thinking of that last night together at Satucket? Was he thinking: *Ah, so you decide for yourself the newspapers lie?* Well, she knew they lied, knew because of her own supposed "accosting" by the sentry. But there she thought of Otis, the accounts in the paper of Otis, and of the very real accosting at the ropewalks. She turned away and felt Phinnie again—those same light fingers—on her arm.

"The thing is over, Jane. Blast Knox for getting you in it, but 'tis done now; 'tis naught to do with you and you mustn't think on it anymore."

Jane picked up the pamphlet that had somehow fallen to the floor. "I must read the rest."

A second line formed to join the first across Phinnie's brow. "Whatever for? 'Tis naught to do with you. Four men died, yes—"

"*Four* men? Do you mean to say one of the wounded has died?"

"He has."

Jane's eyes slipped toward the door beyond which her brother lay. Her brother, who might have been five.

"Have you seen Mr. Revere's rendition of the scene?"

"I have."

Jane wanted to ask what he thought of it but knew better than to try.

"'Tis not how it was. And yet all the town will see it, and all the town will read this pamphlet. What hope have those soldiers of a fair trial?"

"Their hope rests in Adams."

"And will Mr. Adams be vindicated this time?"

Phinnie looked at her in something like alarm, and for once Jane could see—she could clearly see—the workings of his mind: Was she reminding him of their last conversation, their last falling-out over her father's case? Jane raised the pamphlet and tapped it against the air to reassure Phinnie that she had only the one case on her mind—the case against the soldiers—that she wanted to know only one thing: *Was* there the least hope that Adams might win? Phinnie saw, and understood, and shook his head slowly side to side.

JANE READ ALL the depositions through, and even found some delivered by women, although the women only testified to rumors they'd overheard leading up to March the fifth; no woman had testified to the night itself, to the "massacre" itself. And of the eyewitness accounts, all but one put the blame for the massacre on an unprovoked assault by Preston and his men on a perhaps unruly but harmless group of townsmen. If this message had not been brought out in the body of a particular deposition, an editorial note in the form of a "memorandum" often followed, such as the one tagged to the deposition of Josiah Simpson: *the deponent further saith that he is satisfied there was not more than seventy or eighty people in King Street, who offered no violence to the soldiers or to any other persons, nor threatened any.* An editorial note had even been appended to the lone dissenting voice, warning against the credibility of the witness.

Jane read the accounts again and again, trying to find in them something of the night as she remembered it—the crowd taunting the soldiers, a club being thrown that in fact knocked a soldier to the ground, the stick hitting Preston, a townsman slipping from the crowd and behind the soldiers, urging them to fire. How was it possible no one but Jane had seen this man? How was it possible no one had noticed Preston standing in *front* of his men, the last place he would stand if he had any intention of ordering them to fire? And hadn't anyone noticed Preston's mouth fixed in that hard, tight grimace as the persistent commands to fire had come from *behind* the line?

All the while Jane struggled to preserve the night as she remembered it, her brother grew stronger, more lucid, more talkative—about the night as *he* remembered it, about Hugh White gunning him down.

"I knew the minute his head came around. I knew when he spied me. I should have dropped to the ground. He saw me, he raised his musket, it was like I saw it twice—once when I knew it was to happen and once when it, happened. And then I was down."

He closed his eyes. Opened them on Jane. "And then you came." The mad, white tightness in his features eased. "Do you remember when Father whipped me and you stole the whip and threw it down the dung-hole?"

"And he blamed you and whipped you again."

Nate grinned. "We'll fix the blame right this time."

Chapter Twenty-three

THE NEWS CAME first from John Adams, second from Jane's grand-parents, and third, as it seemed, through every crack in the door and wall. On the afternoon of March the eighth there was to be a massive funeral procession for the four men who had died victims of the "Bloody Massacre." Having read the depositions through, having seen the Revere print, having heard from Prince the minute description of the funeral for the boy killed by Richardson, Jane felt she knew well enough what this funeral procession might be like and would have been happy enough to stay at home. But to Jane's alarm, Nate had risen from his bed, his arm still strapped across his chest, insisting on going out to watch the show; Jane could not let him go out alone. Aunt Gill was as alarmed as Jane and only subsided in her protests when Nate startled her into silence by kissing her cheek; Jane might have kissed her aunt too had she prevailed in detaining Nate, but she had not done so.

As Jane assisted Nate in hanging his coat over his bandaged shoulder, she thought for a minute his fever had returned, so bright had his eyes become. At the corner of Royal Exchange and King they pulled up; indeed, they were forced to by the crowd; the taverns and shops had once again emptied, and the mass of inhabitants pressed thick along each side of the street to await the procession. As they waited, Jane lifted her voice over the constant tolling of the bells to ask her brother, "Have you read the pamphlet with the depositions in?"

Nate pulled his eyes off the street and onto Jane. "*You've* read it?"

"Why should I not read it? Or do you forget I was there too?"

He stared at her. "Indeed, I do forget you! Now this is a happy thing! We must get your deposition taken down. I see nowhere in any statement that White drew down on me—'twas all my word alone till now. 'Tis too late for the pamphlet, but no matter. It was kept out of the papers, anyhow, so as not to influence the trial."

Jane looked at her brother, unable to decide if he spoke in jest, or if he was in fact so naive as to believe that as long as the paper hadn't printed it, the pamphlet might float around town without harm to the soldiers' cause. Or was Jane the naive one to think for a minute that her brother cared a whit about the soldiers' cause? Again she wondered why *she* should care about their cause. They'd held and beaten Otis into madness; they'd tussled her about outside the ropewalk; the soldier she'd defended for months had clubbed a small boy to the ground and tried to murder her brother where he stood in King Street. Or had he? Jane stood taking birdlike glances at her brother's profile, trying to find in him the answer to her question, but all she saw was the angry whipped boy, the angry boy-man standing in King Street dressing down Hugh White, the injured man lying in bed lifting his gaze to Miss Linnet. Which of those brothers was the one she looked at now?

"I must get to Adams's office tomorrow and see how he gets on," Nate continued. "And I must get my own deposition taken down; blast this arm! 'Tis a thing I should like to write out myself." He shrugged his shoulder, which no doubt set loose new pain—some of the brightness and color drained out of him, but not the mosquitolike obsession with the subject at hand. "You must go to the clerk's, Jane, and get your deposition taken down too. But no, as I think on it, you must come to Mr. Adams's office with me tomorrow and let him take a draft before you go to the clerk's."

"But Mr. Adams works *against* your side."

Nate smiled. "Mr. Adams never works against our side."

Jane looked across the road and spied her grandfather and grandmother in the crowd; her grandmother saw her and lifted her hand, in much the same pledgelike manner in which she'd said good-bye to her at Satucket. A pledge. An oath. Jane turned toward her brother. "Nate, I didn't see Hugh White shoot at you. I didn't even know you were in the crowd."

He looked down at her. "And you didn't see my father whip me."

Indeed, she had not. She remembered the whip, Nate's red face, the raging tears, but she could not remember what had been his crime, or why she hadn't simply told her father she'd tossed the whip in the dung-hole and saved her brother the second beating. That had been *her* crime.

The funeral procession had at last made its turn onto King Street—the four coffins of Attucks, Maverick, Caldwell, and Gray at the fore, behind them a stream of mourners that widened with the road, like a snake swallowing a rat whole. Jane spied many of the Sons of Liberty in the crowd directly behind the coffins, including Henry Knox, but after them came wave after wave of the town's inhabitants, high and low, rough dressed and well dressed; the dead boy's parade could have been nothing compared to it.

As the coffins passed by, an appropriate deathly hush befell the crowd. After a time Nate whispered into it. "Do you see, Jane? Have you ever seen such a crowd collected anywhere? If anyone doubts the Sons control the town now, they're as thick as the governor."

APPARENTLY THE CUSTOMS COMMISSIONERS were not as thick as the governor; two days later the *Gazette* reported that they had sailed for England. Nor could Captain Preston be called a fool, as he had submitted his own advertisement to the paper:

My thanks in the most public manner to the inhabitants in general of
this town who throwing aside all party and prejudice have with the
utmost humanity and freedom stepped forth advocates for truth in
defense of my injured innocence. I assure them that I shall ever have the
highest sense of the justice they have done me.

But printed farther along:

Capt. Preston with his soldiers took place by the Customs House and,
pushing to drive the people off pricked some in several places with
their bayonets, on which they were clamorous and, it is said, threw
snowballs. On this, the Captain commanded them to fire; and more
snowballs coming, he again said, Damn you, fire, be the consequence
what it will!

AGAINST JANE'S AND AUNT Gill's arguing, Nate returned to his rooms
at Cold Lane. His arm was no longer pinned to his chest, but he couldn't
yet write a clear hand, and would not be taking his place as Adams's clerk
anytime soon. The thought of being kept out of Adams's most famous case
had him spewing the kind of language at an invisible Hugh White that
Jane was not happy for Aunt Gill to hear, although she looked to be of like
enough mind.

ON MARCH FOURTEENTH THE last massacre victim, an Irishman named
Patrick Carr, succumbed to his wounds and died. Prince carried the news
home, along with a rumor that on his deathbed Carr exonerated the soldiers, declaring they had borne more than he'd seen any soldier bear in
England and Ireland combined. That same day the newspaper reported
that Preston and the other soldiers had been indicted before the grand jury;
someone named Robert Goddard had even been brought to the jail and

positively identified Preston as the man who had ordered the soldiers to fire.

Jane had slept poorly since the fifth, but that night she believed she might have counted every minute from ten o'clock till dawn. She'd been so sure that Preston had not issued the call to fire; she'd had her eye on him, standing in front of the soldiers right up until the second call came, his mouth always in that hard silent line; could the single word have slipped from his mouth in one of the split seconds when Jane blinked her eyes? But why should she believe this Robert Goddard any more than she believed the other reports in the paper? Why should she believe a Goddard over her own eyes? She had seen what the witnesses had done with the other facts of the night, how they had shrunk and castrated the crowd—even Henry Knox, open, honest Henry Knox, had done so. *Was* she wrong? She wished to talk to Henry, but for once, he didn't come.

PHINNIE PAINE CAME. He'd come again to see how Nate fared, but Jane could only direct him to Cold Lane. Phinnie had turned to go when Aunt Gill chirped from the front room for Jane to bid him sit and take a cup of labrador with her; Phinnie was, of course Phinnie would be, happy to oblige.

Another listener might have been amused at Aunt Gill's effort to determine Phinnie Paine's political frame of mind.

"What think you of the recent events in King Street?" she asked.

"I think them unfortunate."

"Do you know this Captain Preston they speak of?"

"We've met from time to time."

"What say you of the soldiers being ordered from town?"

"I see both dark and light in it, Miss Gill."

"But what of Mr. Adams's defense of the soldiers? What kind of show do you think he might put on?"

"I'm quite sure Mr. Adams will defend his clients, guilty or innocent, with all the skill he owns."

Did Phinnie speak of Jane's father now? Jane looked at him, stared at him, willed him to look at her. He sipped his labrador and smiled at Aunt Gill.

SOONER THAN SHE COULD have expected, Jane received a letter from her stepmother. Jane had written nothing since the night of the fifth, unwilling to alarm her parents over Nate, equally unwilling to falsify by omission. That Mehitable had received news of the troubles was evident in the first paragraph, but no one seemed to have included Nate in the list of wounded. Mehitable urged Jane to keep herself safe; she urged her to avoid all those types who might expose her to the tempest. *The loss of your person to this house has been a great enough grief to me; the loss of you to this life could not be borne. If I could describe to you how alone I feel since you've been gone you would weep for me.* She closed with, *I've not said nor will I say anything to you of Mr. Paine. I will say only that a letter to your father at this time might work toward seeing you safe home, considering such additional proof as he now possesses of the situation in town. In the meanwhile you must go to my mother if you find yourself in any difficulty—it much relieves my mind to know she's near. God bless you and watch over you—Your Most Affectionate Mother.*

Jane spent a fair time reading over this letter in some amazement. It was as if she'd never heard her stepmother's voice before. And yes, Jane could weep for her, but not over the loss of Jane. *How alone I feel,* she'd written, as her husband sat by her side.

HENRY KNOX CAME AT last, full of apology for events keeping him too occupied for too long. Aunt Gill interrogated him much as she had interrogated Phinnie: she wanted to know what was being said in town about Mr. Adams's defense of the soldiers; she wanted to know how it was on the streets; she wanted to know how long the soldiers were to remain in jail. Unlike Phinnie Paine, Henry was more easily drawn.

"Indeed, Mr. Adams is much vilified through the streets of town, and this on top of the death of his little daughter has him walking about a most glum creature."

"Not Susanna!" Jane cried. "'Tis not his little Susanna who's died?"

Henry gave a nod.

But Aunt Gill had never seen Adams cradling Mehitable's babe in his arms, as if such care of a stranger's child might keep his own safe from harm; the old woman continued on without pause. "What of the trials?" she asked. "When do they commence?"

"Preston is to be tried first and separately from the soldiers. The mood is high; the time is now; 'tis imperative the trials begin soon. Instead we have judges disappearing, falling ill, court postponed. These are the tricks worked by the Crown, Miss Gill."

Such news was too much for Aunt Gill; she called for Martha and retired.

As soon as she was out of sight, Henry said, "Should you like me to read something more from Pope?"

"No," Jane said. She was no longer as fond of Pope as she had once been. She said, "I've something to read to you." She picked up the pamphlet that Phinnie Paine had brought around, turned to Henry's testimony, and began. "'While I was talking with Captain Preston, the soldiers of his detachment had attacked the people with their bayonets. There was not the least provocation given to Captain Preston or his party, the backs of the people being toward them when they were attacked.'"

Jane stopped reading. Henry's eyebrow rose. "You have a concern?"

"A concern! Yes, indeed, a concern. It was nothing like. You saw the crowd attacking the sentry before Preston came; you saw them press in on the grenadiers as they tried to march along; you saw the sticks, the great chunks of ice—"

Henry crossed to Jane and removed the pamphlet from her hand, tossed it on the table, and claimed the hand. "Jane, how long since I've been with you! Must we waste time on this talk?"

"Waste time! My brother wants my testimony against Hugh White. He says the sentry took careful aim at him in an effort to shoot him down. To kill him. Over some words exchanged on the street over half a year ago. Hugh White, the fellow you walk past each week when you come to call, the fellow who twice tried to keep me from harm."

"The fellow who split open a small boy's head with the butt of his musket."

Jane fell silent.

"I can't tell you where Hugh White aimed his musket," Henry went on, "but I can certainly tell you he discharged his musket into the crowd. I can further tell you the soldiers should not have been sent here, but the minute that order was given, the events on King Street were ordained, and now the soldiers have done what they've done and must be tried, as would any citizen of this town. I, for one, shall give my testimony, keeping in mind the best outcome for my town and for my country, and I should hope you would do the same."

"And if Hugh White killed no one? If he discharged his weapon at the ground or at the gutter or at the moon? You make no allowance for such an occurrence?"

"By discharging his weapon he put at risk the lives of the innocent inhabitants of this town. What matter whether he in fact struck any of them down? The guilt is the same."

"Under law?"

For the first time since Jane had met Henry Knox, he looked on her with something that was not entirely admiring. "I am no lawyer, Jane. I cannot argue law with you. I'd prefer not to argue with you at all. I can only speak my mind to you as I've always done, and 'tis now your choice whether to come here and prove us still friends or bid me go home."

It was true, Jane thought—she couldn't dismiss Henry for doing the very thing she had once begged Phinnie to do, but it seemed now as if there were a great weight, like a pendulum, hanging between them in the room. But what was this weight made of? A man and a woman, a husband and a wife come to that, needn't always be of the same mind. There would be fundamental things they must agree upon, no doubt, but was the direction of a British sentry's aim such a fundamental?

Jane looked across the room at Henry. He had fallen silent, and without the dangerous words she saw only the things that had so often comforted her—the great shoulders, the solid chest, the gentle brown eyes that she knew if she drew close enough would hold nothing but her image. She crossed the room.

Chapter Twenty-four

AFTER PATRICK CARR'S funeral a peculiar calm dropped over the town like a still, cool snow. Nate came to fetch her to work out her deposition at Adams's office, but it so happened Jane's excuse was ready at hand and true to boot—Aunt Gill was not well, in chills and shakes and confined to her room. Jane sent her brother back with a note for Adams instead, expressing her great sorrow over the death of his child.

Nate came again the next day, and Aunt Gill having returned to her parlor chair, Jane's only excuse was her indecision, if it could even be called indecision. She had thought of the whip; she had thought of Henry's words; she had felt that small, hard thing inside her that wanted the soldiers to pay for what they did—to Otis, to her, to her brother, to the five dead. It seemed it was only the will she lacked. She got up and followed Nate out the door, into Royal Exchange Lane, as far as the corner of King and the scene of the violence.

Jane had spent so many nights lying with her eyes closed, seeing the thick snow turned blue with moonlight, the soldiers' red coats, the multicolored jackets of the crowd, the yellow flash of the muskets, the red blood, so much redder on the snow than on the clothes. Her brother's clothes. Hugh White. Bloody White? What *had* he done? Jane could see the line of soldiers as clearly as she could see her hand in front of her face, but the hand was too close; she couldn't see all the fingers. She knew that Preston had stood in front of the line and the man in the cloak had slipped behind. She could see the man in the cloak, his mouth moving, urging the soldiers to fire, Preston's mouth still fixed and grim. But what of Hugh White? He'd stood near her; he'd urged her back to safety. And then what? She didn't know.

Jane stopped. "Nate. I don't know where Hugh White aimed his musket. I don't indeed know that he fired his musket."

"Don't know that he fired! Were you deaf and blind? And I told you where he aimed. Do you think I lie to you?"

"No. Nor should I like to think you would ask me to."

That quieted him, as she knew it would; he was not that far a stranger to her. She said, "Come. I'll walk a way with you. We have other things to talk of. Tell me of Miss Linnet. I know nothing of this woman who comes to see you in your distress, who clearly cares for you very—"

"She's no Miss Linnet, she's Mrs. Lincoln; she stops with me while her husband travels the country with his concubine. You see, Jane? I don't lie to you. Not about her, not about White."

He picked up his pace and left her behind.

THAT NIGHT JANE WROTE her longest letter ever to Bethiah. She of course had Mrs. Lincoln on her mind, but in no long time she realized that was not a story that served any purpose in its telling. There was another story, though, that she was anxious to get down. She began by laying out the barest, bluntest version of events, hoping that to do so might clear up matters in her own mind, but after a very few lines her pen seemed to dash off on a road of its own. When she finished she discovered she'd laid out all—what she saw, what the ninety-some-odd deposers said they saw, what Nate and Henry wished her to say she saw, what Phinnie wished her not to say at all—and yet as she read over what she'd written she found herself less sure of things than when she'd begun. In any case, it was no letter to send to Bethiah. She closed her letter book on it but could not close her mind on it. She lay awake, seeing it, doubting what she saw.

THE NEXT MORNING JANE woke realizing that if she wished to sort it, if she wished to sort herself, she must revisit the scene. She'd stood near enough to the spot twice now, but each time she'd been accompanied by Nate—preoccupied by Nate—she needed to be alone with her memory. She hastened herself into her clothes, hurried Aunt Gill into hers as much as it was ever possible to hurry Aunt Gill, and urged her down the stairs to her breakfast. After breakfast, as Jane settled the old woman in the front room, she explained that she needed to make an emergency errand to the apothecary for some catnip to treat a toothache.

"Ah!" her aunt said. "I saw the shadow of your candle last night. I thought you keeping overlong at your letters, but it was, after all, a tooth."

"*And* an overlong letter."

"But you leave nothing on the post table."

Jane smiled. "Overlong letters must never be sent."

Aunt Gill patted her arm. "Well then, you must hasten out and take care of your tooth."

Jane wrapped herself up in her cloak and stepped out. The wind that ripped down Royal Exchange Lane reminded Jane again of Satucket, made her think in a way she hadn't thought in a while about returning home. What if it did require only a simple letter to her father, as Mehitable had implied? What if she *could* go home? What then?

Out of nothing Jane recalled a time when the family had gone in a carriage to visit a relative at Yarmouth; Jane could not remember what had happened to the carriage or the relative, but she remembered the long carriage ride coming home from that visit, her parents sitting in the front seat, Jane and Nate and Bethiah curled up on one another like puppies in the seat behind. The dark and damp had come down before they'd reached home and Jane's mother had pulled a bed rug over them, tucking it around. The touch of the rug had wakened Jane, and she'd lain with her eyes open for the rest of the ride, looking at the dim silhouettes of her parents, feeling the warmth of her siblings, listening to the *whoomph whoomph whoomph* of the horse's hooves as it pulled them closer to home. Over all the years Jane had remembered that ride home and the utter sleepy contentment of it: there were her father and mother just there; here were her sister and brother just here; here too was the maple sugar in her stomach and the warm rug over her, and what a fine thing it was to be just who she was and where she was—curled in the nest of her rug with her mother on the watch, her father at the reins.

Except. It could not have been her mother on the watch beside her father or Jane would have been too young to remember it, and Bethiah would not have been born. Yes, now Jane remembered it had been *Bethiah's* mother on the watch, and she remembered another thing too—when they reached Nobscusset Jane had puked up the maple sugar at the side of the road. Her father had said, "You do that again and you'll do it in your shoe—we're an hour behind time." But then he'd reached behind and tugged her hair and said, "My poor Jane."

Jane pushed back against the wind and trudged on, but at the corner of Exchange and King a queer thing happened; the wind grew less, as it often did when channeled from narrow tunnel to wide expanse, but Jane's feet struggled twice as hard to move. Around that corner lay the spot where someone had shouted *fire* and someone else had shot her brother through the shoulder, and Jane found she could not push ahead. She turned around and made her way home. *Home.* Jane had called Aunt Gill's house *home* before, but was it? She supposed she could love Aunt Gill well enough; she supposed she could fill her days with what passed for nursing, writing letters and reading, and perhaps in time all those things would make it home.

Or perhaps not. The wind and Jane's thoughts converged to start tears in her eyes; she dashed them away, but more came, in a horrifying torrent.

When Jane reached the house she crept through the door and past the front room in hope of slipping by her aunt unnoticed; she took care to avoid the two cracked treads on the stairs and crept upward. She had been so sure of Aunt Gill's still sitting in the front room where she'd left her that as she passed her aunt's chamber door and saw her at the small table by her bed, she started. Aunt Gill, too, seemed startled. She drew in a sharp breath. She picked up her letter book and attempted to slide it under the bolster.

"'Tis only I, Aunt," Jane said, but her aunt continued her fumbling, and only then did Jane realize that the letter book her aunt was struggling to conceal looked very much like her own.

Jane crossed to the bed and pulled the letter book free of the bolster. It *was* her letter book. She looked down at her aunt in puzzlement. "What on earth do you want with my letter book?" She looked down at the paper her aunt had half covered with ink. The old woman grabbed at the paper and attempted to conceal that too; Jane snatched it out of her hands, knocking the inky pen to the floor. She looked down and read in disbelief: *Sir: The girl remains in confusion yet—it is not clear what if any testimony she might offer. The brother will declare that White aimed at him with intent. Knox continues to disguise any provocation by the crowd. I have not yet learned anything from the brother about how Adams intends to proceed. Otis I think you may safely dispense with.*

Jane read and did not understand it. She looked over the paper at her aunt. "Why do you write about me in this way? Who is it you write to?"

"'Tis not your concern."

"Not my concern! When you write all I put down in my letter book? All I talk about with my family and friends? Is it my father you write?"

"Your father!"

"Who else would want to know what I write to my sister? Who else would care what I think or what Nate says or what Knox says or what Adams or Otis might do? Stop smiling at me as if I were a child and tell me who you write!"

"And why should I not smile at you as if you were a child? Is it not a child who thinks all the world spins around its father? Your father!" She broke into bright, rippling laughter, as if her father were a joke, as if Jane were one. But if not her father, *who*?

Jane looked down at the paper in her hand. Knox. Adams. Otis. Well, of course. "You write to a king's man," Jane said. "You *spy* for them."

"Spy!" Aunt Gill spat. "The people you write about don't deserve the word! Look what they do! Look what they write! They represent no government. They represent only themselves and their false ideas and their own puffed-up importance. That they could think themselves equal to a king, or a Parliament!" Aunt Gill pushed herself to her feet with a strength that Jane hadn't seen in her. She walked in perfect steadiness to the window and pointed at the street below. "I've lived here the length of my life. First with my parents and sisters and brothers and now alone. In all those years I've never felt fear at opening my door till now. Do you think I should sit about and let them rule my street?"

Jane followed her aunt across the room and gripped her arm. "Who is it you write to, Aunt?"

Aunt Gill whirled around. "You think a name will help you? You think you would even know it? What do you know that isn't vomited out of that paper? A paper run by my own cousin! I do naught but even the scale in my family's name."

Jane stared at her aunt. The old woman appeared to have grown taller and stronger as she spoke. "And you have no qualm at taking my private words and sending them where I might have no wish for them to go?"

"*Might* have no wish? You think I don't know how joined you are to your brother? You think I don't know the things your brother does? And him clerking for that Adams! Why, if he'd done his duty to me I'd have had no need of you, but as it was, when your father wrote to me, I thought, now there's a fine thing! Send me the sister! That will bring the brother around! And then you bring me Henry Knox! Whore that you are, you bring me Knox too!"

Jane looked at her aunt, at the yellowed teeth exposed in her gloat, and felt the twitch in her hands, the twitch to slap the mouth closed. She looked down at the letter book she held in one hand, the paper she held in the other. She set down the letter book and ripped Aunt Gill's paper straight across, lined up the halves with care, and ripped it across again. And again. She opened her clenched fingers and let the pieces drift over Aunt Gill's floor, a useless and unsatisfying act. She picked up the letter book, left her aunt where she stood, and went to her room.

JANE SAT ON HER bed, leafing through the pages of her letter book, her fingers and the papers she turned in them trembling. What else had Aunt Gill copied out and passed along to her king's man? What had Jane written to Bethiah? This of the boys tormenting the sentry? This of the false account in the paper of her being accosted by him? Or this of Nate's unreasoned anger, or the celebration at the Liberty Tree, or Henry's poem that she'd copied in . . . Henry. What had her aunt done, hovered listening on the stairs as she visited with Henry? Yes, of course she had—twice Jane had caught her lurking there and only thought her confused in her mind. Jane thought of her aunt listening to her talking with Henry, not talking with Henry, and a hot, bitter fire erupted in her, the like of which she hadn't felt since Otis had been beaten by the soldiers. She had once defended those soldiers as she had supposed she was defending this woman, watching and worrying over her day after day, allowing an affection to spring to life in her, more and more each day as the months wore on. And all that time the old woman had been sitting there like a turkey buzzard, watching and waiting to pick out Jane's heart as soon as she dared to expose it. Well, the buzzard could sit there. Jane could not. She leaped off the bed, pulled her cloak off the peg, tumbled down the stairs and out the door, still gripping her letter book in her hands.

THE WIND SEEMED LESS than it was, due, no doubt, to Jane's heat within. She pushed across King Street with little regard now for what offense had transpired there and beat against the wind toward the Town House. She had no great idea where she was going, but as she walked she found she was thinking of Henry Knox, and imagined that a calmer part of her mind had directed her feet toward the store. But there the not-calm part of her mind began thinking of Henry, what she had done with Henry, with Aunt Gill listening from the hall. She slowed, her face, her chest, her ears—indeed, all that Henry had ever touched—in flame. She stopped in the street across from the empty whipping post, unable to move. An oxcart swung wide around her on one side; a couple pushed past on the other. They were in their middle years, their faces crosshatched with the appropriate lines; there was nothing in either to remind her of her parents, especially her youthful stepmother, except for the woman's silence as the man talked on and on. But Mehitable had not been silent in her letters. *You must go to my mother if you find yourself in any difficulty.*

Jane turned around.

Water Street

Chapter Twenty-five

J ANE TRAVELED THROUGH the streets locked inside her own rage. She
saw nothing of the remains of King Street or Quaker Lane or Water
Street until she'd reached her grandparents' door and realized that the
street had been swept clean, the top of the elm that had fallen had been
chopped and stacked, the shutters rehung, and the windows repaired.
The sight of such redemption soothed her only enough to bring her into
something that resembled calm as she knocked on the door. Mrs. Poole
answered, but Jane's grandmother was close behind; Jane had given no
thought as to how she might explain herself, but when she saw her grandmother's face she understood there was no need. Her grandmother cupped
a strong hand under Jane's elbow and drew her to the keeping room without a question asked.

No fire had ever felt so comforting as the hissing logs on her grandmother's hearth, no fine imported Bohea so welcoming as the piss-yellow
swamp tea her grandmother served. Jane wrapped her hands around the
stoneware mug and leaned over the steam; her grandmother busied herself

over a plate of bread and butter, and by the time she'd delivered it to the table, Jane felt ready to begin. But she hadn't gotten far before her grandmother stood up and walked to the foot of the back stairs. "Eben!" She called.

Jane's grandfather mumbled an answer.

"Best come now!"

He came, still holding an open book in his hand. "Why, Jane! How did I not hear you arrive?" He stepped up to her and dropped a kiss on the part of her hair, a thing he'd done often enough without causing that hot press of tears at the back of her eyes. He looked from Jane to his wife and back again at Jane. "Have we some trouble here?"

Jane began again. The part she knew was short; the part she began to suspect and piece together grew longer as the short part got told, and her grandfather interjected a number of questions that pieced together more; the fuller the picture appeared, the greater the fool Jane appeared. Had it not been clear from the minute Jane had arrived at her aunt's home? The old woman's great concern over Jane's father's Tory views, not because she disagreed with them but because she was afraid they would give her away. Her collapse the morning after the tarring and feathering of the customs informer. Her intensified fears when the royal governor left town. The money in the desk, not inherited from her family but paid to her for information by a representative of the Crown, paid out to Prince no doubt. Prince who came and went as he pleased, carrying only the aunt's letters and never Jane's. Once Jane discovered the cache in the desk they must have changed their hiding place, of course, and so the coins always remained, fooling Jane into believing *she'd* fooled Prince and Martha, while protecting Aunt Gill. Protecting Aunt Gill! That she could think she had come along and made it their two against the other two, when all along it had been their three against her one.

"I wonder what other papers she might have hidden away that would be useful to us," Jane's grandfather said after a time, and the single remark caused another wave of recollections to flood in.

"None, now," Jane said. "The night the governor left, Martha took a leather case out of the house, right under my eyes. To protect it from fire, she said, my aunt said. To protect it from any rampaging mob, more like, now the governor was gone!"

"But in truth, Eben," Jane's grandmother cut in. "What of value could that one old woman pass along?"

"The cache of arms at Faneuil Hall," Jane said, thinking furiously now. "The planned signal to raise the countryside with a flaming barrel on the beacon hill. She heard the first from Henry. She heard the last from Nate, right here in your home."

"And she heard things from Adams and Otis as well," Jane's grandfather added. "No doubt she used you, Jane, for access to news of such men through your brother—indeed, for access to the men themselves; I'd never heard of her entertaining in such fashion before." He turned to his wife. "And as I included the aunt in my invitations to Jane, I abetted her as well. We must think now. What besides the arms, the beacon, did we disclose?"

Together Jane and her grandfather attempted to reconstruct the conversations they'd shared with Aunt Gill, but Jane could recall only the things that she should have seen before: her aunt's insistence on including herself among the rebels in her talk with that pompous and artificial *we*; her agitation, not fatigue, when the talk had turned to hanging traitors; her false concern over Otis after the beating and for her grandfather after the storm; the glee she had been unable to disguise over a British soldier becoming Otis's son-in-law. Jane thought of that smile she had described as a child's but now saw as a cat's, a smile that had met Jane every time she offered up evidence that her affection had been engaged, the wool successfully drawn.

After a time Jane's grandfather stood. "I must speak to some gentlemen about this. I trust, Jane, you will now stay here with us. On my return I shall call upon your Aunt Gill and ask for your things to be sent along."

And no doubt he would ask other things as well. After he left, Jane's grandmother, proving her thoughts once again in line with Jane's, said, "He'll get what he can, make no mistake. But he'll see no harm comes to her."

Jane searched, but could find nowhere in her that she cared.

JANE'S GRANDFATHER RETURNED LATE, long after Jane and her grandmother had eaten a scrabbled-together supper before the fire in the keeping room. They had cleared away the effects and settled back to talk away what they could of the day's grime when he entered the room. He was not at ease. He talked for a time about Aunt Gill and the abuse she had vomited his way, but she had told him all he needed to know. They had been correct in all their suppositions—she had been in constant communication with an aide to the governor; Jane had been right about Prince as well. He was no slave; his name was in fact Prence; he was descended from one of the colony's first governors. At first Jane thought such a disagreeable interview must be enough to account for her grandfather's state, but it proved not to be so.

"I spoke to the gentlemen I mentioned before," he began. "I must tell you, Jane, I'm not always in accord with these gentlemen; but I must also tell you that I see the purpose in what they ask of me now. In what they ask of *you*. They ask to see your letter book. They wish to discover what else Aunt Gill might have passed along, things that you might not consider compromising, not having the larger picture in mind. I offered the alternative that you might allow me to see it and me alone—flattering myself that you would honor me with a greater degree of trust than you might a stranger—they accepted the plan on condition that if you didn't voluntarily hand me the book I must examine it in secret. I promise you that will not happen. Either you agree or you do not, and so it will rest."

Jane's grandmother said, "'Tis no time to ask this of the girl."

"Indeed, it is not, if it ever would be. They wanted to come and confiscate the book at once, but I put a stop to that only by suggesting this alternative." He stood up. "But now we are done with the subject, and Jane may think on it, and in due time inform me of her wishes. Your trunk has already been brought upstairs, Jane; best make sure all is as it should be. Now if you would excuse me please, I've work—" He left the room, his mind already gone on ahead of his tongue.

JANE TOOK A CANDLE above-stairs. She had been too distressed earlier to take much solace from her room, but now she took it in and was surprised—pleasantly so—to feel how familiar it had already become. It could not be called home any more than Aunt Gill's, but what could be now? Perhaps her trunk. She opened it and checked through all her belongings; her pouch with her earnings was the first thing she sought out, and she took a long, relieved breath at the sight of it. Next she looked for the letters from her family, her paper and ink, the books she'd either bought or received from Henry as gifts. She rifled quickly through the clothes without removing them from their storage place. But what now? The trunk held her life as it had been, without any hint of what it might become.

Jane sat, at great waste of the candle, pondering her choices. She supposed she might count on her grandparents to keep her, but for them to be forced to do so out of necessity rather than generosity seemed unfair to all three. She supposed too that she could write her father the letter that Mehitable had suggested she write. Jane had been away from home a long time; her father's bluff had been called and hers in due turn; surely by now they might consider all debts paid? Surely Mehitable would not have suggested such a letter if she weren't confident of her husband's willingness to suffer her return? And now there was no question that her father *knew* of the dangers of town. A small corner of her mind, the child's corner, wondered if a letter should not be traveling the other way, demanding that she return home, but the adult Jane pushed that wondering aside.

Jane collected her writing things and arranged them on the small table by the window. She sat down, adjusted her candle, dipped her pen, and opened her letter book. Her letter book. She laid down the pen. She began turning pages in the book, stopping at this or that place as her eye got captured. Sometimes she had used the book to compose a draft of a letter that she planned to copy over; sometimes she had used it to make a sketchy copy after the fact of a hastily written effort, in order to remind herself where she'd left off in the correspondence; but sometimes—she could better see it now where she hadn't before—sometimes she'd used her letter book as a journal.

The pages that were journal were the pages that concerned Jane the greatest. The reason they'd been kept as journal and not sent as letter was because their content had proved either too confused or too troubling or too private to share. Now she was to hand these pages to her grandfather? Or wait for them to be confiscated by one or another of the famous Sons—perhaps an Adams or a Molineux or even a Knox? No. Before they did that she'd let the fire take them. Indeed, why *not* let the fire take them? Why allow her grandfather, however trusted he might be, to wander about inside her private musings?

Because Aunt Gill had already wandered there. Because no doubt half the governor's men had wandered there. And if Jane wished to undo any of what Aunt Gill had done, not just to this already disordered cause but to Jane, she must let at least one other person wander there. And there was one other reason to allow the thing, and in the end that was the reason that carried Jane to the stairs: her grandfather's careworn face. Jane had only the barest idea of what he dealt with in the legislature and with the Sons and in the town itself, especially now with Otis out of it, but she had a fairly good idea of how small her own embarrassment stood beside it. She picked up her letter book and went below.

JANE FOUND HER GRANDFATHER sitting at the keeping room table alone, hands splayed flat on the bare boards, eyes fixed on the single log that sighed weakly atop the embers.

He lifted his head. "Why, Jane, I should have thought you long asleep." He smiled. "Or perhaps not."

"And you, sir."

Jane's grandfather made no answer. He pointed to the chair opposite; Jane sat down, setting the letter book on the table. Her grandfather looked at it, and at her. "This shall be returned to you on the morrow. And I promise you, Jane, no eyes shall touch it but mine."

"Thank you."

"No, Jane, 'tis we must thank you." He paused. "I took the liberty of stopping at your brother's and acquainting him with the situation regarding your aunt. I felt a word of caution might be wise."

Jane nodded. "He was angry enough before; 'twill be worse now. There's one soldier he believes took deliberate aim at him to repay him for some past words. He's made out a deposition that condemns him." There Jane paused. It was late. Her grandfather was no doubt near exhaustion. And yet she added—she couldn't help but add—"Now he awaits mine."

"I see. And perhaps yours might not agree so precisely with your brother's?"

"Or many of the others that are being passed about town."

"Which should not have been passed about," her grandfather said with some heat. "Which you should never have seen." He drew up his shoulders and let them fall. "There have been times as a lawyer, Jane, when it has been necessary for me to ask a juror to ignore a particular testimony, as if his ears had not heard the very thing he'd just heard. 'Tis a difficult thing to do. But this is what you must do now."

"Phinnie Paine sees no need of me giving testimony at all. He says it doesn't concern me."

Jane's grandfather smiled. "Mr. Paine's opinion must be adjusted to account for his bias concerning the witness, as your brother's must likewise be adjusted to account for his bias concerning the accused. Are there any other opinions troubling you just now?"

Just as he seemed to know all about Phinnie Paine, so he seemed to know about Henry Knox too. And why should he not? She'd been seen all about town with the man; his deposition had been spread out in print for all to see. "Mr. Knox and I arrived together at the scene," she said. "I didn't see all that led up to the shooting in just the same light as Mr. Knox saw it. He believes the larger good outweighs a strict rendering of facts."

"And do you believe so?"

"I don't know."

"Well then, you must think on it. And as you think on it, you must think on this too. Do you believe Mr. Knox has a greater right to his opinion than you have to yours?"

"No doubt the judges would think so."

"I'm not concerned with judges at this moment, Jane. I'm concerned only with the question at hand, and this question is the only one I am in fact able to answer for you. The answer is no, Mr. Knox does not have a greater right to his opinion than you have to yours. And once you understand that, it becomes simpler, does it not?"

Yes. No.

Jane said, "May I ask you your opinion of what happened in King Street, sir?"

"I don't know what happened. I wasn't there."

"I mean to say—" Jane stopped. What did she mean to say? "I only wonder, sir, what you think of the situation in general. Of the soldiers. Of . . . of—" She stopped again.

If Jane's grandfather had looked tired before, he looked beyond it now. "I think the taxes Parliament has imposed on these colonies are unlawful. I think it our right—no, indeed, our obligation—to protest against these unlawful taxes. As the soldiers were sent here to stifle that right, I think their presence unlawful, and they should be called home." He shook his head, as if to clear it. "Home. There is all of it in a word. England is too distant from us for us to call it home anymore. And England has no idea of the thing that America has become. They don't realize that we've grown. They don't realize we're not their children anymore."

"But what of those who do think England home? What of those who wish to stay her children?"

"Well, then," her grandfather said, "they'd best go home."

CURIOUSLY, JANE DID SLEEP, mental and physical exhaustion swallowing her up the instant she lay down. And when she woke in the middle of the night she found herself remembering, not the massacre or her aunt's betrayal or any of the events that had occurred in town, but that long-ago carriage ride. Suddenly, however, the memory had changed. The three children had not curled up like puppies in the backseat—Bethiah had been little more than a toddler and fidgeted about from seat to floor; Nate had wanted the whole seat and more than once had used a heel to push Jane away; twice, the carriage had veered dangerously off the road, causing Bethiah's mother to cry out, "Nathan, pay heed!" And if even that old, cherished memory was a lie, Jane must keep watch that no such lie would survive over Aunt Gill. She must remember these many months with her aunt, not for what she'd wished them to be, but for the lie they truly were. The whole of it, even the old woman's supposed need of her, had been proved a lie the minute she'd gotten up and walked unaided across her chamber. But for the aunt to have allowed—or even cultivated—an affection in the niece was the greatest deceit of all. The greatest humiliation of all. Was nothing as it seemed? Aunt Gill wasn't. Prince wasn't. The massacre wasn't. Miss Linnet wasn't, nor was her brother. Or Henry Knox. But what of her father? And Phinnie? Phinnie had never seemed anything at all except in love with her, but even that had melted away like a spring snow.

And what of Jane? What could Jane claim to be, as she twisted in the face of every wind that blew?

Chapter Twenty-six

THE NEXT MORNING Jane wrote to her brother: *I have considered long and am now firm in my mind. I am unable to offer any testimony regarding Mr. White. I know you will accept this decision from your sister who loves you and prays you will continue to love her in return. I am staying with our grandparents for a time, as a result of a situation of which you have been apprised. I remain, as always—Your Most Affectionate Sister.*

Jane read it over and felt as good as she'd felt since the events in King Street. She had, at last, left the "Bloody Massacre" behind.

A knock sounded on her door. Jane opened it on her grandfather, her letter book in his hand. She took it from him.

"What other trouble did it cause?" she asked.

"None we hadn't already discovered."

Hearing her grandfather's words, the lingering tightness behind Jane's eyes eased; knowing the bound of the trouble had diminished it somehow. She returned the letter book to her room and tucked it away in her trunk;

she carried her brother's letter below-stairs, and found her grandmother in the kitchen alone, gutting a chicken with what appeared to be unnecessary violence.

"I should like to know what Mrs. Poole was thinking when she brought this bird home. Look at these legs! Speckled! Rough! This bird is older than I am! Why is it not possible in this town to step out the door and return with a young and healthy bird? If I but had my coop at Satucket—"

"Can you not have a coop here?"

Jane's grandmother sent the knife hard into the table. She looked at Jane in such a way that Jane wondered with an insane alarm if she was entirely safe from the blade. Well, of course her grandmother might have a coop if she'd only stay in town long enough to tend it.

Jane picked up a turnip and began peeling, and for a time she was able to leave off thoughts of letters written and unwritten, but not for long. The letter to her brother crackled at her from where it lay on the post table. The potential letter to her father started and stopped with each slash of the knife.

Jane's grandmother lopped off the bird's neck with a single blow, stared a minute at the offending legs, and lopped those off too.

THE NEXT DAY'S *GAZETTE* carried the news:

> A group of patriotic citizens of the town, being informed that a woman residing at Royal Exchange Lane having informed against them, called on the house and not being received took up stones, then breaking the windowpanes on both floors. The woman and her servants subsequently fleeing to a neighbor's house, the citizens followed but were turned away by a presentation of arms. The household's attempting to leave for the country being discovered, they were escorted on their way by a number of patriotic citizens of the town.

Along with a tar pot and feathers? Or the contents of their night jars? Even the *Gazette* might exhibit some reticence in reporting such treatment of a woman so old, traitor or no. But reading the story, Jane discovered that there was, after all, a reason to write a letter to her father.

THAT LETTER WAS NOT so difficult. Jane put down what had happened at Aunt Gill's and what had happened to Aunt Gill; she informed her father where she currently resided; no more was required. But as Jane laid down her pen she discovered there *was* something about the letter that troubled her; she began to feel that it was half-done. Her father had sent her away to what he had no doubt hoped, and what had indeed proved, to be an unhappy experience, but that was not the whole. She dipped her pen and put it to the paper again. *I send with this letter something to liven your bookshelf. I purchased this book from my friend, Mr. Henry Knox, the bookseller at Wharton & Bowes—perhaps you have visited this store on one of your trips to town, but if not, I recommend you visit it on your next one. Mr. Knox would be most happy to attend you, if only on my account alone. You see that thanks to your clever negotiation of my wage I am able to supply myself with many fine things I could not afford before, although these things not being available to me at Satucket, I should hardly have known the lack.*

Jane read over what she'd added and was pleasantly surprised at her own cleverness—to disguise so thick a vein of bitterness under so thin a skin of magnanimity was something perhaps only Phinnie Paine might appreciate. She copied the letter out, added her best hopes for the family's health and her great affection for all, signed her name, and sat back, exhausted.

JANE AND HER GRANDMOTHER were out in the garden, picking over an old, neglected bed of herbs, when Jane's grandmother said, "I must put a choice before you, Jane. Should you like to return to Satucket with us when we leave or should you prefer to stay in town? You must know our house is yours."

Jane said, "My father—" but found herself unsure of how to go on. All just seemed to begin with him. Or end there. She began again. "Until I receive my father's answer to my letter—"

Jane's grandmother rocked back on her knees and dusted her hands on her skirt. "When I say our house is yours I mean this house and *that* house, Jane. Your returning to Satucket does not depend on him unbolting his door to you."

Jane sat back on her heels too. It had never occurred to her that she could return to Satucket on anything but her father's terms. She imagined greeting her father not as a beggar but as a visitor, free to come and go as she chose.

Jane's grandmother said, "You needn't decide the thing now," but of course it was decided the minute her grandmother mentioned it.

"When do you plan to return?"

Jane's grandmother's eyes changed focus, from near to far. She said, as her husband had, "Soon."

JANE HAD LEARNED FROM her grandfather what "soon" did and didn't mean, but it didn't matter. It would take little time to pack, as her trunk had never been unpacked. As she waited she resumed her place beside her grandmother in the kitchen and soon discovered that the job was not as simple as it had first appeared. As many times as her grandfather made it to the table for their dinner, as many more times he sent a note saying he was delayed and could not attend. When he did arrive for dinner he was often not alone, and besides seeing old acquaintances like John Adams, Jane met other lawyers involved in the upcoming trials. And so the "Bloody Massacre" wasn't left behind after all.

The two most interesting men who came to call, aside from Adams, were a pair of brothers Jane had never met before—Josiah and Samuel

Quincy. Josiah possessed a crossed eye and would appear for the defense, despite his father's violent objections; Samuel's eyes sat straight, but he would appear for the prosecution. The more interesting thing about the brothers, however, was that their political inclination should have put each on the other's side. A true loyalist named Auchmuty filled out the defense team, and it was this man who caused Jane the greatest unease.

"The evidence is very strong that the firing came by Preston's order," he declared one day as Jane worked around the table, filling platters. "We must therefore build up the case of the soldiers' provocation. The outrageous reports in the papers, the long months of orchestrated attacks by the inhabitants, the unrelenting efforts to provoke the soldiers into just such an event as has now transpired."

"No, no, no," Adams cried. "We must have no talk of orchestration! No long months of attacks!"

"What?" Josiah Quincy put in. "Against the kinds of witnesses the prosecution will provide?"

Adams shook his head. "The eyes of every friend in all the colonies and abroad are now fixed on us and will be fixed so throughout these trials. If the inhabitants are perceived as the instigators of this event we lose them all. This cannot become a trial of the town."

"Then it shall be no trial," Auchmuty said.

"And you'll hang the lot," Josiah Quincy added.

Adams, all there was of height and width and breadth to him, drew himself up. "If such an effort as just described is made by either of you, I shall stand down as counsel for the defense."

And thus the matter was closed.

IT WAS NO CONCERN of Jane's. So Phinnie had said, and so Jane agreed; with her brother's letter mailed there was no reason on God's earth for Jane to be thinking about the massacre at all. She told herself this as she lay in bed, and she told herself this as she woke in the morning, and she told herself this as she labored over the dough tray beside her grandmother. It was no concern of hers, and she almost hoped Phinnie would stop by so she could admit the same.

But it was Henry Knox who stopped by. It was different with Henry at Water Street—he wasn't ushered into any formal parlor but brought into the keeping room and set down among the bustle there. Jane's grandmother asked a number of questions, the kind Jane's father might have asked, and Jane discovered a number of things she was embarrassed to learn she hadn't discovered before. Henry was the seventh of ten sons and the oldest now at home, supporting his widowed mother and the remaining three siblings; he only managed Wharton & Bowes for his employers, but one day he hoped to open a bookshop of his own. One thing about his visits, however, remained the same: after due attention was paid to their guest, Jane's grandparents made their excuses and left the pair alone. It was there Jane might have told Henry about her letter to her brother, but somehow she did not, and when he reached for her she felt hollow under his hand, as if the core of herself had been left behind in the silence.

WHEN PHINNIE PAINE DID stop by at last, it was over business with her grandfather. Jane was in the keeping room peeling and chopping onions for a soup and she heard his voice—the unmistakable lift in it: *Good-day, Mrs. Poole, how do you fare?*

Phinnie had come, he told Mrs. Poole, to see Mr. Freeman about some shingles. Jane heard the pair of footsteps move off in the direction of her grandfather's office, heard the rich, deep rise and fall of male voices, heard a laugh—her grandfather's laugh—and a possessive wave of gratitude swept over her; it had been some time since she'd heard her grandfather laugh. Jane's grandmother, just returned from the cellar, paused when she heard it too and smiled. She cast an eye at Jane and said, "Best bring that man a cider."

Jane went to the jug, poured two tankards full, carried them down the hall and into her grandfather's office. The room was like and not like her father's in that the books that lined these shelves were most certainly full of words, words of which, no doubt, her father would not approve. As Jane entered, Phinnie rose to his feet and accepted his mug with a silent nod. Jane's grandfather took his mug and peered inside.

"I've an earwig swimming in here."

Jane reached for the mug, but her grandfather held it away. "No, no, I'll tend it." He left the room, leaving silence behind.

After a time Phinnie said, "An earwig. I thought him cleverer than that."

Jane said nothing.

Phinnie said, "You might as well sit down, Jane. He'll not be back soon."

Jane stayed standing.

Phinnie said, "When I was last at Satucket your sister Bethiah engaged me in a private word. She said your father sent you here because of me."

"I sent myself," Jane said, which was, and wasn't, true.

"To hide from me?"

"No." True? Not true?

"When I saw you at your aunt's I behaved poorly. Perhaps I understand something better now of how you felt. The difficulty I caused you. I would cause you no difficulty, Jane." He stopped. He leaned over and set his tankard on the table. Jane looked at his back and remembered all the times she thought she'd seen it through the crowds. A wild, meaningless desire to lay her hand on that back rose up in her.

Phinnie turned to Jane again. "I wonder if you remember the day I met you, Jane. I was in your father's office; I don't believe you knew anyone had even entered the house. You tapped on the door and called out, 'Papa?' Your father called you into the room, beckoned you to his side, and circled your waist. 'Mr. Paine,' he said, 'you now have the great honor of meeting my eldest daughter.' How your face glowed! How happy you were to be inside the circle of that man's arm, to be presented by him so proudly! 'Twas a thing I could not forget." Phinnie paused. "Remembering such a thing, how could I answer your questions of that last night in Satucket, Jane? How could I say to you I thought your father self-serving in his politics and well capable of any number of dishonorable acts? Was he capable of cutting off a horse's ears? I don't know. I do know I could not work under a man of his temperament, nor would I care to live across the road from him, nor could I ever love him as you do. Is that what you would have liked me to say to you that night? Would that have swept you happily into our marriage? Tell me, Jane. What should you have done that night if I had said such things? Would you have gone ahead and bedded me, all in accordance with your father's plan?"

"My *father's* plan!"

"I'm not a fool, Jane. I knew well enough he would never allow me to lie with you under his roof and then remain a single man. I knew he pushed you into my bed to put the final seal on his scheme. But understand, your father's plan and mine were up until a particular point one and the same. Aside from the usual passions at play, I was in even greater haste to see the thing done, before you discovered that I could not love your father as you should like me to do, before you discovered I could not agree to the second part of his plan. The plan for my future. For our future."

Our future. The words hung in the air as dead as the thing itself, dead as a thing never born. Phinnie had stopped speaking, no doubt waiting for Jane to answer, but she couldn't raise a single word—Phinnie had said too many of them for her to sort them through. He had drained his tankard and picked up his hat when the first ones came to her.

"And how my father loved *you*."

It sounded bitter and cold, not the way she wished it to sound, but she couldn't think how to sweeten or warm it, because it was true.

———

THE NEXT DAY A note arrived from Jane's brother. *Dear Sister—I am in receipt of your letter; 'tis just as well; Mr. Adams should have made a hash of you. Indeed, if you can't speak to the cause, best you don't speak at all. I remain as I always have remained and always shall remain—Your Most Affectionate Brother.*

There was no letter from her father.

Chapter Twenty-seven

A T THE FIRST of April Otis came by. In all Jane's brief acquaintance with the man he had been finely dressed; this day he came in a soiled shirt, without a coat, his knee buckles unfastened. They were at supper when Mrs. Poole ushered him in; he stood at the keeping room door and peered at them as if he'd somehow arrived at the wrong dwelling.

"Welcome, my friend," Jane's grandfather said. "Will you join us?"

Otis looked over the table. "I will make thee think thy swan a crow."

"You might at that," Jane's grandmother said, "but I believe you'll find 'tis tasty just the same."

Otis stared at her. "The devil can cite scripture for his purpose."

"Come, sir," Jane's grandfather tried again. "'Tis no devil here—none but old friends."

Otis looked in evident perplexity from face to face. He came around the table and leaned down until he could claim a fairer view of Jane's. Did he know her? Jane was not at all sure of it.

"Truth is the trial of itself," he said to her. "What can we know or what can we discern when error chokes the windows of the mind? No pleasure is comparable to the standing upon the vantage-ground of truth!"

"Mr. Otis," Jane's grandmother tried yet again. "If you please, it would be our greatest pleasure if you would sit and take some food with us."

"I must cudgel my brains no more about it!" Otis cried and bolted out the door.

Jane's grandmother started to speak and faltered. "'Tis . . .'tis all nonsense he speaks now."

"Not all," Jane's grandfather answered. "He gave us Ben Jonson; Shakespeare. 'Tis Sir John Davies, I believe, who speaks of windows of the mind; Francis Bacon the vantage-ground of truth; he came back to Shakespeare at the end. 'Cudgel thy brains no more.' Poor, tormented creature; if only he could do so. I fear . . . I fear—" He stood up. "I must see him safe." He followed Otis's path out the door.

Near midnight Jane's grandfather sent a note that he would be in attendance until Otis's brother arrived, that plans were under way to deliver Otis into the care of his family at Cape Cod. Jane woke to her grandfather's tread on the stairs in the early hours, to low voices coming from behind her grandparents' chamber door. It went on long, but it didn't keep Jane awake; she was now awake on her own account, thinking of Otis, unable to free her mind of the man. He had leaned down to *her*. He had spoken to *her. What can we know or what can we discern when error chokes the windows of the mind?* The solitary sentence held in it all that Jane had wrestled with since March the fifth. But she had put the fifth behind her along with her decision about Hugh White. Why must *she* cudgel her brains about it so?

Because of Captain Preston. Jane's brother might think it all about Hugh White—Jane might once have thought it all about Hugh White—and her brother might absolve her from testifying about him, but he couldn't absolve her from testifying about Captain Preston. But why must she care about Captain Preston when others didn't? The captain stood so close to hanging he might look up and see the shadow of the rope, and his lawyer had voluntarily tied his own hands in Preston's defense. And yet she must care. And why? Because Phinnie was wrong. It *was* her concern. If they hanged a man for a thing he did not do, it might be because of a thing she did not say. It didn't matter who Captain Preston was or what he stood for or even whether or not Jane liked him, although, in fact, she did. She must say what she believed she saw. And she must soon discover if Otis—or Bacon—was right: that there was no pleasure comparable to standing upon the vantage-ground of truth. Judging by the great wave of nausea rising up in her chest, she held her doubts.

JANE ROSE EARLY, WASHED and dressed herself, made up her bed, and sat down on its edge. She listened and heard her grandmother's steps on the stairs; she continued to sit. When she heard her grandfather's heavier tread, she leaped up and opened her door, giving her grandfather a start.

"Jane!"

"I'm sorry, sir. But I have a question I needed to ask, and I wanted to ask it before you left on your business. It concerns Mr. Adams."

Jane's grandfather looked his surprise, but without hesitation he folded up like a crane and sat down on the next step. Jane sat on the step above, the better to even their heights. "I once talked to you about making a deposition at my brother's request. I told him I could not say what he wished. He accepted that answer."

"Then I would call the matter settled."

"That aspect of it is. But I might be able to give some other testimony in favor of Captain Preston. My brother knows nothing of this."

"I see."

"Don't mistake me, sir. My brother is not my concern. Or rather, he is not my *total* concern. I have some concern over Mr. Adams."

"Mr. Adams!"

"I well know his political sympathies do not lie with the soldiers. If I were to go to him with something I saw that aided Captain Preston, if I were to take the trouble to myself, knowing I should make unhappy those I love—" Jane paused. "I only wonder if Mr. Adams is sincere in his effort."

"Ah! I see. There, perhaps, I may be of some help. I have known Mr. Adams some years now and may say without reservation that he is the hardest-working, most honest man I know. You may have no fear that he will apply all of his considerable talents to freeing Captain Preston."

Except if it required putting the town on trial along with the soldiers. But *that* could not be Jane's responsibility. In truth, she'd known her responsibility from the minute Otis had peered into her face and begun to speak.

JANE AND HER GRANDFATHER conspired together. Mrs. Poole was sent with a note to Adams's office which would occupy Jane's brother on an errand and leave Jane free to speak without him present. Indeed, when she arrived, the lawyer was alone at a desk so covered with books it required him to hold his elbow in the air as he wrote. On seeing Jane his eyes first widened in surprise and then dampened. "Miss Clarke! How touched I was to receive your most expressive letter on the loss of my darling Susanna. You, who never laid eyes upon her!"

For a minute Jane stood puzzled. Of course she'd seen her, seen her in Adams's arms—and then she remembered. It was only the father's love she'd seen as he'd held Mehitable's babe and thought of his.

Adams blinked, regaining himself. "I do hope you don't come to me with some trouble of your own, Miss Clarke."

"No, sir, I come to you with some help for Captain Preston."

She explained herself. Adams's round eyes grew rounder as she talked, first with disbelief, then with relief, and finally with an honest man's joy, which she wished with all her heart she could better share.

HENRY KNOX CAME, and the minute he stepped into the keeping room Jane knew she could not tell him of her visit to Adams. He would learn of it in due time—that was the way of things in town—but he would not learn of it today, from her. This self-imposed silence pressed so heavily on her that it took her some time to catch up to what Henry was saying to *her.* Jane was working at pies, and Henry had come around the table to examine her work. She'd just laid out the pigeons, peppered and salted her lumps of butter and stuffed them inside; as Henry lifted his eyes from the pie to her she at first mistook one kind of hunger for the other.

"Times are coming to a head, Jane," he was saying. "Times are dictating a man's behavior, prompting him to think ahead of himself and his circumstance, suggesting to him that the day must be seized before all is swept away before him." He paused. "Perhaps, Jane, you recall something of my living situation. Perhaps you remember that I live with my widowed mother and younger siblings and work to provide their keep and care. One might think this left no room for another, but such is not the case; my mother has reached that age and state of health where she is ready to sit back and let another take her place at the hearth." There Henry paused and looked at Jane, waiting for her to speak.

Jane looked at Henry and saw again her image in his eyes, but somehow her image had now taken on the coloration of her stepmother Mehitable. She said, "So you are in need of a housekeeper, then? Perhaps my grandmother would know of someone who might suit."

Henry blinked. "Well . . . yes. Thank you."

JANE'S GRANDFATHER BROUGHT THE talk home to dinner—Preston's trial was to take place at the May sitting of the court—and it was as if his words sailed through the air and got caught in Jane's throat.

But out of that same air Jane's grandmother said, "Perhaps after the trial we might return to Satucket."

Jane's grandfather's eyes came up from his pie to fix on her. He said, "'Tis impossible for me to leave town at present. You know this."

"Indeed I do. I was thinking to take Jane. Only to see how the house fared over winter. 'Twas more work last spring than I anticipated."

A canopy of weight, heavier than cheesecloth but lighter than a bed rug, draped itself over the table. At length Jane's grandfather said, "You've not been here six months."

"Long enough for an empty house to need tending. Lord, when I think what might await—why, it has suffered a hurricane since I last saw it! And only think of Jane. When has she last seen home?"

Jane's grandfather turned to her. "'Tis true, I don't think of you, Jane. Your work here is ended—no doubt you're anxious to return to Satucket."

She was. She wasn't. She'd by now received her father's answer to her letter, which was that he had chosen not to answer it. She had heard from Bethiah and Mehitable and neither had made mention of it. If she returned to Satucket it would be as her grandmother returned—for a visit. Her grandmother wanted desperately to see her home, but what did Jane want? It would be necessary to see her father, of course, but she had no idea how he would greet her. She thought of Phinnie's description of them that day in her father's office—it had seemed like such a simple affection as he described it. But it would not be a simple thing now, if it were a thing at all.

She said, "I should like to see Satucket and help my grandmother if you would permit it."

Jane's grandfather smiled. "Ah, Jane. You do not escape so easily. I do not permit or deny—you must consult your own wisdom in this."

Jane tried to imagine such words issuing from her father's lips and couldn't.

THE MAY TRIAL WAS postponed. At the end of the month the news arrived from England that the Townshend duties had been repealed, all but the tax on tea, and talk of it consumed the dinner table for weeks. Jane could see some gain for the pocketbook but little for the principle and was pleased to see that for once her brother, Henry, and her grandparents were all in accord with her view of it.

Talk of the trial resumed in June and continued through July and August, trapping Jane and her grandmother in town. Jane did her best to keep hands and mind occupied, and her grandmother saw that she was fitfully if not steadily employed—she nursed the neighborhood children through a dysentery epidemic, poulticed a chest and an ankle, lanced an abscess, salved some burns, and treated any number of cases of worms.

Nate began to come by more often, Mrs. Lincoln's husband having come to collect her at last—he seemed in better spirits than he had all through the fall, winter, and spring, but Jane could find no reason for it. She had refused to offer up testimony incriminating Hugh White. She had told him of her pending testimony regarding Preston, and he had said only, "Mr. Adams informed me of it." Afterward it occurred to her that Nate might not want Captain Preston handed all the blame for the assault, leaving Hugh White guilty of nothing but obeying his officer's order, but she was too glad to have her old almost-happy brother back again to cudgel her brains long about it.

Henry Knox continued to stop by. He must have heard of her pending testimony in favor of Preston, but he said nothing of it. Neither did he speak again of his housekeeping. Now and again he looked at Jane as if he were waiting for her to either send him away or to offer to engage herself, but Jane wanted neither thing, without entirely understanding why. She could not brand him with the Phinnie complaint; he spoke openly and honestly to her, and she felt she knew him well enough, but day by day as she observed her grandparents in their ordinary relations, she began to learn something of another kind of marriage than the one she'd observed

in her father's house. What she did not know was what it was that made
it that kind of marriage, but before she entered into one herself she was
determined to find out.

Phinnie Paine did not come at all, which was just as Jane expected.

WHEN THE TRIAL WAS rescheduled for October, Jane paid little heed,
assuming it should be pushed off again as it had been so many times before.
When it wasn't she felt almost as betrayed as she'd felt when she'd discovered Aunt Gill copying out of her letter book.

Chapter Twenty-eight

THE NEW COURTHOUSE on Queen Street had put its courtroom above-stairs; Jane climbed the steps as if they led to her own personal gallows. Once inside, the size of the crowd and the number of uniforms in it further alarmed her—a thick bar ran the length of the room, separating the onlookers from the principals, but nothing separated the two sides of the audience, and so many members of the army and navy and customs mixing so tightly together with the town's inhabitants seemed sure to promise a brawl.

On the other side of the bar Preston stood in the prisoner's box, his coat appearing to glow redder than those of his fellow soldiers, being set off to itself as it was. Next came the lawyers' tables, almost as congested as the onlookers' area, with three barristers for each side; next came the clerk's table, the jury box, and the judges, seated in the prime location before the fireplace. The five wigged and robed justices might have seemed to Jane all that the law should be had she not remembered Henry's stories of contrived illnesses and disappearances, and when she looked at the jury she could only remember that they came from the streets of Boston, with their minds as set against the soldiers as the cobbles on which they trampled. So Jane thought until she heard her grandfather whispering to her grandmother about one juror from Braintree and another from Dorchester and one who made his living baking bread for the Fourteenth Regiment.

Jane took up her station near the bar, a grandparent on either side; she had expected some jostling and even taunting, but the crowd—inhabitants and soldiers alike—were solemn and courteous. So, this was not the street. This was the world of law. She looked again at Preston, wanting very much to know what he was thinking. Was it: *Here now is my sham trial begun,* or was it: *Here is Jane Clarke to speak of the man in the cloak, and here on the jury is the man who bakes my bread; perhaps I will have justice done me after all.* Nothing in Preston's face or carriage gave the least hint of either. He stood tall, his mouth again fixed in that grim, hard line Jane had come to know so well from her dreams. All Jane might venture to read in him was that he was done with begging. Whatever happened, Jane doubted there would be any more letters of gratitude printed in the paper.

The first of the Quincy brothers—the loyalist Samuel Quincy—opened the prosecution's case with a description of the night of March the fifth much as the papers had described it: roaming bands of off-duty, armed soldiers looking for trouble and finding it at the corner of Exchange and King, the noisy but harmless crowd gathering, Preston ordering his men to load with powder and ball, to fire and fire again. Jane watched Preston as Samuel Quincy spoke and saw in him no change.

Samuel Quincy's first witness, Edward Garrick, the young apprentice wig maker who had tussled with White, told what he had to tell with fervor, but it had little to do with Preston. The second, Thomas Marshal, stated with certainty that whoever had given the order to fire, it made little matter, as Preston had had enough time between the first and later shots to order his men to recover and thereby prevent further bloodshed—an opportunity he had ignored. The next witness, Peter Cunningham, could only insist he'd heard Preston order his men to prime and load.

But the next witness, William Wyat, caused the first rumble through the courtroom.

"I heard the defendant give the orders to prime and load. I heard him give the order to fire. I heard him say, 'Damn your bloods, fire, be the consequence what it will!' "

The other Quincy brother, the cross-eyed patriot Josiah Quincy, arose from his seat and approached the witness.

"This was the only cry for fire you heard, sir?"

"Yes, sir."

"You heard no calls for fire coming from the crowd?"

"Well, some."

"People in the crowd calling on the soldiers to fire."

"Well, to tease them, like."

"Knowing they could not fire without an order. The crowd calling over and over, 'Damn you, fire'?"

"Words of that sort."

"Damn you, damn your eyes—"

"Well, yes. But it was Preston gave the order."

"And which order would that be?"

"All of them! To prime, load, fire."

"And how did you know it to be Captain Preston giving the orders?"

"I've seen him enough on his way to his parties about town, haven't I? And he had his captain's sash and epaulets on, hadn't he? How many captains do you think there were out there on that corner?"

As if only to get the last word, thin as it was, Josiah Quincy said, "This we shall determine, sir."

THE NEXT WITNESS, JOHN COX, came up to the bar and gripped it as if he'd like to leap over it in his eagerness to help get Preston hanged. "It was the captain ordered the soldiers to fire," he said. "The captain in his sash and epaulets. He said it once—he said 'fire'—and then he said it again: 'Damn your blood, fire, let the consequence be what it will!'"

The witnesses spoke so closely to their depositions that Jane felt as if she was at one of Henry Knox's play-readings. She looked again at Preston—if he had read the printed accounts none of this would surprise him—and indeed, he remained as impassive as before. Josiah Quincy rose again—a handsome man if it weren't for the eyes—but all he did for Preston was to draw out of Cox an even more vigorous repetition of what he'd already said—more harm than help to Preston.

After Cox, the justices decided the day was too advanced to go on and that court would be adjourned until the next morning—the news brought Jane's grandmother leaning across Jane to her husband. "I've never heard of such a thing! A trial gone beyond a day? Whatever will those poor jurors from the outlying towns do?"

"They'll be sequestered in the gaol-keeper's house."

"The lot of them? To sleep on the floor?"

"Bedding will be brought in. Food and liquor as well; 'tisn't the old days where they were starved till the verdict was delivered. But the one who will suffer greatest from such a hold-over is Captain Preston."

Yes, thought Jane—the words that will hang in the jurors' minds all night will be: *Damn your blood, fire!*

ON THE SECOND DAY it was as if someone had wrapped each member of the courtroom in string and pulled hard on the end, the inhabitants bouncing upward while the soldiery dragged down. Preston in his box had grown, if possible, more grim; he did not look at Jane. Of the five judges and six lawyers on the opposite side of the bar, only Adams looked serene. Did he think to win either way?

The first witness of the day was a man named Bliss, who testified with certainty that someone in the soldiers' line had indeed called out the order to fire, but he could not say that it was Preston. When he recalled that Preston had been standing in front of the guns most of the time, Jane looked to see if the jury had made note of the significance; half the men looked blank; the other half looked bored.

The second witness was Henry Knox. The loyalist Samuel Quincy began by asking Knox to describe the scene as he'd arrived, and there Henry looked at Jane, as if in some sort of signal. Or was it a warning? "I was escorting a friend to her home on Royal Exchange Lane. As we came upon the sentry at the Custom House he was being pestered by a group of boys. He was scared, but in no danger, and there was no need for him to raise the alarm."

Jane looked to John Adams, waiting for him to object to such an over-stepping, but he did nothing. Henry went on to describe his conversation with Preston and the events as they had been recorded in his deposition. Samuel Quincy then rose to thank him, not only for his testimony, but for his noble efforts to forestall the crisis that had nonetheless befallen the town.

Josiah Quincy rose. "Could you tell me, Mr. Knox, how many times you heard the call to fire?"

"It came twice from the soldiers' line."

"And how many times from the crowd?"

Henry hesitated. "I don't know."

"But you heard the crowd so call."

"I did."

Josiah Quincy likewise thanked Henry, but he hadn't helped either, or so Jane believed.

And neither did Benjamin Burdick, who only reiterated what Henry had said—that a call to fire had come from the soldiers' line, although he couldn't say for sure that Preston gave it. Robert Fullerton was much the same. Daniel Calef was not.

"I heard the officer who stood on the left in the line give the order to fire, twice. I looked him in the face and saw his mouth move. He had on a red coat, yellow jacket, and silver-laced hat." It was the perfect description of Preston's uniform. He went on, in case there was any question: "The prisoner is the officer I mean. I saw his face plain, the moon shone on it. I am sure of the man."

Robert Goddard came next, the troubling Robert Goddard who had identified Preston in gaol as the officer who had given the order to fire; at first Jane was unconcerned, as he seemed to be slow-witted, but when it came to the important moment, he grew all too clear.

"A sailor or a townsman charged up and struck the captain," he said. "The captain leaped back, drew his sword, and cried, 'Damn your blood, fire!'"

There John Adams stood up. "What makes you say the man might have been a sailor, sir?"

"'Spose it was how he looked."

"How he was dressed?"

"Like that, yes."

"So he was dressed as a sailor."

"I said so, didn't I?"

"Yes, you did, sir. Thank you."

Adams sat. Jane was not awed. He had achieved his goal of establishing that at least one of the troublemakers had come off a ship, likely from outside the town, but Goddard's identification of Preston stood firm. Perhaps deadliest of all, so did a motivation: Preston had been struck and thus would demand his revenge.

Nine more witnesses were brought to the bar, but they neither added nor subtracted to what had gone before. They didn't need to. Samuel Quincy reminded the jurors in his summation of the damning testimony by Calef and Goddard. He spoke of the massacre as an act "accompanied with those circumstances that show the heart to be perversely wicked," and so the Crown closed.

John Adams rose to open the case for the defense and no doubt he gave a stirring speech, but Jane heard none of it—it was as if Samuel Quincy's words, "perversely wicked," had clamped her ears closed. The words had brought her again to Winslow's horse. Why had Adams declined to accept that case when he had agreed to accept the *qui tam*? Perhaps he thought her father guilty of that particular crime and not the other. Perhaps he thought her father too "perversely wicked" to deserve his skill, a skill of which Jane continued ignorant thus far.

Jane came alert when the first defense witness was called, but there too it seemed to Jane that John Adams fared poorly. He called up the importer from the Brazen Head, whose entire purpose, it seemed, was to testify to the summons for Preston and the Main Guard. The next two witnesses attested to like matters. The fourth witness testified to Preston knocking up the soldiers' muskets after the firing had occurred, and perhaps there some valuable momentum might have been gained, but there the court adjourned.

Chapter Twenty-nine

J ANE EXPECTED TO appear among the witnesses the next day, and the thought of it brought on a Mehitable-style headache that carried her away from the supper table. She lay down on her bed in all her clothes, unequal to all the extra movements required to undress. She closed her eyes and immediately saw the moonlit snow, the snapping jaws of the crowd, the line of soldiers, Preston's red coat. Then what? There was what she believed she'd seen and heard. There was what her brother wished her to have seen and heard. There was what Henry Knox and, to a degree, John Adams wished her *not* to have seen and heard. And there was that merciless, grinding, pounding between her ears.

JOHN ADAMS CAME TO greet her as she entered the courtroom. "Ah! My favorite witness! Are we ready to do battle?"

No, thought Jane; never had the events of March the fifth jumbled about so in her mind. She knew that a sleepless night could jumble things well enough by itself, but there was this other thing, this sense that she was being asked to carry something large and she was too small to even see around it. If Hugh White had indeed attempted to slay her brother, should she not thirst with him for his revenge? If Preston had indeed given the order to fire, must she not judge it a transgression of the severest kind and wish him punished accordingly? If, however, Preston had not ordered his soldiers to fire, but in the normal bedlam had failed to collect his men in time, should he not pay some price for that as well? But if he were to pay a price, should that price be his life? She looked at John Adams. She said, "I fear, sir, you expect too much."

"Why, I expect you to say what you saw and no more." He peered down at her, every bit the foremost lawyer in town now. "And no less." He walked away.

ADAMS'S FIRST WITNESS, JOSEPH Edwards, testified that it was the corporal, not the captain, who had ordered the soldiers to prime and load their muskets.

"And what makes you certain it was the corporal?" Adams asked.

"The chevrons on his sleeve, sir," Edwards said. "In the moonlight they looked like rips."

Jane looked at the jury and could see the image printed across every single face: the moonlight, the sleeve, the "rips." Two other witnesses came forward and testified to Preston's attire—the sash, the silver georgette, the officer's sword—and Jane saw that imprinted as well; they would not be confused.

"Jane Clarke!" Her name had been called. She stepped forward. Adams approached and smiled at her, and with the smile a strange thing happened—she no longer saw the foremost lawyer in Boston but the man who had cradled Mehitable's babe, the man whose night jar she had emptied, and the thing he had asked her to do seemed instantly simpler. To say what she saw. Not to judge Preston's act, or to decide on the price that should be paid for such an act, but to say what she saw. Jane laid her hands on the bar; to her great amazement, they lay still.

"Would you be so kind as to describe for me, Miss Clarke, what you observed at the corner of Exchange and King on the night of March the fifth?"

Jane began. The boys pestering the sentry, the name-calling, the challenge over the bill. She described Hugh White striking the boy, the increasing crowd, the chunks of ice being thrown, the appearance of clubs, one club being thrown and striking a soldier. Adams never stopped her, even as she described the attack by the crowd, until she described the man in a dark cloak moving behind the soldiers.

"Can you better describe this cloak, Miss Clarke?"

"It was blue or black. A material like velvet or plush." As she said it Jane saw that the jury saw it, and Jane saw exactly why Adams had brought up so many witnesses to testify to Preston's uniform. There was the red and the silver and the yellow on the one hand, and the blue or black velvet or plush on the other; they could not be confused.

"And what did this gentleman do when he moved behind the soldiers?"

"He walked back and forth behind them, encouraging them to fire. The captain was at least three yards distant and for most of that time standing in front of his men. It was only when Captain Preston was struck that he stepped back. This was at the same time that the man in the cloak touched one of the soldiers on the back and said 'Fire, by God I'll stand by you,' and immediately upon his speaking the soldiers fired. That is to say the main of the soldiers fired. There had been a single shot fired previously at the time the soldier had been knocked to the ground."

"And you're positive this man who touched the soldier and spoke these words was not Captain Preston?"

"I am. He was at a good distance from the captain. He wore a dark cloak, as I said. He worked his way out of the crowd and behind the soldiers, no doubt with such intention in mind." She had gone too far, to even it up for Henry Knox having gone too far, but again, no one objected. Indeed, around the courtroom skirts and shoes and coat sleeves scraped and rustled and an involuntary murmur broke loose; inside the noise Jane heard for the first time the very great importance of her testimony for Preston. This or that or the other one could say that Preston had not given the order to fire, but if he hadn't, who had? Jane was the only one thus far who had been able to offer an alternative. She was the only one who had spoken out loud the obvious motive of some in that crowd, to incite the very incident that some had prayed for, the incident that would get the soldiers removed.

Adams said, "And after this unfortunate incident, after citizens and soldiers alike had been brought to the ground, what happened then, Miss Clarke? Tell us, please. Tell us, what did you do?"

"I tended to the wounded inhabitants."

"And among the inhabitants, did you find anyone you knew?"

My brother.

"I found my brother."

"You found your brother wounded by these British soldiers."

"Yes, sir."

"You found your brother wounded by these British soldiers," Adams repeated. He walked the length of the jury box, and returned to Jane again. "You found your brother lying bloodied in the street, and yet you came here to testify on Captain Preston's behalf. Why, Miss Clarke?"

"Because the truth of it should be known."

"*Because the truth of it should be known.* Thank you, Miss Clarke. For your testimony, and for the human decency that brought you here. We all thank you."

Jane stepped back and waited for the pleasure that was to overcome her there on her lofty vantage-ground of truth, but the only thing that overcame her was an exhaustion so complete she could barely stand.

———

THERE WAS MORE TESTIMONY. To Jane's great relief a sailor named James Waddell now remembered that he had also seen the man in the dark cloak slip behind the soldiers. A Richard Palmes testified that at the time of the command to fire he stood next to Preston with his hand on his shoulder, and although he couldn't say for certain the captain hadn't given the order, he had not heard the words. A slave testified to the general unruliness of the crowd, their threats and assaults on the soldiers; the slave's owner testified to the trustworthiness of the slave. Two more slaves and their owners testified in like manner. Several more witnesses, military and civilian, testified to Preston's mild-tempered, prudent, and discreet nature. No doubt all of these witnesses greatly aided Preston's cause, but Jane had felt and heard what had happened in the courtroom when she spoke and knew that her words had effected the great turn. The thought made her feel lighter and heavier in one.

ON SATURDAY JOHN ADAMS gave his closing argument. The legal precedents he quoted were lost on Jane until he pulled something from a thing called *Pleas of the Crown:* "It is better five guilty persons should escape unpunished, than one innocent person should die." He followed it with a man named Blackstone: "Self-defence is the primary canon of the law of nature." Next Adams proceeded to rip asunder each witness of the prosecution, and those he couldn't rip apart he explained away as in error. But once he had done all that, he turned around and forgave them. "Man is a social creature," he said. "His passions and imagination are contagious. The circumstances in King Street had a tendency to move all the passions. They have had a tendency to produce gloom and melancholy in all our minds. This may account for the variation in the testimony of honest men."

He next reminded the jury of all the important points of the testimony for the defense, Jane's central among them, but now she saw better the limits of her own importance. She had helped, yes, but if Preston were to be saved, it would be Adams who had saved him. Vindicated him. Or vindicated himself.

Jane thought—again—of Phinnie Paine.

THE COURT BROKE for the Sabbath. For Jane, the day wore away as slowly as the cobblestones on the street, and she could only think how it must have passed for Preston in gaol, the jurors at the gaol-keeper's. Jane's grandfather attended meeting, but as was her usual habit even at Satucket, Jane's grandmother stayed home. Ordinarily, Jane would have gone with her grandfather, but this day she decided to stay behind—there would be too many in the pews who disapproved of what she'd had to say in the courtroom.

THE TRIAL, THE FIRST ever to go beyond a day, had now done the unheard of—it had gone into a second week—but when court resumed on Monday all that remained was for the prosecution to make its closing remarks and the jury to be charged. The jury retreated, but no one else left the courtroom. People began to mill about and greet their neighbors, but little of the chat had anything to do with the trial; it was as if all were afraid their talk might cast the wrong kind of spell.

Jane saw her brother Nate working his way through the crowd toward her. He came up and gave the smallest bow. "You did well."

"I suppose from you that must mean I did not do well."

Nate gazed at her with something almost of hurt. "I mean you did a difficult thing and you did it well."

Jane laid a hand on his sleeve. "I suppose we shall see how well."

Nate smiled and shook his head, as if there were no doubt, but no doubt of which verdict? He moved off.

Jane looked through the crowd, wondering if she might see Phinnie Paine. Surely if he were in town he would attend? She spied the kind of tapered back she had taken so often for his but refused to be fooled again. It turned and was Phinnie. The weight of her parting remark to him still heavy on her mind, she searched for some sort of greeting that might lighten it but could think of nothing fitting—to wave seemed too little, too call out seemed too much. Afterward, after he'd stared a time and turned away, she realized she'd left out the one thing that would have fitted best— a smile.

IT TOOK THE JURY three hours to return Preston to his freedom. It took Sam Adams three minutes to begin his attempt to take it away. Jane had seen nothing of the man in the courtroom; he could not have expected John Adams, representing the defense, to have given his rebel cousin the floor, but perhaps he resented the prosecutors' denying him a word to the cause. He stood now on the courthouse steps, his too-short arms waving, his voice pitched to a catcall, describing the jury's verdict as the latest and grossest of all the recent miscarriages of justice the town had lately borne.

Satucket

Chapter Thirty

A S IT HAPPENED, Jane and her grandmother were still in town when the soldiers were brought to trial and defended, again, by John Adams. Henry Knox testified again, but in another of the many queer and inexplicable twists of the trials, this time he testified for the defense. Jane heard this news from her grandfather—Henry did not call—and she puzzled over it long. The news was almost enough to bring her to attend the trial, but in the end she elected to stay at home, waiting for her grandfather to bring her the news of Henry's testimony—the same as before—and of the verdict as well. Two of the soldiers were convicted of manslaughter, and pleading benefit of clergy proving that they could read their Bible and were therefore Christians worthy of saving, were excused the hanging and branded on the thumbs. The rest, Hugh White included, went free. Jane could only imagine how this must please Aunt Gill and enrage her brother, how strained his relationship with his mentor must have grown.

As for the cousin, Sam Adams, he took to the courthouse steps again, just as he had after Preston's trial, but now that the dual verdicts were in he could additionally set about retrying them all in the newspaper as well. Unbelievably, it was his version of events that began to take hold; soon, it was as if the verdicts at the trials had never been handed down.

NATE CAME TO SEE Jane before she left for Satucket. They talked, of course, of Hugh White. Jane said, "Are you very angry that Mr. Adams set him free?"

Nate took his time in answering, which was a new thing in him. "Mr. Adams talked to me after the trial. He spoke of a longer view, of how worthless our words become if we can't stand by the principles behind them while under fire." There he lifted his eyes and grinned, the old Nate again. "But perhaps he also knew his cousin Sam would get what he needed of it. The cause is not lost with the case. In fact it is reborn."

Still, Jane could not quite believe her brother's new loftiness. She said, to test him, "And Hugh White wins."

"What does he win? His life, no more. The true victory is mine. He's gone from here. They're all gone from here. 'Tis *my* town again."

My town. Jane heard the words and should not have been surprised but was so. "Do you plan to live here always, then?"

"Where else could a lawyer wish to be in these times? Where else could I take part? Satucket?"

No.

Nate peered at her. "But what of you? Do you leave here forever now?"

"I go home as guest of our grandmother and stay only till she returns to town."

Nate squinted at her. "And if Father begs you to come home?"

"Father, begging?"

Nate laughed. "All right, then. If he says to you, 'Well, Jane, 'tis about time you came home. Now get to work mending my breeches.' You would mend them, I suppose. God in heaven! Our father was mad for sending you here at such a time. But now 'tis different. The soldiers are gone, and I might unselfishly wish you here to keep me company."

Yes, thought Jane, but only now that Mrs. Lincoln is gone. And no doubt it would be someone new soon. Or perhaps Jane's life would have filled too much to allow room for any greater number of visits between brother and sister. She tried to imagine such a life and could not. She could not imagine her life at all.

DETERMINING TO GO to Satucket was one thing—getting there was another, especially with winter coming on. Jane's grandfather had not recovered from the thought of his wife being caught up in the fall storm, and now December was closing in—he began to talk of hiring a carriage, but there Jane's grandmother grew warm.

"And spend three nights in strange inns along the road?"

"You know the inns well enough."

"Yes, I do, and the last time I was in one I slept with an army of bugs and a rum bottle, or so I thought till it rolled over and puked into my hair. I'll take my single night at sea and home."

Jane's grandfather gazed on the pair of them as if they were already gone. "Then go before the ice forms."

THEY WERE PACKED and on board on the eleventh of December, later than all had hoped, but still well before the ice. Jane's grandfather stood on the dock with his hands jammed in his pockets, his lips moving in some final argument no one could hear. He looked so thin and alone, despite the comings and goings of travelers and hawkers and mariners around him, that Jane was not surprised when her grandmother's talk took a turn.

"Mrs. Poole is a good-hearted woman," she said, "but she does not know how to pick a bird."

"She'd not find one in winter anyhow," Jane offered; it was one of her first lessons learned—that poultry did not survive a winter trip to town—but Jane's grandmother went along as if she hadn't heard.

"A good chicken pie with a nice, thick gravy is all I ask. And a dinner consumed without a political maelstrom swirling around. But will he get them? Will he even—" She stopped there.

THEY WERE TWO HOURS out of the harbor when the weather turned. Jane's first hint of its seriousness was when her grandmother said, "I've had poor luck with the sea." The second hint was when all Harry Nye's efforts at cleverness disappeared into the wind. Sail was taken in; the sea began to crash over the deck; the women were sent below and the hatches closed. The easiest way to avoid being tossed about was to get into their bunks, and they did so. It seemed to Jane that the thunder of the waves was louder from below, but it didn't mask the other sounds—carefully lashed objects on deck breaking free and crashing about, the shouts of the men and the pounding of their heels. It would have been one kind of thing if the raging winds had pushed them faster toward home, but when Ned Crowe and Joseph Woollen came below for a new sail to replace one that had been torn, she heard them remark on being pushed off course. In the end the trip that should have kept them over one night kept them over three.

On the fourth day the thunder of the waves softened, the rolling lessened, the hatches opened. Jane and her grandmother sprang onto the deck like escaped geese and could not be persuaded to go below. Soon enough Jane recognized the spit that curled out around Barnstable Harbor; next the stand of trees at Freeman's Point; finally the marsh and inconsequential strip of beach that marked their landing at Satucket. At last the ship was brought about and anchored, the dory was lowered over the side, Jane and her grandmother were helped into it. Joseph Woollen was one of the rowers, but Jane no longer cared; indeed, it seemed a child's version of herself who had once been so troubled by his presence. She fixed her eyes on the shore, and the images of sedge, scrub, and landing road began to erase the other images: the Boston street, the snow, the moon, the blood. Her brother.

The boat scraped sand; the men leaped out and pulled it up on the shore. Jane's grandmother hiked up her dress without caring for effect and climbed over the gunwale before helping hands could reach her; Jane followed her. They trudged together over the sand to the landing road and on through the mud. Jane looked sideways at her grandmother and caught all the apprehension in her face, but they rounded the turn and there was the house, appearing much as they had left it. Her grandmother caught up Jane's hand, dragged her across the dooryard, and through the door.

Dust and mouse nests and cobwebs and dead insects and an aching, pounding cold greeted them. How odd, thought Jane, that she could stand in the middle of a room in such a state and feel, again, that utter peace come down on her. She would have liked to stand so forever, let it curl around her forever, but her grandmother had already dropped her cloak where she stood and crossed the room to the shelf that held the tinderbox. Jane went to the wood box and laid the kindling down; her grandmother set to work with the tinder, and after a time the chimney began to draw. Jane added the first logs—pine for the quick, bright flame—and felt the heat, first on her, then in her.

Jane's grandmother had brought some cheese, bread, and dried apples—enough to make a supper with the blackberry tea from the tin. That night Jane shared her grandmother's bed for warmth, and she slept deep and long, but in the morning she woke and mistook the warmth for her sister. The heart-soreness that filled her when she discovered it was not Bethiah surprised her.

THEY FINISHED THE BREAD and cheese for their breakfast, and Jane's grandmother set off for Sears's store. Jane began the cleaning—first knocking down webs, next dusting walls and shelves, last sweeping up the detritus and scouring the floor. She was just finishing when her grandmother returned with salt fish and potatoes and onions and Indian meal—it would be corn bread and fish stew for their dinner. As they cut up the vegetables Jane's grandmother said, "Your presence is already known here. Already talked of at the store. You must prepare what you wish to say if your father decides to pay a call."

"He won't," Jane said.

"He won't if you call there first."

Jane looked at her grandmother, this woman who had come in a storm and returned in one and remained uncowed by any number of other disturbances that had blown up in between. Was this the thing that made her marriage what it was, this life in her, this strength? Was this what gave her such an unfettered voice in that marriage? Perhaps, Jane thought, but part must come from a husband strong enough in himself to greet such life without attempting to beat it down, to silence it. Jane thought there of her father. Perhaps this supposed great strength in him was in fact something less than strength; perhaps it could only thrive in the fetid bog of his wife's diminishment, her silence. And—perhaps—the no longer silent daughter's absence.

But perhaps Jane's grandmother was right—better to meet her father while it remained her idea, not his, even though it seemed a great deal to ask on this first afternoon in the peace of her grandmother's house, after so trying a sea voyage.

THE SKY HUNG the color of ice. Jagged, white shards of it, like the blades of knives—or swords—lined the stream. Jane could not have said there was one thing warm and welcoming in the sight of it, and yet as she stood gazing over the mill valley she felt the width and depth of its comfort. Even Winslow's fulling mill and her father's grist mill lay as still and peaceful as if all the trouble they had caused had been nothing but lies.

Lies. Oddly, the word brought Phinnie Paine to mind. But wasn't that what all his agreeableness amounted to, now that Jane knew his true feelings about her father—lies? No marriage could thrive on such deceit. But as Jane walked and thought, she was forced to think, perhaps for the first time—of what Phinnie had said to her in her grandfather's office. There had been no deceit in *that*. And how had Jane responded? First, with silence, even as Phinnie waited in all patience for any words she would offer. And what words *had* Jane finally offered? *How my father loved you.* Perhaps, after all, there was the biggest lie of all of it. Her father wanted Phinnie's means and Phinnie's talents, talents that included his ability to create more means, to create an air of agreeableness out of adversity. Which meant . . . more lies.

Jane continued walking until her father's house rose before her, tall and square and solid and immovable. She stepped into the dooryard and halted. Once, when she was so young that she could remember nothing before it, her father had carried her into the dooryard and pointed upward. "Look, Jane, at the moon. Look how it watches over you. As I do." Or *was* that what he'd said? Or had her corrupted memory added the "As I do"? Whether she correctly remembered hearing the words, it made little difference, for she could still feel their meaning—that she was loved and cherished and safe in her father's arms.

Jane stepped across the dooryard and opened the door. Bethiah saw her first. She stumbled up from her knees in front of the fire and threw herself at Jane, shrieking enough to dull both their eardrums. The sight of the two sisters joined brought Hitty and Anne into it, and altogether the noise brought Mehitable down the stairs with the babe—so grown he could no doubt walk down on his own if Mehitable hadn't gripped him so hard— and Neddy hanging back behind. Neddy *would* hang back; he would know the trouble her visit would cause, as would Mehitable, even as she reached over the clinging girls to lay a hand on Jane's hair.

"My dearest Jane," she said, the words matching what Jane had first taken for meaningless addresses in her letters; now Jane could look at her stepmother's face as she said them and almost believe they were true. But she had little time to study the look before it was gone, replaced with the old, familiar mask, as Mehitable's eyes moved from Jane's face to something behind. Jane turned just in time to catch the closing of her father's office door.

Chapter Thirty-one

To KNOW HOW much one loved a thing one must see it at its worst—so it was with winter in Satucket. A few days after Jane and her grandmother had arrived another gale swept in, ripping a limb off the shadblow and raking a strip of shingles off the barn roof. A week later a northeast storm dropped a foot of snow, trapping the women within doors and burying the wood pile. With the New Year came a bitter, chilling cold.

Despite the adverse conditions, Jane's family came to visit—sometimes just Bethiah but on the better days the three girls together. Mehitable came once and Neddy twice; Jane saw nothing of her father and he sent no message, which was all Jane had expected. She heard from Bethiah that their father spent most days closed up in his office, that Mehitable still suffered from her sick headache, that Winslow had gotten a new horse and there was no talk of anyone's going to court anymore. She said, "Shall you ever come home again?" But before Jane could answer, Bethiah answered for herself. "He must say you can come, mustn't he? He won't, will he?"

When Jane made no answer Bethiah said, "I *hate* him."

How simple it sounded in her sister's mouth.

AT THE MIDDLE of January Granny Hall sent the neighbor boy for Jane as if she'd never been gone. The King's road had been worked smoother than the shore road, the Southside road something in between, but by the time Jane reached the midwife's she was mud to the knees. The old woman greeted her with a list of chores, as if she'd been saving them up for Jane: the dried herbs to be brought down from the attic, the roots to be pounded, the tinctures to be brewed, but at the midday she was sent to the Cookes' alone, to treat a burn. The Cookes lived a good distance east along the King's road, and just walking there Jane rediscovered the beauty of a sparsely trafficked road, the freedom to let her eyes light where they would, the comfort of knowing who and what awaited her around the turn. At the Cookes she discovered seven-year-old Priscilla, old enough to take her place at the fire but young enough to forget what it was; she'd laid the inside of her wrist across the hot iron and was still in tears when Jane arrived. An ointment of linseed oil, beeswax, and resin drew the heat and dried the eyes; it also reminded Jane what had been missing in all her supposed nursing of Aunt Gill: the patient never relieved, or, indeed, even ill.

As Jane worked her way back to Granny Hall's, she continued to think of Aunt Gill, but to her surprise she discovered that some of the heat had been drawn from that too. Perhaps she was not as ready to forgive as John Adams had been, but perhaps she was, at last, forgetting. Or perhaps it was that here in Satucket Aunt Gill mattered so very little, after all.

THE COLD CONTINUED. FIRST the edge of the bay turned to slush, then the well froze, next the ink, and last the clock. By the end of the month the whole of the shore was locked in with ice, taking away any hope of a return to town by sea. At almost the same time Jane's grandmother began to spend a good deal of time standing at the above-stairs window, staring out at the frozen bay. "Look, Jane," she said. "Look there to the westward. Do you not think it shifting?"

Jane looked out and saw the crinkled white surface of the bay solid to the horizon. She looked to the west as instructed and saw only the rippled shadows of the late-day sun turning the ice to slate. She said, "You're not looking to leave so soon?"

Jane's grandmother didn't answer at once. After a time she said, "No, but 'tis an unsettling feeling, knowing that were something to happen I couldn't get to him." She swung around. She gave a laugh that held little humor in it.

Jane said in haste, "Indeed, I do think the ice begins to move." It was the only lie she'd ever told her grandmother, and its falseness rang loud in the room, but curiously, her grandmother appeared to believe her.

When Jane said later, "We've enough grease for candles now," her grandmother said, "Why take the trouble? The mice will only eat them once we're gone."

IN HER GRANDMOTHER'S HOUSE Jane found moments in which the only sound about her was the hissing of the fire. Jane had never experienced such silence in town or, indeed, in her father's house; the silence fueled her, repaired her frayed edges, rested her mind, but it did not seem to have the same effect on her grandmother. She sat down, got up, climbed the stairs to peer out at the ice five times a day or more.

Jane had worked three more days for Granny Hall and the ice hadn't budged when the letters came, delivered by the hand of Seth Cobb, another shipmaster from the village. Cobb was a sociable man with easy, engaging ways; Jane was surprised when her grandmother began to beat him with questions even before a proper greeting had been exchanged.

"These letters came by sea? The shore has opened?"

"No, indeed. They came by road. I met them at Yarmouth."

"But you sail soon?"

Cobb looked with understandable puzzlement at Jane. "No one sails. I must be in town a week next and plan to travel overland."

Jane's grandmother stood in silence, staring at the letter in her hand. It was left to Jane to offer up their fire and refreshment, both of which Cobb seemed to sense it best to refuse. Once he'd gone Jane's grandmother stared a moment longer at the letter before breaking the seal. When she'd finished reading she handed it across. "I feared such a thing," she said. "I feared it as soon as I saw the ice form."

Jane read the letter in her own alarm but had some trouble accounting for her grandmother's concern; her grandfather called it a common distemper and only mentioned it by the way toward the end of the letter: *Being kept within doors several days by a common distemper I managed to miss the worst of the weather . . .*

Jane looked up from her reading. "A *common distemper,* he calls it. No doubt nothing more than his usual winter congestion."

"Or a lung fever."

"Lung fever! He gives no hint of a lung fever."

"He would hint at nothing! Only think of the look of him when we left. He works himself to illness. I know him. Indeed, I knew this would come."

"But look what he says—he was kept within doors a few days only."

"And which few days was that? Perhaps he wrote in the throes of it. Perhaps he's not yet recovered."

"But look at the date of the letter. Surely by now he's recovered."

"Or dead. And when should a letter with *that* news reach me?"

Jane's grandmother got up and climbed the stairs. Jane followed and found her as she knew she'd find her, peering out the window at the ice-choked bay and breathing deeply, as if she were suffocating under the weight of it. Jane looked out at the sea with her; she could glimpse a narrow ribbon of blue on the horizon, but no motion in the ice. This time, she stayed silent.

JANE HAD RECEIVED a letter too. *My Darling Jane,* Henry had written, and Jane knew the rest without reading on. He had not enjoyed a day since she'd left town. He could not rest for thought of her. He must beg that she return to town and marry him without delay. He added: *Town is much the same since you left it—the deficiencies of the Massacre trials continue to be the first subject. Mr. Sam Adams and Mr. John Adams each walk about in a fine heat but for contrary reasons.* He signed it: *Your Greatest Admirer—HK.*

The letter worked a curious spell on Jane; she sat down in all conscientiousness to contemplate the advantages and disadvantages of marriage to Henry Knox, but in turning her mind to Henry now she discovered how completely he had been absent from her thoughts since she'd arrived at Satucket. She was able to draw up his physical form easily enough, but she couldn't seem to hear him. She turned again to the letter and reading it a second time was reminded of a long-ago letter from Phinnie Paine, in which a question had arisen in Jane's mind whether she was indeed first in his thoughts. Even in Henry's letter proposing their marriage, the politics of town had intruded.

Henry's letter proposing their marriage. This was what Jane was to think about, and again she tried to do so, but again found herself thinking of Phinnie Paine, of the *no* she'd delivered to him with such ease. Was this a sign, the fact that she hadn't yet managed to offer that word to Henry? Had the comet indeed been a sign? And what if she did offer another *no* to Henry? Was that what her life was to be, a series of *nos* until nothing but the life of an Aunt Gill remained? But as Jane sat and thought more she realized that her view of Aunt Gill's life had somehow now changed. Aunt

Gill had believed in a thing and had set about to be of use to it. She *had* been of use to it. And was that not all Jane had asked?

JANE WAS IN HER shift and readying for bed when her grandmother burst through her door in her own shift, her shawl wrapped around her, her gold and silver hair let down out of its knot and streaming behind. "When did Cobb say he must to be in town?"

"A week next."

"And how does he travel?"

"Overland."

"Yes, yes, I mean by horse or by carriage?"

"He didn't say."

"We must find out. We must find out if by carriage, and if so, what room there is in it. You must take him a note in the morning."

Jane looked at her grandmother in surprise.

She said, "I no longer have the will to be apart from him."

And there, so simply, so clearly, was Jane's answer for Henry, without a father to demand it, without a comet to signal it. She could not, she should not, marry any man she could so painlessly leave behind.

Jane's grandmother returned to her room. Jane burrowed under her coverlet but soon tossed it back again. When she knew the thing to do she needed to do the thing. She returned to the keeping room and went through the old routine—blowing up the fire, lighting the candle off the coal, setting the inkwell on the hearth to thaw, laying out paper and pen— and as she did those things she thought how this was to be a part of her life now, no matter whether she lived in Satucket or town, that "home" was now a fractured thing, that someone she cared about should always be away from her, and only letters would allow of an exchange between. Might she one day become her brother, who could forsake a home for a cause? Or her grandmother, who it now appeared would at last forsake her home for a husband? Yes, Jane thought, she might do such a thing. But not for Henry Knox. She picked up her pen.

> *Dear Henry,*
>
> *No doubt you ask me to be your wife because you believe me to possess those qualities you should require in a wife, but as I have not yet determined for myself what those qualities should be, or, indeed, what qualities I should require in a husband if I should indeed require one, I must refuse your kind offer. Please know that I shall long treasure the honor of your proposal and shall remain always,*
>
> *Your friend,*
> *Jane Clarke*

THE NEXT MORNING JANE set out to be of use to her grandmother with the call on the Cobbs but was disappointed to discover that already her new philosophy had failed her—she wanted to be of use to her grandmother and secure her a carriage ride to town, but she did not want to get into that carriage herself. She trudged on, with her heart trailing behind. The Cobbs lived along the shore road that ran from the landing to the meetinghouse, no great walk for Jane in easy weather, but hobbling over great chunks of ice and potholes made it another matter. Indeed, it was hard to look at the bare fields covered in their silver-gray sheen and remember the summers she'd spent there watermeloning.

Mr. Cobb read her grandmother's note and passed it to his wife. She said, "Well, of course, Seth, you must take the carriage and bring them with you. Poor Mr. Freeman."

By the change in Mr. Cobb's features it seemed clear enough to Jane that he'd harbored no intention of bringing the carriage, but by a hasty adjustment it became equally clear that he would do so. "Indeed, I should be happy to carry Mrs. Freeman to town."

"And Jane," his wife added.

And Jane.

The plan was laid out for the next day's departure, and Jane thanked both Cobbs heartily on behalf of her grandmother, but there in the shadow of the thing all the noise and anger and dirt of town came crashing back at her, a great bleakness opened inside her. She must return to town and fall again on her grandparents' mercy for her keep until she might find some reasonable employment, perhaps with another Aunt Gill, perhaps, if she were lucky, with someone truly ill.

And there Jane remembered Granny Hall.

THE OLD WOMAN SHOWED little surprise at Jane's appearing unsummoned. She said, "Wood first. Then I'll need a syrup of vinegar and onions for Mrs. Hopkins."

Jane said, "I'd be happy to do those things. I'd be happy to come every day and work at whatever you wish, and I shall only charge you a shilling a day for it."

Granny Hall closed her eyes and tipped her head to the ceiling. She let out a sound like a crow, which Jane didn't at once identify as laughter. "More like I'll charge you a shilling a day for the teaching."

"Without the expense of my keep and care?"

"You would keep yourself! Where? In your father's barn?"

"I would keep myself at my grandparents' house and look after it while they're gone. But I suppose ten pence, with the noon meal provided, would keep me fed and warm."

The old woman studied her. "Six pence."

"Eight. And the meal."

The old woman turned back to her kettle, which was all Jane would get for a nod on the deal.

Jane collected the wood. She made up the syrup, carried it to the Hopkins house, and administered it to Mrs. Hopkins, who was so glad to see

Jane she gave her an extra twopence of her own, making up for the first day's twopence Jane had lost in her deal, which Jane decided to take as her own kind of sign. She left the Hopkins house feeling both heavy and light—eight pence a day was in fact more than she had expected to receive from Granny Hall, and the work would be much as she *had* expected, but she felt the weight of it just the same.

WHEN JANE RETURNED SHE found her grandmother bent over the oven, scraping a spill off the bricks. Jane took the knife from her and began to chip at the mess, explaining the arrangement with the Cobbs as she worked. She looked sideways and saw her grandmother's shoulders loosen in relief. Jane continued, "I wonder what you should think if I were to stay behind in Satucket. I might keep the house for you till your return, put in your garden for you once it thaws, perhaps get in some chickens. I've spoken to Granny Hall and have work there if I wish it."

Jane's grandmother's shoulders stiffened again. She stared at Jane in silence. What was she thinking? Of Jane, alone at Satucket? Of Jane in town? Of Jane's father? Those were the things Jane thought of.

After a time Jane's grandmother said, "You feel quite sure of this?"

"I feel quite sure I should like to try."

"You do know you might return to me at town at any time?"

"I know it."

"Well, then."

To Jane's great surprise her grandmother's eyes filled with tears.

JANE'S GRANDMOTHER HAD SAILED out of Satucket in a storm and sailed back to it the same way; ironic that the day of the carriage journey the bay sat as still and bright as a silver bowl. Mrs. Cobb had decided to take advantage of the carriage and accompany her husband to town; Jane was glad of it, for her grandmother's unease had not dissipated, and Jane suspected she would have made Mr. Cobb a poor traveling companion alone. The carriage was already in motion when Jane remembered Mehitable's old request for a letter confirming her safe arrival; she shouted the same request after her grandmother, and her grandmother raised her hand in the old pledge. Again, Jane raised her hand in return.

Chapter Thirty-two

I T HAD BEEN a long day. She'd spent the first part of it peeling, cutting, and boiling onions; she'd spent the second part of it blistering her fingers making up Granny Hall's turpentine and mustard poultice and attempting to apply it to the chest of the demented Mr. Earle. The experience with Mr. Earle would of course bring Otis to mind, which would of course bring her a little low; she'd stopped by the Cookes' to check on the child's burn and was brought lower. The girl's skin looked healthy; Mrs. Cooke paid promptly into Jane's palm, but she then said, "Heard you're living alone out at the landing road."

"For a time."

"How long a time?"

"I don't know, Mrs. Cooke. I imagine my grandparents will remain in town a good while; I keep their house while they're gone."

Mrs. Cooke planted her chin on her chest in a way that allowed her eyes to bore into Jane's. "An unmarried girl should be living at home."

Jane pushed on to her grandmother's house, the going that much harder as she now pushed against Mrs. Cooke all the way, to find a cold house and a basket of seed cake on her table, a sign that her sister had been and she'd missed the call. Jane shouldn't have greatly minded the missed visit—Bethiah came often and like as not brought seed cake, thinking it a favorite of Jane's, although in fact it was Nate who had preferred it above all—and yet she felt lower still. She built up the fire and made herself a supper of toast and tea; she sat with her shoes to the blaze and waited for the peace and comfort of her grandmother's house to take hold.

Jane could not say she was lonely. She saw Granny Hall and at least one or two of the village inhabitants every day, although a quarter of the women she saw looked their disapproval and perhaps half their men looked away. She saw Bethiah every few days and Neddy and the little girls once a week or so; Mehitable stayed away, but Jane couldn't blame her—her absence at home would be noted much faster than a child's. Jane might have *liked* her stepmother to call, she might have *liked* a letter, but she was *not* lonely. It was the commonest of courtesies only that drew her to invite Harry Nye inside when he arrived with the long-awaited mail.

He came in shaking off the cold like a dog shook off water and stepped up close to the fire. Jane offered him a hot cup from the kettle, and he accepted, sniffing at it, again like a dog.

He sighed. "I had hope of something beside this bog brew."

"Perhaps at your next stop."

"Oh, no, I stop nowhere else this day." He set down his cup, stepped closer to Jane, grinned. "As you seem so willing to keep me warm."

Jane's instinct was to back away, but as with any dog she suspected it would only draw him on. Instead she leaned over, picked up the poker, and jabbed it hard into the front log on the fire. Sparks shot into the air, and it was Nye who leaped back. She said without looking up from the fire, "Thank you for the letter, Mr. Nye. As you don't care for my tea and I've nothing else to offer you'd best get on." She didn't turn around until she'd heard the door close.

THE LETTER WAS FROM Jane's grandmother. In it she announced that she had not found her husband well, the paper front and back filled with a long list of complaints, but the complaints all hers: he did not eat as he should; he did not sleep as he should; he answered to any call in any weather; he came home from every meeting with his humors violently disturbed. From all this Jane concluded that her grandfather was much as he had been and that her grandmother was . . . home.

THE PRESENCE OF HARRY Nye in the village caused Jane to wonder if the bay had indeed opened while she'd not been paying attention; she went to the above-stairs window and was at once disabused. Nye could not have landed in Satucket by sea—the February bay was still too full of ice—but the shift had begun, and rivers of blue now appeared between the giant ice islands. Jane gazed at it for some time—the option of travel to town must require of her *some* consideration—but those blue rivers didn't draw her.

It drew others though, and either a horse and rider or walker took the trip down the landing road each day. It was perhaps five days after Nye's visit when Winslow came by. He was mounted on his new horse and trotted past Jane with hat lifted, but Jane almost didn't notice the hat, so blinding was the horse—the finest animal Jane had ever seen. Its coat was the black of charcoal with the shine of glass, its legs were as long and finely turned as the railings in the courthouse at Boston; it looked down its long nose at Jane with dancing eyes full of contempt for such a poor, two-legged sufferer. All that Jane had thought of Winslow in the past changed as horse and rider pranced along the road; the man who had so proudly ridden a horse with no ears had now passed that creature by. A battle lost for a battle won.

AT THE END of March Bethiah smuggled her father's *Boston Gazette* out of the house and delivered it to Jane. Jane hadn't seen a newspaper in so long that she nearly snatched it from her sister's hands, but when she saw that the entire contents was a celebration of the events of the previous March the fifth, she handed it back again. The celebration of August the four-teenth had been supplanted for all time.

Mrs. Cooke and her ilk aside, Jane began to have other callers besides her family. Temperance Collier was the first, coming by to ask Jane for Granny Hall's headache decoction, Jane being nearer to hand. The request thrust at Jane her first moral dilemma—it was, after all, Granny Hall's decoction. Jane solved the problem by offering to make up her own decoc-tion for Temperance; she had long thought that Granny Hall's recipe was short on mustard and long on rum; she had long thought some sage would improve it. If it worked as well as Granny Hall's, all would gain by the experiment; if it didn't, best that Jane discover it now.

AT THE FIRST of April, just after Jane had swept away the last crumbs from her supper, she heard a forceful but uneven knock at her door. She picked up the poker, thinking of a drunken Harry Nye, and flung the door wide with a bang and a scold all prepared.

Her father stood there. He looked at the poker in her hand and said, "So this is how you live? Arming yourself just to open the door?"

Jane said, "Come in," but kept hold of the poker. Her father went up to the keeping room table where Jane had been composing a letter to her brother. He leaned over the page. Jane snatched it up. Her father straight-ened.

"I suppose you hear what's said about you. Entertaining the like of

Harry Nye. You can't be so great a fool as to think you'll marry *him*."

"No."

Jane's father brought his hands down flat on the table and leaned across it. Jane touched the table too, bracing for her father's roar, but instead his voice came at her deep and low—like the shocked and pained voice of an animal that had received a surprise wound; like a horse, perhaps, whose ears had been cut off.

"What the devil do you think to do, Jane, humiliate me by setting yourself up here alone?"

"*I* humiliate *you*?"

"God's breath! Do you think—?"

"Do *you* think I was not humiliated when you shipped me away to a town in the throes of bedlam, into the home of a woman without a moral scruple to her name?"

"You dare talk moral scruple to me?"

"*You* dare?"

"You watch how you go!"

"Did you cut off the horse's ears?"

She'd had no idea of asking it, but there it was, after all that time. And there it sat; Jane's father was not a man who shifted from thought to thought with any great speed. First he had to stop his speech; next he had to shut up his gaping maw; third he had to decide if he had indeed heard what he couldn't possibly have heard; fourth he had to respond. Most times the fourth stage followed hard on the third as her father spewed out whatever thought happened to arrive first, but now he took the time to round the table to the fire and hold out his hands to the flame. When he spoke at last he spoke in utter calm.

"For you of all people in this godforsaken village to ask me this—" He turned, took a step toward her. She didn't move.

He smiled. "Very well, I shall answer what I shouldn't need to. Not to my own daughter. Not to *you*. 'Twas your cousin Silas, the lad I took on as tanner's apprentice, who butchered the horse. He'd ruined a vat of hides and thought to get in better with me, to put the Clarkes one up for a change. I always thought him half idiot, but there I knew him to be the whole. When he told me what he'd done I packed him off. There. Does this satisfy you?"

Did it? "But Winslow threatened to sue *you*."

"Of course he threatened to sue me. What's he like to get from a tanner's apprentice? And the boy was in my charge. Acting on orders, they might say."

"But the suit was called off."

"And Winslow has a new horse. Or didn't you see?"

Yes, Jane saw. Her father stood backlit by the fire, his features a wash of gray, but without the individual bits of him, Jane saw, for the first time, something of the whole.

When her father spoke again he spoke softly, as he had done that night in the dark when she was a child. "Jane. Do you know what it cost me having you gone? Do you know what it costs me now? Never mind the fool you make of me living here alone; I'm telling you now—I want you home. Do as you like with Paine." He stepped up to her, laid a hand on her hair. "I'll send Jot with the cart on the morrow."

He left.

JANE SAT AT THE KEEPING room table, her brother's letter pushed aside. *I want you home.* She thought of her sister Bethiah and all the letters full of heart and mind that they had learned to share. She thought of the comfort she hadn't identified as such while she'd had it—the comfort of a shared bed. She thought of Mehitable, of the heart and mind she'd shared with her pen and might yet learn to share with her voice. She thought of Neddy, of what he might need of her in the years to come, and the little girls and the babe she should like to know as it grew. To love as it grew. She thought of her father, a man she had long loved and who had loved her in return. Jane had lived nearly two years in town and had seen the many parts that could make up a man, good and bad, right and wrong, all the parts necessarily cemented together to make the whole. Why should she have thought her father made up of only one of those parts? Perhaps the whole that she now saw might get another man cast from church or flood his mill in the throes of an impotent rage; perhaps it might impede the flow of herring for personal gain. But was it something that might cut off the ears of another man's horse? Did he tell the truth about her cousin Silas? Did it even matter now? What Jane needed to know she already knew, and she'd learned it from her father and brother and Aunt Gill and Henry Knox and Phinnie Paine and even John Adams, the day he'd stood in her father's house cradling Mehitable's babe: she could not look to her father's arms to keep her safe anymore.

Jane sat at the table long, thinking of all that had transpired in all the days since she'd left Satucket, thinking of all the people who had passed through those days, and after a time a new thought came to her. Even though her father had been wrong in so many things, was there a place where he may have been right? She thought then—as in truth she'd been thinking for nearly two years now—of Phinnie Paine.

Jane got up and went to the chest in the room her grandmother had allotted her. Jane had brought all she owned to Satucket; by contrast, her grandmother had brought very little, which might have told Jane a thing or two had she considered it beforehand. She found her bundle of letters under her summer petticoats; Phinnie's, so old now, was nearest the bottom. She picked it out and read it through.

Sum over parts.

But were not they all the sum of their parts?

Jane pushed the letter back onto the top of the bundle and dropped it into the drawer of her grandmother's chest. She returned to the keeping room, pulled out a fresh piece of paper, and picked up her pen. As she did so she couldn't help but smile—she was, at last, obeying her father's wish.

Dear Phinnie,

*If I properly recollect your ways, you and your barrel staves should
be arriving at Satucket with the herring. So as not to take you by
surprise should you come upon me along the road, I write to inform
you that I too am returned to Satucket, although I no longer live at my
father's house—I live now at my Grandfather Freeman's on the landing
road. I make my way out of work for Granny Hall and plan to remain
here at least until my grandparents return from town, which judging by
the situation there will not be soon. I hope this letter finds you in health.
I am—*

Jane lifted her pen. What was she? In truth, what was she? She put the
pen to page.

In hope of seeing you again—Jane

Historical Note

Although the Clarke and Winslow characters referenced in this novel are entirely fictitious, the legal feud between the families that swirled around the Satucket mill valley for generations is fact. Some of these cases may be found in the Massachusetts Archives/Judicial Archives, but the *Winslow v. Clarke qui tam* was considered interesting enough to have been included in *The Legal Papers of John Adams,* where Adams's successful defense of Clarke is documented. Josiah Paine's *A History of Harwich, Benjamin Bangs' Diary,* and Dean Dudley's *History and Genealogy of the Bangs Family in America* all give brief but colorful accounts of other cases between the families, including the one involving Winslow's horse.

In 1773 John Adams wrote of the trials of Captain Preston and the soldiers involved in the Boston Massacre: "The death sentence would have been as foul a Stain upon this country as the executions of the Quakers or Witches, anciently. As the Evidence was, the Verdict of the Jury was exactly right." Adams's fellow townsmen disagreed. Writing again in 1815 Adams said, "To this hour, my conduct in [the trial] is remembered, and is alleged against me to prove I am an enemy to my country, and always have been." But Adams always believed that his participation in the trial was "one of the most gallant, generous, manly and disinterested actions of my whole life, and one of the best pieces of service I ever rendered my country."

In the course of Thomas Preston's trial John Adams was greatly helped by the testimony of one Jane Whitehouse, who lived near the British sentry, Hugh White, on Royal Exchange Lane, and was present at the scene; she cast the first strong doubt that it was indeed Preston who gave the order to fire, giving vivid testimony of the townsman in the dark cloak. Hugh White, in the thick of his own troubles, reached out to Jane Whitehouse to protect her from harm.

After his trial Thomas Preston wrote a warm thank-you to Auchmuty but none to Adams or Quincy. Many years later, when Adams was serving in London as minister for the newly formed United States of America, he and Thomas Preston passed in a London street without speaking; Preston had greatly resented Adams's refusal to "try the town."

John Adams's career being so well exposed of late, there is no need to list his accomplishments here, but Henry Knox's are perhaps not as well known. Knox's testimony at the massacre trials may have been somewhat partisan, but his efforts to avert the carnage were acknowledged by both sides. The year following the massacre Knox opened his own bookstore, spending his spare time in an intense study of military science and artillery. In 1774 he married the daughter of a confirmed Tory, but this did little to sway his politics. He volunteered for service in Washington's army in 1775, and his incredible feat of transporting the cannon captured at Fort Ticonderoga to Dorchester Heights was in large part responsible for driving the British from Boston on March 17, 1776. From that point on Knox was one of George Washington's most trusted henchmen—his artillery played large roles in the battles of Princeton, Brandywine, Germantown, Monmouth, and Yorktown—and he served as secretary of war from 1785 to 1794.

My two previous historical novels, *The Widow's War* and *Bound,* highlighted James Otis's rise to political fame, beginning in 1761 with his famous speech arguing against the Writs of Assistance and promoting Man's natural right to life, liberty, and property. The young law student, John Adams, in attendance at the speech, called Otis "a flame of fire," and later declared that on that day "the child independence was born." Otis was the driving force behind the boycott of British goods, and his speeches and pamphlets and other writings greatly influenced the course of American politics through the 1760s. But by 1769 Otis's career had begun its reverse trajectory. Although Otis's conflicted mind had already begun to slip prior to the attack at the British Coffee House in 1769, that event dramatically accelerated his decline. He began to waver in his convictions; his behavior grew more erratic; by the time of the Boston Massacre he was no longer an effective participant in the political scene. His family found it necessary to remove his firearms, and later that spring it was announced that he had "retired" to the country; in fact he had been carted out of town in a "straight-waistcoat" and left in his family's care at Great Marshes, or West Barnstable, on Cape Cod. In 1771 Otis's friends and relations petitioned the court to have him declared a "Non-Compos Distracted or Lunatic Person and a proper object for a Guardian." His brother Samuel served as his legal guardian for most of the remainder of his years. At one point Otis paid a visit to his old enemy, Governor Thomas Hutchinson, and apologized for "ruining the country," but by 1775 his politics had come around again. He is listed on the official roster of militia from Barnstable who set out for Lexington in support of the minutemen who stood against the British there.

Otis exited the political stage much as he came onto it. In 1783, shortly after the peace treaty between Britain and America had been signed, he was standing in the doorway of his custodian's farmhouse, watching an approaching storm, when he was struck by a bolt of lightning and killed.